3/7

Igarashi. Y 2450
3-31-88   16⁵⁰
Berkeley   Ⓐ

D1522653

FIVE POLITICAL LEADERS OF MODERN JAPAN

FIVE POLITICAL LEADERS
OF MODERN JAPAN

Itō Hirobumi, Ōkuma Shigenobu, Hara Takashi,
Inukai Tsuyoshi, and Saionji Kimmochi

Yoshitake Oka
Translated by
Andrew Fraser and Patricia Murray

UNIVERSITY OF TOKYO PRESS

Translation supported by a grant-in-aid from the Ministry of Education, Science and Culture, Japan, and publication supported by a grant from The Japan Foundation.

Translated from the Japanese original KINDAI NIHON NO SEIJIKA (Iwanami Shoten, 1979)
English translation © 1986 UNIVERSITY OF TOKYO PRESS
All rights reserved. No part of this publication may be reproduced or transmitted in any form or by any means, electronic or mechanical, including photocopy, recording, or any information storage and retrieval system, without permission in writing from the publisher.

ISBN 4-13-037014-6 UTP 37146
ISBN 0-86008-379-9

Printed in Japan

CONTENTS

Preface   vii

Itō Hirobumi: Father of the Constitution   3

Ōkuma Shigenobu: Champion of Democracy   45

Hara Takashi: The "Commoner" Prime Minister   85

Inukai Tsuyoshi: Frustration, Triumph, and Tragedy   125

Saionji Kimmochi: Last of the Genrō   177

Notes   225
Index   231

PREFACE

This book singles out five political leaders who, although their roles were different, each played an important part in shaping modern Japan. I have sought to examine how, and with what results, they exercised their leadership.

In the preface to the Japanese edition (1979) I wrote: "Itō Hirobumi, Ōkuma Shigenobu, Hara Takashi, Inukai Tsuyoshi, and Saionji Kimmochi were all familiar names before the Second World War. But the era when they occupied the spotlight of their world now seems long past. The bewildering and irrevocable changes in Japan's politics triggered by the Manchurian (1931–33) and May 15th (1932) incidents, and the disaster that came a few years later, have created a gulf between us and such political leaders that is a great deal wider than just the passage of years would merit. Quietly, without our knowing quite when, they have withdrawn into the shadows of history, where their features have become dim and blurred. Here, I have sought to bring the lives of these five men back into the light, retracing their political careers and seeking to recreate an image of each man as he was during his time of active political leadership."

Examining the character of each of these leaders is an important concern of this book, but I have also stressed the ways they responded to circumstances, their political roles, and their final fate. My purpose was not to write short biographies or to pass judgment on them. Nor have I sought to fit their character, actions, and roles into any given pattern or model. Rather, the five chapters of this book are case studies in political leadership, a long-standing interest of mine, as seen in terms of specific historical events and people.

If, in addition, my book sheds a little more light on the politics of prewar Japan and prompts some useful reflections on our present or future political situation, I shall be very satisfied.

Yoshitake Oka

Itō Hirobumi

Ōkuma Shigenobu

Hara Takashi

Inukai Tsuyoshi

Saionji Kimmochi

Photographs of Itō, Hara, and Inukai courtesy of Kensei Kinenkan; of Ōkuma courtesy of Waseda University; and of Saionji courtesy of Harada Keisaku.

FIVE POLITICAL LEADERS OF MODERN JAPAN

ITŌ HIROBUMI

Father of the Constitution

1841–1909

In the mid-nineteenth century Japan was governed from Edo (now Tokyo) by the Bakufu, a military regime headed by the Tokugawa shoguns. Excluded from active participation in national affairs, several of Japan's most powerful feudal domains were growing restless, impatient with the Tokugawa regime's indecisive measures against mounting pressure from the Western Powers, while looking increasingly toward the emperor in Kyoto as a new focus for loyalty and national unity.

Young Days

Chōshū, in western Honshū, was one of those domains, and there Itō Hirobumi was born in the autumn of 1841, the son of a low-ranking samurai. In 1857 he entered Shōka Sonjuku, the academy founded and run by Yoshida Shōin, an inspired teacher and pro-emperor loyalist, executed two years later by the Bakufu for unauthorized political activities. With many other young Chōshū pupils at this academy, Itō fully espoused the cause that gave rise to the famous rally-cry: "Honor the Emperor, Expel the Barbarians!" His deep respect for Yoshida Shōin never waned throughout Itō's life. As the years passed, demands to replace the Bakufu with a government headed by the emperor and to rid Japan of an encroaching foreign presence grew more and more strident. Then in 1862 a group of Chōshū activists—Takasugi Shinsaku, Kusaka Genzui, and Inoue Kaoru (then named Shidō Bunda) among them—attacked and burned the British Legation at Gotenyama temple in Shinagawa, the southwest gateway to Edo. Itō, then aged twenty-two, also took part in the attack. A year later Itō was persuaded by Inoue to join him and three other young men of the Chōshū domain on a voyage to England to study naval affairs. At the time of his departure in mid-1863, Itō composed this verse:

> Be assured—it is for the emperor's realm
> That I embark on this journey,
> Shamed though I am in my manly pride.

The main object of this small group was to learn as much as they could about conditions in enemy countries. Five days out of Yokohama, their steamship docked at Shanghai. All of them were immediately struck by the imposing sight of warships and steamships all around them, thronging the harbor in a continual procession of arrivals and departures. To Inoue, this was a daunting scene. When such a concentration of naval power had already gathered at so little distance from Japan, he reasoned, defense of the nation's coastline was well nigh impossible. Attempting to expel the foreigners was a dangerously mistaken policy; rather, Japan should plan positively, opening its doors in peace and amity, while steadily building up a strong naval defense and a modern commercial and industrial base. But when Inoue voiced his apprehensions, Itō turned on him in a fury. Only several days out of Japan, how could Inoue so quickly abandon his fierce determination to rid their country of foreigners, merely at the sight of a few warships in Shanghai harbor? Yet after heated arguments, Itō finally came to see that any attempt to push the foreigners out by force was doomed to fail and would lead Japan to disaster.

Later that year in their London lodgings, the four young men from Chōshū learned that artillery batteries of their domain had opened fire on foreign shipping in the Straits of Shimonoseki. This news plunged them all into deep anxiety, coming as it did after reports of hostilities between Britain and Satsuma, in the course of which a squadron of British warships had bombarded and devastated Kagoshima, the castle town of the domain. They feared that Japan, by warlike measures against the foreigners, was running headlong down a path to self-destruction. Convinced that Chōshū must change its policy immediately and support opening the nation in peace and amity, they debated what to do. Hurriedly, Itō and Inoue returned to Japan. They arrived at Yokohama in mid-1864, just as a fleet of seventeen warships—British, French, American, and Dutch—prepared to set out on a punitive expedition against Chōshū in retaliation for the artillery attacks on their ships the previous year. Itō and Inoue then tried desperately to persuade the domain to seek a peaceful solution, but to no avail. Shortly afterward, the foreigners arrived and their bombardment of Shimonoseki inflicted a truly humiliating defeat on Chōshū.

The events of the next few years moved forward with mounting violence and bewildering rapidity. Satsuma and Chōshū formed an alliance that in 1866 successfully resisted a military expedition mounted by the Bakufu to punish Chōshū for taking unauthorized initiatives in national affairs. The Bakufu's defeat led swiftly to the shogun's resignation and the assumption of ruling power in November 1867 by the fifteen-year-old emperor. Bakufu supporters made a final attempt to wrest the political advantage from their Satsuma and Chōshū opponents early in 1868 but were defeated at the battle of Toba Fushimi on the southern outskirts of Kyoto. The way was now clear for Emperor Meiji to lead the era that bears his name. During these upheavals, Itō was fully occupied trying to secure unity of purpose and cooperation between Satsuma and Chōshū, but until early 1868 he was still in a comparatively junior position. The main roles were played by Kido Takayoshi of his own domain, together with Ōkubo Toshimichi and Saigō Takamori of Satsuma—the "Three Great Heroes" of the Meiji Restoration.

Under the titular sovereignty of the young emperor, the Meiji government was directed by a Council of State, with both deliberative and executive functions, presided over by two prominent court nobles, Sanjō Sanetomi and Iwakura Tomomi. Itō's first post was as an executive official in charge of foreign affairs. Next, at the age of twenty-eight, he was promoted to junior councillor and a secretary of the foreign ministry. In 1871, a mission headed by Council of State Vice-president Iwakura Tomomi was sent overseas to negotiate a revision of the unequal treaties forced on Japan by the Western Powers between 1858 and 1866, while also making a study tour of Europe and the United States. Iwakura requested Itō, by then working as vice-minister of public works, to join the mission. Thus Itō became one of his four assistant envoys, along with Councillor Kido Takayoshi, Finance Minister Ōkubo Toshimichi, and Foreign Minister Yamaguchi Naoyoshi. Clearly, Iwakura had developed a deep trust in Itō by this time. As a result of political maneuvers since the early 1860s, Iwakura had developed close ties with the Satsuma leaders but was rather reserved toward those of Chōshū, so this high esteem for Itō was quite exceptional.

During the course of the mission, while seeming to distance himself from Kido Takayoshi, his senior colleague from Chōshū, Itō drew closer to Ōkubo of Satsuma. Henceforth, Ōkubo put great trust in Itō. The respect was mutual, and to the end of his days Itō held Ōkubo in the highest degree of affection and esteem. Holding strong even throughout considerable Satsuma-Chōshū competition for supremacy after the Restoration, that bond was all the more remarkable. After the mission returned to Japan in 1873, disagreement over the issue of war with Korea split the government into two bitterly contending factions. Ōkubo and his allies successfully quashed the pro-war faction, who all resigned from the government. In the reshuffle that followed, Ōkubo assumed a new post as home minister and now came to wield decisive influence in the government. Itō was made councillor and minister of public works. Together with Ōkuma Shigenobu, councillor and finance minister, Itō now became one of Ōkubo's most loyal and capable colleagues. When Ōkubo was assassinated in 1878 by a small group of former samurai angered by his policies and seeming monopoly of power, Itō succeeded him as councillor and home minister. Meanwhile, in 1877 Kido had died of illness and Saigō had perished in the Satsuma Rebellion. Itō took over as the leading minister under Council of State Presidents Sanjō Sanetomi and Iwakura Tomomi. Along with Ōkuma, he was now the most senior of the councillors.

As Ōkubo's assassination demonstrated, the Meiji government had aroused widespread discontent in its hasty drive to transform Japan into a powerful industrial state within a single generation. Former samurai on reduced incomes and farmers subject to heavy taxes were particularly hard hit. When the defeat of Saigō Takamori and the Satsuma rebels in 1877 put an end to armed uprisings, this discontent found an outlet in political agitation. A

[6]

Freedom and People's Rights movement began to spread with dramatic speed, coming to a head in 1880 when delegations from all over Japan arrived in Tokyo to press petitions for a constitution and an elected legislative assembly.

The leaders of this movement were Itagaki Taisuke and Gotō Shōjirō of the former Tosa domain. Tosa had joined Satsuma and Chōshū in spearheading the Restoration and subsequently received a lesser share of the spoils of victory. In 1873, Itagaki and Gotō both held high government posts but left office with Saigō Takamori and other prominent officials when Ōkubo and his allies vetoed the decision to go to war with Korea. Unlike Saigō, who looked to armed rebellion as a weapon against the government, Itagaki and Gotō set out to launch a political opposition movement as champions of the common people. In 1875, their challenge had already induced the government to issue an imperial proclamation foreshadowing gradual constitutional progress. Thereafter, they continued to press the government to honor this pledge, and in October 1881, as the petition movement rose to a climax amid mounting public excitement and agitation, they formed Japan's first people's party, the Jiyūtō.

Government leaders were forced to respond. Itō, together with Inoue Kaoru and Ōkuma Shigenobu, had already begun to hold discussions on drawing up a constitutional regime. But then Ōkuma was forced to resign after the political crisis of October 1881, when Itō and Inoue suspected him of trying to seize the initiative from them on the issue of constitutional progress. At the same time, to allay public agitation, an imperial edict was issued declaring that a constitution would be promulgated by 1890. After this crisis, Itō had the highest seniority among the councillors. His place in the government was now stronger and more vital than it had ever been.

Enactment of the Meiji Constitution

The next task was to draw up the constitution. Council of State Presidents Sanjō and Iwakura had now been joined by Imperial Prince Arisugawa; they all advised the emperor to entrust this important commission to Itō. He spent one year from 1882 to 1883 in Europe, studying the organization and working of con-

[7]

stitutional systems in the leading Western nations. Two years later, in 1885, concrete preparations began when the structure of the government was changed to a modern cabinet system. Sanjō Sanetomi moved aside to a palace post as Lord Keeper of the Privy Seal. Itō was appointed Japan's first modern prime minister and formed its first real cabinet. Some years later the historian and critic Tokutomi Sohō commented on Itō's rise:

> Very few statesmen had such a brilliant career as Itō. He rose from humble origins to become prime minister. Since Fujiwara Kamatari in the seventh century A.D. until 1885, only four men outside this emperor-related family rose to be chief minister of state—Ashikaga Yoshimitsu, Toyotomi Hideyoshi, Tokugawa Ienari, and Itō Hirobumi.[1] Itō's achievement must be acclaimed as the hallmark of greatness.

At the time, Itō's appointment as prime minister was regarded as an epoch-making event. The drafting of a constitution began in 1886 under his direction. When it was completed two years later, Itō relinquished the prime ministership to Satsuma leader Kuroda Kiyotaka and became the first president of the Privy Council. After a draft had been submitted to the Privy Council for discussion and amendment, the constitution was promulgated in February 1889.

Itō's role in formulating the Meiji Constitution was thus of supreme importance and exercised a dominant influence on the political history of Japan after 1890. During his trip to Europe the lectures of Rudolf von Gneist and Lorenz von Stein in particular had convinced him that the Prussian Constitution and its methods of operation offered the best model for Japan. Itō was thoroughly convinced of the virtues of a supreme monarchy, and so placed a high priority on establishing a firm legal and institutional base for the emperor system. Writing to Iwakura Tomomi in August 1882, Itō declared that he had reached a clear understanding of how to make "the emperor a cornerstone, secure in his grasp of sovereign power." That was all the more necessary, continued Itō, because the advocates of Freedom and People's Rights mistakenly hailed the writings of radical liberals in England, America, and France as golden rules, and they had become

[8]

a force that could lead virtually to the overthrow of the state. But Itō had discovered principles and means to overcome this trend and believed he had rendered an important service to the nation. "I feel inwardly that I can die a happy man," he told Iwakura, in the famous phrase expressing complete confidence that the constitution he now proposed to draft would be the best for Japan.

As the sovereign who had granted the constitution to his subjects, the emperor was supreme, sacred, and inviolable. By 1889, the assets of the imperial household had been boosted to give him a large measure of financial independence. In matters of government, the emperor was a constitutional monarch who reigned rather than ruled directly. The constitution established a number of state offices and corporate bodies, each with its own specific powers to advise, direct, and assist in the totality of imperial rule. Checks and balances within and between these bodies were designed to ensure that no individual or group could monopolize the emperor's counsels or deprive him of all initiative in state affairs.

The imperial household department was run by the Lord Chamberlain, a minister without cabinet portfolio, thus keeping palace affairs apart from actual politics. In addition, the Lord Keeper of the Privy Seal—usually a distinguished nobleman, elder statesman, or ex-prime minister—acted as the emperor's closest adviser on matters of government. Throughout the Meiji era and beyond, these posts were not important in politics, but became much more so in the troubled years of the mid-1930s and early 1940s.

A corporate body of advisers, the Privy Council, met whenever ordered to do so by the emperor. Responsible to him alone, it could be consulted on all important affairs of state. Under a president and vice-president, the twenty or so Privy Councillors were appointed for life. Most of them were retired officials or military officers of rank and distinction. Ex officio, ministers of the current cabinet attended deliberations of the Privy Council, giving its resolutions added weight. Although of little importance in politics for many years, the Privy Council played a more active role during the 1920s, when it often met to review treaties with foreign nations during this decade of active diplomacy.

[9]

At the very center of government, directing the executive, stood the cabinet, with the prime minster and ten or so department ministers all directly appointed by the emperor and individually responsible to him. Any Japanese citizen—nobleman, bureaucrat, military officer, or commoner—could become prime minister or hold a cabinet portfolio on receipt of the emperor's mandate. Cabinets often resigned collectively, but there was no rule that if the prime minister left office, all his colleagues must do so too.

When proposing new laws or yearly budgets, the cabinet had to secure the approval of both chambers of the Diet. The House of Peers numbered around 300 members. Half of these were noblemen, sitting either by right or by mutual election from the lower grades of the peerage; the other half were selected by the emperor from distinguished persons in all walks of life, together with fifty or so high taxpayers, one from each metropolitan city and prefecture. Members of the House of Representatives, at first 300 in number but increased after 1902 to 464, were elected from standard constituencies throughout the nation. Suffrage rights were restricted to male adults, and tax-paying qualifications kept the voters limited to just under half a million (1 percent of total population). The electorate was extended twice after 1890—to 3 million (5 percent) in 1919 and then to just over 12 million (19 percent) in 1925 when the Diet finally passed a manhood suffrage law.

The two houses of the Diet had important powers to check the cabinet, both by rejecting proposals for new legislation and by withholding approval of the budget. In the latter event, the cabinet could make do with the current budget, but in times of rapidly rising expenditures, this restriction was a serious handicap and usually precipitated a change of government. In addition to their power to initiate legislation, both houses could send reports directly to the emperor, and Diet motions of no-confidence or impeachment were a grave embarrassment that could force a cabinet to resign.

Two other groups were of crucial importance in politics, though in ways not formally prescribed by the constitution itself. First, six or seven Satsuma and Chōshū elder statesmen, known by 1900 as the genrō, wielded tremendous influence in national affairs and were invariably consulted by the emperor on the choice of prime minister. In effect, they were the nominators and guardians of cabinets up until the mid-1920s when the last of them died, leaving their chosen heir, the court noble Saionji, to perform this role on his own. Second, especially after the victories over China in 1895 and Russia in 1905, the army and navy enjoyed great prestige and had important privileges in government. Together, they formed a kind of "establishment" that can be called the military. After 1890, the military exercised "rights of supreme command," maintaining that they had powers under the constitution to advise the emperor on strategic affairs without cabinet or Diet interference. Further, it was an accepted convention after 1890 that the army and navy ministers in any cabinet must be serving officers with the rank of lieutenant general, vice-admiral, or above. This privilege was confirmed by an imperial ordinance in 1900. From 1913 to 1936 the field was widened to include officers on the retired list, but from the outset of the constitutional regime the military had a virtual veto over cabinet formation and strong bargaining powers in budget allotments. No wonder, perhaps, that so many prime ministers after 1890 were army or naval officers.

The unenfranchised masses were apparently excluded from national politics, but they, too, were a force to be reckoned with. Many of them had electoral rights in their town, village, district, and prefectural assemblies, where politics were conducted at the grass roots. Despite the fact that the electorate to the national assembly was so restricted, the Diet representatives could not afford to ignore the common people. Even before the constitution came into force, most of the larger political organizations dubbed themselves "people's parties," and after 1890 often appealed to the masses for support in their drive to gain greater power at the expense of entrenched forces such as the genrō, the military, the Privy Council, and the House of Peers. At any time, outbursts of public indignation could shake the cabinet, or force it to resign if things got out of control. Cabinets were expected to take responsibility even for unforeseeable events such as assaults on prominent people.

Confronted by such a complicated medley of political forces, cabinets were perhaps bound to be shortlived. Diet dissolutions

[11]

followed by general elections were also fairly frequent, as cabinets sought to gain more influence over the House of Representatives. Both before and after 1890, government leaders occasionally attempted to set up subservient political organizations, but they were never able to deprive the people's parties of their importance in politics, until the 1930s when the military overawed them by violence and intimidation.

Such, in sum, was the balance of forces that any prime minister under Itō's constitution would have to reconcile and manage. Forming a cabinet and keeping it in office was a complicated and difficult matter, requiring much political bargaining and intrigue. As for the constitution itself, Itō had looked to Prussia as a model, and conservatives of all sorts continued to interpret constitutional government in authoritarian, militaristic, and bureaucratic terms. To the leaders of the people's parties, constitutional government meant something very different—they looked to other Western nations for models, in particular to the parliamentary democracies. From the outset, Itō's constitution was open to a variety of conflicting interpretations that no amount of political bargaining or accommodation could hope to resolve.

A Door for Party Politics

When the Diet opened in 1890, Itō chalked up a new appointment as president of the House of Peers. Then he served again as prime minister from 1892 to 1896. Among several noteworthy achievements, the second Itō cabinet gained partial revision of the unequal treaties that had vexed the nation for so many years. Extra-territoriality was abolished, and Japan secured tariff autonomy in several categories of imported goods. Also under this cabinet, Japan waged a war against China and surprised the world by its rapid and decisive victory. The Treaty of Shimonoseki in 1895 concluded the Sino-Japanese War; but almost immediately after it was signed, Russia, France, and Germany, in what was later called the Triple Intervention, combined to coerce Japan into restoring to China the strategic Liaotung peninsula of South Manchuria. This diplomatic humiliation provoked widespread anger in Japan, and in August 1896 Prime Minister Itō resigned with all his cabinet.

Now, for the first time since 1868, Itō held no official post; but he did not stay out for long. In January 1898, he was back as prime minister for the third time. In 1900, he set up a political party of his own, the Rikken Seiyūkai, and became its president. Although other parties had formed by this time, the Seiyūkai was the first of them to have really strong ties with government. Originally, when the constitution was first promulgated, the Satsuma and Chōshū leaders rejected the notion of party cabinets. They maintained that the new regime implied government by a cabinet that should govern over and above political parties. At the time, Itō fully supported the idea of keeping the government aloof from party politics—the so-called transcendence principle. But after the opening of the Diet in 1890, when the realities of running a constitutional government became clear and Itō himself had run up against some trying situations while prime minister, he began to feel a strong need for a political party of his own. So in 1900, ten years after the opening of the Diet, Itō set up the Seiyūkai and, predictably, encountered considerable opposition from several of his fellow Sat-Chō veteran statesmen, now known as the genrō, who held fast to the transcendence principle. That year he formed his fourth cabinet, using the Seiyūkai as its base. This fourth cabinet was shortlived, holding office for little over seven months, and was Itō's last.

Confronting Russia

About the time when the Boxer Rebellion was gathering steam in China, Russia exploited the turmoil to march in and occupy Manchuria. That was in 1900. When the Russians made no move to withdraw their troops once the crisis in China had passed, and, rather, seemed intent on expanding their influence over Korea, Japan's leaders began to worry about what grandiose designs their huge neighbor had. General Katsura Tarō of Chōshū became prime minister in 1901 after Itō's cabinet had resigned. Supported by a majority of the genrō, Katsura's cabinet decided that Japan should form an alliance with Britain, but Itō and Inoue did not concur with this. They feared that an alliance with Britain would only provoke Russia further. In their opinion, Japan's best policy was, rather, to negotiate with Russia toward an understanding contingent upon mutual concessions regarding Manchuria and Korea, and thus resolve the looming confrontation. Itō himself went to Russia in an attempt to gauge the workability of that approach, but despite his efforts the Katsura cabinet, backed by a majority of the genrō, formally entered into an alliance with Britain.

The Anglo-Japanese Alliance did not deter Russia; mounting tension led to the outbreak of war in February 1904. Much to the surprise of many, Japan proved stronger and Russia was defeated. Under the Treaty of Portsmouth of September 1905, which formally concluded the war, Korea became a Japanese protectorate. Itō was sent to Seoul as the first resident general, an office that gave him the power to plan the control of Korea.

Itō remained in his post until June 1909. Four months later, while on an inspection tour of Manchuria, he stopped at Harbin, and there a bullet fired by a Korean nationalist killed him, ending his life at the age of sixty-nine.

Political Adversary: Yamagata Aritomo

Throughout Itō's career in politics, the man who put up the most persistent and powerful challenge was Yamagata Aritomo. They had been fellow pupils at Yoshida Shōin's academy, Shōka Sonjuku, and were equally acclaimed as the two most powerful genrō. From the outset, Itō advanced steadily upward as a civil official. After the Restoration, he became the first to hold the offices of prime minister, president of the Privy Council, and president of the House of Peers. In contrast, Yamagata was above all, as he liked to describe himself, a soldier. It was Yamagata who was responsible for creating Japan's modern army. Thus, in 1873 he became the first army minister, and in 1878 chief-of-staff, rising in 1890 to field marshal. On the establishment of the Supreme Military Council in 1898, he became one of its first members, together with Imperial Prince Komatsu no Miya Akihito and Satsuma leaders General Ōyama Iwao and Admiral Saigō Tsugumichi. Yamagata's influence within the army became so strong that he was widely dubbed its "supreme deity."

Having begun as a soldier, Yamagata naturally emerged on the political stage somewhat later than Itō. He was appointed home minister in 1883, prime minister in 1889, and president of the Privy Council in 1893. However, he had the advantage of army backing, and unlike Itō he surrounded himself with a large clique of personal followers that extended widely across palace, political, and official circles. Constantly working on strategies to maintain and extend this clique network, Yamagata used it as leverage to strengthen his control over politics and government. He was eminently successful; in time, he became powerful enough in the political world to confront Itō directly.

Itō and Yamagata differed not only in their personal character, but also, on many occasions, in their opinions about politics. One of the most bitter collisions arose when Itō, more and more convinced of the need for a political party behind him, set up the Seiyūkai. With his rigid and lifelong commitment to the transcendence principle, Yamagata found Itō's ideas and actions repugnant. Thereafter, the gulf between the two men grew even wider. They also directly opposed each other on foreign policy when the Anglo-Japanese Alliance of 1902 was being discussed. Some heated exchanges ensued, Itō pressing for peaceful relations with Russia, and Yamagata the spokesman for close ties with Britain. The alliance eventually went through, and Yamagata then set about curtailing Itō's influence. With assistance from Prime Minister Katsura, the leading member of his clique, Yamagata was able to gain the emperor's agreement for his plans. So in 1903, Itō was suddenly appointed president of the Privy Council, the emperor's supreme advisory body, by imperial mandate, making it obligatory for him to give up the presidency of the Seiyūkai. That was a carefully contrived stratagem. At the time, Itō was a genrō while also president of the Seiyūkai, which enabled him to exert power on two fronts. To Prime Minister Katsura, Itō's strategic position was an insufferable obstacle to his administration. From Yamagata's point of view, forcing Itō to relinquish the presidency of the Seiyūkai would boost his protégé Katsura and also check the growth of party influence in government. Yamagata's stratagem worked, leaving Itō furious, but powerless to disobey imperial orders.

Enmity between Itō and Yamagata surfaced on many other occasions, but the net effect was to make Itō always deeply suspicious of Yamagata and to put him on constant guard against

[15]

the moves of this introspective and calculating man. In return, Yamagata disliked Itō with unusual intensity. Ozaki Yukio, a famous politician who knew both men well, relates that one day while talking about the past Yamagata suddenly began to speak more heatedly, using oddly polite expressions to describe a difference of opinion. "My superior did not like it," "my superior disagreed," he kept saying. Ozaki thought for a moment that he was talking about Emperor Meiji, but listening more closely, he realized that Yamagata was describing a quarrel with Itō. Yamagata's unnaturally polite tone was laced with bitter sarcasm. Whenever the conversation came around to Itō, Yamagata invariably stiffened, and he was always antagonistic.[2]

Highly Conceited

Itō's character undoubtedly had qualities that provoked such resentment. Major General Miura Gorō, a fellow Chōshū leader, once commented that Yamagata always referred to himself as a simple soldier and never affected to be more than a very ordinary man. In contrast, said Miura, Itō believed the world did not appreciate his great qualities, and he was always harping on them.[3] Itō was well known for his conceit. At best he could be called openhearted; at worst, childish. But in any event he was generally guileless and straightforward. He made little effort to suppress his sense of self-importance but rather, openly displayed it. Among the Chinese poems that he loved to compose, many express pride in himself. In one, he writes:

> With high spirits soaring to the heavens,
> Who under the rising sun
> Has exalted the emperor's honor?
> At work in my fine mansion, draining three cups of wine,
> I have as my friends all the Great Heroes of the nation.

This well-known verse was composed while Itō was governor of Hyōgo prefecture in 1869, when his memorial on national policy provoked a fierce uproar among other domain leaders of the time. Again, when the constitution was promulgated on 11 February 1889, the emperor's birthday, Itō wrote:

[16]

After twenty years of service in state affairs,
I have submitted a draft constitution to the emperor.
Looking toward the West, assessing both merits and
    defects,
My mind has ranged extensively over past history in
    detailed and exact study.
A great restoration has been achieved, linking the emperor
    with the Sun Goddess.
To open up the nation was a decision with grand results
    beyond all the expectations of wise men.
Now it is the emperor's wish to carry on government
    in collaboration with the people.
Everlasting honor and devotion to His Imperial Majesty!

Here is another. In 1905, after signing the Treaty of Portsmouth, Itō went to Seoul as special envoy to negotiate with the
Korean government and sign a convention making Korea a
Japanese protectorate. On his return to Japan after carrying out
this mission, he composed the following poem:

Despite old age, how could I refuse a task of such great
    difficulty?
Having managed to link both nations in a new treaty
After an absence abroad of thirty days,
On my return Mt. Fuji beams down a welcome.

Itō greatly admired his four famous predecessors: Sanjō Sanetomi, Iwakura Tomomi, Kido Takayoshi, and Ōkubo Toshimichi.
And he proudly nominated himself their heir. When talking with
people about national affairs, he often admitted that in various
ways he was not up to the standard of the "four great men now
dead and buried."[4] In the garden of his summer villa Sōrōkaku
at Ōiso, a coastal resort southwest of Tokyo, he constructed a
sanctuary in their honor, calling it the Hall of Four Heroes. With
the characteristic cigar still between his fingers, Itō often entered
the hall to linger a while in meditation. On the main wall was
a tablet inscribed by the classical scholar Mishima Chūshū with
a paean entitled "Ode for the Four Heroes Hall: Composed at
the Request of Prince Itō." It reads:

[17]

Who has built the Hall of Four Heroes? Lord Itō, president of the Privy Council. The Four Heroes in their portraits high up under the roof beam are splendid models, honored at all times. Princes Sanjō and Iwakura were superb noblemen, harmoniously directing the government with gentle warmth and sterling strength, like pearls and jade with gold and iron. They selected talent and promoted merit. Of course, they raised to high office lords Kido and Ōkubo, who served the government with virtuous knowledge and consummate skill, and whose great achievements rank with those of ministers Fang and Tu,[5] so renowned since antiquity. Looking back, we see that destiny entrusted power to simple soldiers, and so for over six hundred years there was rebellion and strife in the land. But now it is our good fortune that these Heroes have cleared away all the storms; the sun and moon shine once more, and the emperor's government blazes with glory.

To whom does the mantle pass, to take their achievements even further? At long last, fulfilling the people's dearest hopes, our Prince Itō has drawn up a constitution and enlarged the bounds of civilized government. By assisting Korea and curbing China, he has also elevated the military. May this edifice long endure, and when later joined by Itō be acclaimed as the Hall of Five Heroes!

Journalist Yamaji Aizan remarked about this flowery tribute, "Even if not composed by Itō himself, he must certainly have given tacit consent for it to be displayed on the wall. . . . To have had no qualms about putting up such a self-eulogy— clearly he was a very conceited man."[6]

Hida Chiho, a favorite mistress of Itō, in her later years recalled that "he never finished a letter the first time round, but would always amend one part or another. When I asked him, 'Why, Sir, do you so often correct what you have written?' He replied, 'You will probably not understand how I feel about this, but people are always likely to preserve my letters with great care. If they tore them up and threw them away, well and good. But if they insist on keeping them, my letters will remain for future ages to see, so I must not write carelessly.' "

After Itō's death, a series of memoirs under a pen name appeared in the *Tokyo Asahi* newspaper. The author is reputed to have been stenographer Hayashi Shigeatsu. Writing about Itō's speeches, he observed that Itō was very fond of the word "great" and constantly used expressions such as "greatness," "great achievement," "great, distinguished service." Even when writing the compound word "unusual," he had a quaint habit of following early Chinese variants to use "great" as the first calligraphic sign.[7] It is very interesting to speculate on the underlying reasons for Itō's delight in epic poems and heroes, and his constant use of the word "great."

When talking with visitors, too, Itō tended to be contentious and bombastic, expounding his views with intense conviction and giving full vent to his feelings. Mutsu Munemitsu, who rose to high office under Itō's patronage and knew him well, wrote an anonymous article in 1897 entitled "The Conversational Habits of the Genrō." According to Mutsu, Itō loved conversation and could go on for hours, never seeming to tire of talking with his visitors. But his manner of conversation "was largely like a lecture; he loved having others simply listen and gave no chance for them to say anything. Many people truly enjoyed his talks. They admired his brilliant arguments and found them instructive, but now and again his long-winded monologues just tired people out, especially when, as often happened, he kept coming back to a review of his own career."[8]

Right up to his final years Itō's inclination to vaunt his own importance did not diminish. Yamagata presented himself very differently. He had a habit of calling himself a "simple soldier," too naive to be deeply versed in politics, and in conversation he remained reserved, modest, and taciturn. He preferred to listen solemnly to what his visitors had to say—or at least appear to listen—which made a pleasant impression on them. Itō's undisguised pride in his own merits led him to make boastful statements unthinkable from Yamagata.

As his poems suggest, Itō felt that the fate of the nation rested on his shoulders and that he was a kind of people's saviour. In 1891, when as prime minister he decided resign, to Yamagata recommended Itō as his successor. When summoned by the emperor and asked to form a cabinet, Itō refused. He explained that although the constitution was now in force, "the people are still in a backward condition and to carry on constitutional government remains exceedingly difficult. Whoever is made prime minister will find it hard to stay in office for very long. If I, Hirobumi, am appointed prime minister, I shall either be assassinated or blown up by a bomb; after such a calamity, who would there be to assist the emperor in carrying on the government?" Tormented by deep anxiety about the future, he could not in good conscience comply. So the emperor, Itō suggested, should ask the Satsuma leaders Saigō Tsugumichi or Matsukata Masayoshi to be prime minister.[9]

Around this time, when talking with Sasaki Takayuki, one of his palace advisers, Emperor Meiji observed that "Itō, supremely confident in his talents, is very self-centered. If anyone else of his caliber could be found, the two of them could check and balance each other, to good effect; but no such person is available. There is a dearth of leading men. . . . Itō has become an overweening egotist, assuming that what Bismarck is to Germany or Li Hung-chang to China, he is to Japan. This makes things very difficult. I would like to find an able person who could act as a foil to Itō, but I cannot think of one."[10] Actually, the emperor trusted Itō deeply, as many examples show, but at times the self-importance of this loyal statesman was too inflated even for the emperor himself.

In their younger years before the Restoration, the Sat-Chō leaders had experienced at first-hand the deep national crisis brought about by the appearance of Commodore Perry's squadron of Black Ships in 1853 to demand the opening of Japan; many of them became fervent nationalists eager to restore the emperor, overthrow the Bakufu, and oust the foreigners. Holding high office in the new Meiji government, they took upon themselves the monumental task of transforming Japan into a modern industrial state within a single generation. Consequently, the new Japan that emerged under Emperor Meiji was very dear to them, as if almost a part of themselves. That sentiment perhaps helps to explain the kind of intense loyalty they felt toward the nation, a feeling much less apparent in the generation of leaders who succeeded them. In Itō's case, this spirit of loyalty gave a higher dimension to his self-importance and generated in him a dedicated nationalism of great strength. His overweening conceit when

[20]

transformed in this way worked to refine and concentrate his devotion toward the nation. The genuine integrity of Itō's patriotism drew praise from many quarters. After Itō's death, Ozaki Yukio observed that despite his mistakes, Itō was above malice or self-seeking. His conduct of public affairs was "fair, impartial, and generous. . . . He must be acclaimed a great statesman."[11] Inukai Tsuyoshi, a consistent political enemy of Itō and a man renowned for his sharp tongue, remarked at the time of Itō's assassination that despite being a member of the Chōshū clique he was comparatively fair in matters of government.[12]

Many years later, Seiyūkai politician Okazaki Kunisuke recalled having listened, during a visit, to a long self-eulogy by Itō of his many achievements, upon which Okazaki congratulated him on having done so much in so short a time. Itō replied that this was simply doing as one should. Many people were too tied up in family affairs. On duty at the office they gave their mind to the nation, yet on returning home they gave all their attention to their own family. In his own case, Itō continued, "Whether I was having fun with geisha, drinking *saké* or joking with people, the word 'nation' was always uppermost in my mind. I never gave any thought to the future of my family. At all times and in all circumstances, I cared only for the nation. No wonder I could accomplish so much."[13] Such bragging statements quite possibly contain a fair measure of truth.

Hunger for Praise

It is not hard to picture Itō as some of his contemporaries saw him—always eager to be admired and lauded as a superior person. He craved praise, honor, and glory in an almost childlike way that colored his behavior and innermost thoughts. In one illuminating anecdote, Ichijima Kenkichi, a follower of Ōkuma, described Itō's arrival at the town of Atami near his home. The residents held a reception for their distinguished visitor. While leading citizens made speeches praising him, Itō sat in a slightly raised chair looking proudly down on the assembly; he simply nodded with approval at the laudatory welcome, uttering not a single word in reply. As a member of the audience, Ichijima found Itō's bearing arrogant and undemocratic, typical of a lordly bureaucrat. To Itō, such praise was apparently no more than his just due.

Another well-known aspect of Itō's character was his penchant for decorations and medals. He loved to attach a gleaming array of medals to his chest and strut around with a self-important air. In his latter years when he became resident general of Korea, Itō designed the official uniforms for the administration. Each rank had its respective gold or silver chevrons and stars; epaulets and swords were prescribed for dress uniform. The dress uniform of the resident general himself was the most splendid of all—wide, gold-braid chevrons, three gold stars, and bushy gold epaulets. Festooned in this showy uniform, jingling with medals and girt with sword, Itō made a triumphant appearance at official ceremonies. He also designed the resident general's flag. As he entered or departed from his official residence, the guard lined up and gave him the salute due a field marshal. This was all very much to Itō's liking. In the mid-1890s, politician Kōmuchi Tomotsune slyly predicted to Ozaki Yukio that one day Itō would fulfill his cherished dream to deck himself out with military uniform and ceremonial sword. Years later, when Ozaki saw Itō in his resident general's uniform, complete with sword, pompously frequenting official banquets, he was much amused to remember Kōmuchi's prophecy.[14]

Granted such tastes, Itō's appointment as head of the Palace Organization Bureau in 1884 comes as no surprise. Then, with the additional post of Lord Chamberlain, he took great pains to draw up a new official system for the palace and to issue an ordinance setting up five grades of nobility. In retrospect, it seems quite in character that Itō formulated a solemn and dignified "Order of Honor" for the palace. Many years later, genrō Saionji Kimmochi said about this, "In Admiral Yamamoto Gonnohyōe's opinion, one of Itō's achievements was to enhance honor and reverence for the emperor, and I agree. But while Itō and I concurred in the merits of this, our approaches differed a little. People like myself had a deep respect for the emperor, both personally and as liberals, but we hoped to make things more friendly and informal. Itō, however, was hopelessly enthralled by solemnity and magnificence; he always used very honorific language when addressing the emperor. Even when it was quite proper to describe himself in the first person, he would say 'Your subject' or 'Your subject Hirobumi.' On one occasion, the emperor playfully remarked that 'when Itō comes for an audience, you need to brush up on your Chinese classics.' Carried away by such feelings, Itō raised the palace official system and ceremonies to new heights of dignity and grandeur, imposing strict lines of definition between ruler and subject, superior and inferior.''[15]

Itō is said to have shown the same combination of submissive loyalty and formal propriety in his relations with the Mōri, feudal lords of the previous Chōshū domain. After the Restoration, he was reputed always to have attended the New Year, birthday, and other celebrations of the Mōri family. On such occasions, when a large number of previous Chōshū samurai gathered together, Itō always took the lowest place, despite being urged to move higher in the seating order. But if his former lord commanded, Itō would hesitantly comply and move up toward the middle.

Itō's attitude to the emperor deserves a few further comments. Together with many Sat-Chō leaders, he had actively participated in the 1860s movement to overthrow the Bakufu and restore governing power to the emperor. To these loyalists, the emperor was an exalted and glittering symbol. After the Meiji Restoration they proclaimed that the new regime was in substance a return to ancient rule; they elevated the emperor to a lofty position as the reigning sovereign of Japan and constructed a massive national regime around him. In reality, domain-centered cliques had exploited the 1860s loyalist movement in their drive to gain political power. Their claim to be acting in accordance with the emperor's will provided a justification for this. Consequently, the Sat-Chō leaders always attributed supreme authority to the emperor. Their ideal of the emperor and their feelings toward him were largely the result of the circumstances in which they themselves had attained power. Itō was no exception. Furuya Hisatsuna, long employed as his private secretary, records that Itō paid five formal visits to the chief imperial shrine at Ise in Mie prefecture. The first was in November 1902. Itō later told Furuya that he went on that occasion because as president of the Seiyūkai he had to voice open opposition to "His Imperial Majesty's cabinet" of Katsura, and needed to report his innermost feelings to the shrine deity. In the light of Itō's ideal of the emperor, his visit to Ise was perhaps not just an empty pose. Again, it is well known that Itō won the deep trust of the emperor. Only Itō and long-serving Lord Chamberlain Tanaka Mitsuaki are said to have been given chairs when received in audience by the emperor. In February 1909 the empress presented Itō with a poem in her own handwriting:

> The Heavenly Gods understand—
> A subject's heart as he serves his sovereign with
>   faithfulness.

Kurihara Hirota, an official of the imperial household department and a personal attendant on Emperor Meiji, recalled another anecdote. Itō liked cigars—he was never without one. One day he was walking along a corridor in the palace puffing away vigorously when a servant, unaware of Itō's identity, stopped him and drew his attention to the no-smoking rule. Itō replied, "You probably don't know the reason why smoking is forbidden in the palace corridors. It is because of the danger from lighted tobacco. But my cigar is not of a cheap variety such as would drop off sparks or ash. It is absolutely safe, so there is no need to worry." He then continued on his way. During his audience with the emperor, Itō reported what had happened. Later he went to the imperial household department and on meeting the Lord Chamberlain, with Kurihara and others also present, he told them of the corridor incident, saying, "I was reprimanded by a servant, but on reporting the matter to the emperor he gave me leave to ignore the rule."

Kurihara also related that one year, on the emperor's birthday, when both civil and military officials attended the palace in ceremonial dress, Itō came in the uniform of the resident general of Korea. A master of ceremonies pointed out to Itō that he was improperly dressed. According to current regulations, the necklet of the Supreme Order of the Chrysanthemum could not be worn together with its grand cordon, as Itō was doing. This reproof

[24]

infuriated Itō, who retorted that if it was improper to wear the grand cordon with its necklet, then he would have to wear the grand cordon of a lesser order. That was most unreasonable. Any regulation requiring such a senseless thing ought to be revised immediately. Afterward Itō sent an opinion on the matter to the throne, and the Bureau of Decorations revised the regulations to allow the necklet and the grand cordon to be worn together. "At the time," continued Kurihara, "I thought there must have been good reason for Itō's opinion, but this aside, I was deeply impressed that in so many matters the emperor agreed to whatever Itō proposed." Yamagata is said to have envied the deep trust Itō enjoyed from Emperor Meiji, and to have questioned the throne on the desirability of granting such special confidence. Be that as it may, Itō gained such trust and often made use of it. Palace Chamberlain Hinonishi Sukehiro remembered Emperor Meiji's deep dejection after Itō's death in 1909, leading his entourage to feel that from then on the sovereign noticeably entered old age.[16]

Not a Clique-builder

Endowed with a substantial ego and abundant confidence in his talent and ability, Itō was inclined to despise other people and regard them as stupid. He tended to deny his trusted protégés freedom to put their talents into full play, but simply used them as tools for the task in hand. Thus it seems no accident that long-term employees of Itō—such as Itō Miyoji, Kaneko Kentarō, Suematsu Kenchō, Inoue Kowashi, Furuya Hisatsuna, and Samejima Takenosuke—were all people who excelled at carrying out orders obediently and efficiently. Itō also paid little attention to the future careers of his employees, and as a result he never became the center of a clique. Furuya Hisatsuna records that when Inukai Tsuyoshi was struck from the register of the Kenseihontō party in 1909, a certain magazine playfully observed that if Itō died, not a single person would "follow him in death by ceremonial suicide," the traditional mark of ultimate loyalty, but at least twenty people would do so for Inukai. Commenting on this article to Furuya, Itō said, "The author intended to criticize me and praise Inukai. But actually I find

[25]

such comments pleasing. What has kept me working for the nation is the thought that if ever a crisis arises, I am ready, with fifty million fellow subjects, to die for the emperor. By putting people under obligation to me I could certainly build up a personal clique. But if I did, what would become of my loyalty to the emperor? I don't want anybody to "follow me in death." I am the emperor's loyal servant. And my most cherished hope is for all my fellow subjects to be loyal and brave servants of the emperor."[17] It is a fact that Itō possessed nothing resembling a clique and made no attempt to form one, in complete contrast to Yamagata. Both his sense of personal loyalty to the emperor and his powerful conceit seem to have worked against this.

Judgment and Adaptability

On the other hand, Itō's sense of self-importance was kept in check by unusually incisive powers of judgment and an elastic ability to adapt to changing circumstances. These qualities often saved him from falling into the quixotic mishaps that his conceit might otherwise have precipitated. Basically uncombative in character, he had a natural inclination for compromise and harmony, which made it easier for him to adapt and change when necessary. He was too open and straightforward to enjoy quarreling with people. There was nothing in Itō of the dark stratagems Yamagata was always devising. As prime minister, Yamagata came prepared with detailed, secret plans when he faced the Diet and skillfully manipulated it. Itō often simply dissolved the Diet to overcome opposition; or if this failed he used imperial edicts to gain control. As a result, he was bitterly criticized for shielding himself behind the emperor and adopting unconstitutional tactics, but no one could ever accuse him of deviousness or subterfuge.

Itō always liked making speeches. These were majestic, powerful, and resonant, but also displayed his talent for compromise and harmony. In delivery, he rarely raised his eyebrows, drew up his shoulders, or ranted—he spoke with half-closed eyes, patiently explaining his views. After his death, the *Tokyo Asahi* newspaper published an anonymous collection of reminiscences that describe Itō's public-speaking style in some detail. One re-

[26]

lated how, when summing up, he often used the words "probably" or "perhaps" to qualify his statements and thus avoided committing himself to hard and fast conclusions. He was a dignified speaker and his pronunciation was always precise; the words gave an impression of strength, but his manner of speaking was suave and careful. In an appraisal of Itō's speeches Ozaki Yukio said that "somehow, it was very hard to tie him down."[18]

As a Domestic Politician

In a compensatory balance of a very interesting kind, Itō's conceit was offset by his ability to judge and adapt. Whenever he foresaw strong opposition, he readily inclined to compromise and his conciliatory side appeared. On the other hand, when he judged the opposition to be weak, he took a tough stance and displayed his sense of self-importance to the full. His behavior in domestic politics demonstrates this flexibility, as when he made a sharp changeover on the issue of how to carry on constitutional government.

Just after the promulgation of the constitution in 1889, when Itō was president of the Privy Council, he made a speech to a conference of prefectural assembly chairmen then meeting in Tokyo. He told them that as an essential prerequisite for imperial rule, constitutional government had to be run on the basis of the transcendence principle. Afterward, Itō met his three young assistants—Inoue Kowashi, Itō Miyoji, and Kaneko Kentarō—in a separate room. One of them took issue with Itō, insisting on the need for a pro-government party. He pointed out that Prime Minister Kuroda, also, had announced recently that the transcendence principle would provide the keynote for constitutional government; this had to be carried on completely aloof from the political parties. But, the young man continued, when elections were held the people's parties were bound to win a majority on their platform of attacking the Sat-Chō regime and destroying clique government. Without a supporting party how could the cabinet hope to overcome the people's parties and control the Diet? Before the first election a pro-government party had to be formed. The other two young men agreed, but Itō contradicted them. Look at Bismarck in Germany, he said; was it not a fact that Bismarck had no party of his own? If the Diet was approached with sincerity, no political party could successfully oppose the government. All very well in theory, his three listeners rejoined, but surely rather specious. For in point of fact, the people's parties were determined to overthrow the Sat-Chō clique, and pleas for government measures, however sincere, would fall on deaf ears. Realistically, it was necessary to command a majority, and only a pro-government political party could do that. "You are infants," Itō countered, "you don't understand the realities of government."[19]

Sure enough, during the first Diet session the people's parties launched a vigorous attack on the Sat-Chō clique, and Itō himself was fiercely denounced. When the Diet reopened under the first Matsukata cabinet in 1891, Itō was already half-convinced that unless things improved the constitution would have to be suspended. Matsukata clashed with the Diet and dissolved it, but the election of early 1892 again resulted in an anti-cabinet majority. Itō thought for a time of resigning from his post as president of the Privy Council and setting up a new political party to support Matsukata. His faith in the transcendence principle had soon been shaken. When Matsukata resigned in 1892, Itō took over to form his second cabinet. By then he was fairly sure that later in the year the bitter struggle between the people's parties and the government would come to a head. Less than two years after his confident assertions to Inoue Kowashi and the others, Itō's attitude had undergone a radical change.

The second Itō cabinet was in office throughout the Sino-Japanese War years, 1894 to 1895, when for a time all political opposition was suspended as a patriotic gesture. When the war ended, under the convenient slogan of "postwar endeavor," Itō negotiated with the Jiyūtō and openly formed a coalition. He then brought Jiyūtō President Itagaki Taisuke into the cabinet as home minister. Itō had in fact established a pro-government party in a notable retreat from the transcendence principle. In the next few years, this new tactic of coalition with the people's parties devised by Itō was adopted by a succession of so-called Sat-Chō clique cabinets.

Further intractable developments in politics, especially during

[28]

his third cabinet of 1898, convinced Itō that such makeshift alliances with the people's parties no longer sufficed to keep constitutional government running well. That is why in 1900 he decided to organize a political party of his own, the Seiyūkai. In his manifesto for the new party, Itō did not openly recognize the principle of party cabinets; but even so, just in setting up the Seiyūkai, he had progressed a long way from the transcendence principle. It was at such times that Itō's adaptability stood him in good stead, allowing him to change tack when necessary to do so.

It is also noteworthy that the Seiyūkai was set up with the aim of controlling and running the Diet; it was not the result of any conviction that public opinion should be represented in politics. As Itō prepared to launch the new party, journalist Toyabe Shuntei wrote an article entitled "Is Itō Qualified to Be a Party Leader?" Hitting close to the mark, one feels, he observed that Itō was then "a politician of the first rank" but did not have the attributes needed to lead the people as a party president. Itō was basically a "prime minister of court government. . . . With his copious self-esteem he aspires to set himself up like some kind of monumental leader and relies too much on his own wisdom. He has scant respect for public opinion and is too engrossed in his own personal concerns and feelings. To lead the people and determine the public issues of the nation hand-in-hand with them is probably too much for such a finicky elitist."[20]

Diplomatic Style

In matters connected with foreign relations, the veteran Sat-Chō leaders were generally much more cautious than their successors. That was quite understandable, in view of the way they had fretted and agonized since pre-Restoration days over how to defend Japan's independence, both in name and reality, against the inroads of the Western Powers. Itō was extremely cautious in diplomacy. Sensitive and intelligent diplomacy, he believed, could disarm the antagonism of the Western Powers, and he never stopped trying to achieve this. Before the Sino-Japanese War, Itō regarded China as a powerful nation to be treated with respect and his attitude toward it was one of prudent caution. In

1894, during his second cabinet, relations between China and Japan deteriorated when both sides competed to intervene in Korea on the pretext of pacifying the Tonghak Uprising. Even so, Itō remained hopeful that the crisis could be resolved by diplomatic negotiations. That hope was dashed when hostilities broke out, as had been planned by Deputy Chief of Staff Kawakami Sōroku, Foreign Minister Munemitsu, Privy Council President Yamagata Aritomo, and others in the pro-war faction. After Russia occupied Manchuria in 1900, Itō clung to the possibility that war could be avoided by peaceful agreement. Both at the time of his appointment as resident general of Korea in 1906 and after he resigned that post in 1909, he opposed the outright annexation of Korea. His position on this issue, also, seems to have been determined by fears of arousing the antagonism of the Western Powers.

In September 1901, Itō went on a tour of Europe via the United States. His chief objective was to sound out the possibility of an agreement with Russia. On board ship from the United States to Europe, late at night in the deserted smoking room, Itō spoke at length and no doubt quite sincerely to his private secretary Furuya Hisatsuna: "Our nation has made great progress in barely forty years. Even more than we ourselves expected. But how will things go from now on? One cannot see two or three centuries ahead. We can only do our best for the future and hope that we will be succeeded by a new generation of able men. Even so, I am concerned about the attitudes of our people. If they are content with small successes and have no great and far-reaching ambitions, if the Yamato race thinks of itself as unique and outside the laws of human rise and decline, if it ignores the proper rights and interests of other nations and behaves outrageously, then national ruin is certain. They said in olden times that 'the proud man is shortlived'; this is true not only of individuals. When one looks in history at the rise and decline of nations, they are not destroyed from without; usually they destroy themselves. . . . Our people must be constantly warned that 'the high tree encounters strong wind.' "[21]

Itō was cautious in diplomacy when he feared antagonizing the Western Powers, but if the opposition appeared weak, he could be arrogant and demanding, fully indulging his passion for self-importance. Immediately after the Russo-Japanese War, for example, Itō went as special envoy to Korea, where he was in a position of uncontestable strength. In 1906, Korea became a protectorate after signing a convention with Japan. In his meetings with the ministers of the Korean government, Itō was completely overbearing, even menacing—no doubt because Russia, the United States, and Britain had already agreed to Korea becoming a Japanese protectorate by successive diplomatic agreements, such as the Treaty of Portsmouth, the Katsura-Taft Memorandum, and the Second Anglo-Japanese Alliance.

Alternating Strength and Weakness

Whether Itō's uncombative, compromising, and harmonizing side took the lead, or whether his sense of self-importance took over depended upon his judgment of the immediate situation. If his first decision proved clearly mistaken or if a major shift occurred, he was able to adapt and make a startling change. Toyabe Shuntei observed that when he felt secure, Itō was bombastic and boastful, but in the face of difficulty he tended to weaken, hesitate, and retreat from responsibility. So Toyabe dubbed him a "parade-ground general."[22] Journalist Tokutomi Sohō recalled that Itō tended to get carried away by his feelings— "when things went well for him, he was exultant, but his mood could change to utter dejection when things went badly; that transformation was even more startling than if spring suddenly turned to winter."[23]

Itō's lack of fighting spirit under trying circumstances and ready resort to compromise led his critics to decry him as "all things to all men," as unreliable, or such like. These strictures may have been justified, but it is also true that in the face of weak opposition he advanced boldly, borne up by his sense of self-importance. At such times his incisive powers of judgment came alive to generate and sustain numerous notable achievements. No matter what Itō's weaknesses were, his great contributions to the progress of Japan after the Restoration are enough to ensure him a secure place in history.

To the end of his days, Itō was as close as a brother to Inoue Kaoru. From the last days of the Bakufu, when they risked their

[31]

lives together as pro-emperor loyalists, these two Chōshū colleagues had been inseparable. No wonder, then, that Inoue joined Itō's first three cabinets and gave him strong support. He did not take office in Itō's fourth cabinet, but that was probably because it was based on the Seiyūkai and Inoue had not joined the party. Inoue was fearless and precipitate; when he put his mind to something he pressed on feverishly until completion, at times seeming reckless and even foolhardy. In these points he was quite a contrast to Itō. Rather than alienating the two, this was probably just what linked Itō and Inoue so strongly. Also, Inoue by nature liked to assist people. He was a true friend to Itō and in many ways helped compensate for his deficiencies.

The Private Man

Itō as a government official was a very different person from his off-duty counterpart. In private life his unaffected and congenial nature came to the fore. He liked to invite local residents to Sōrōkaku, his villa at Ōiso, and drink *saké* with them. He could often be found in his garden entertaining local fishermen, joining in songs and dances and helping to pass around the cups. On his walks he would often stop at the neighborhood sweetshops and stores to gossip, and he liked to discuss how the crops were progressing with farmers he met in pathways through the fields. He talked quite genuinely as an equal with such people, expecting no special respect. He was also known to spread a red blanket on the floor, get out the checkerboard and play *go* with his police guards. In many ways, this was the real Itō. His enjoyment of simple company was quite free from condescension or a "common-man" pose—it was quite genuine.

On the other hand, when he was conscious of dealing with the local townspeople in an official capacity, his self-esteem got to work and his manner changed. On the occasion of Yamagata's death in 1922, Head Officer Kikuchi Yoshiji of the Kanagawa Ashigarishimo rural division recalled his days as chief of Ōiso Police Station. At the time, both Yamagata and Itō had villas in Ōiso, and Kikuchi often called on them. On such occasions Itō usually remained seated, with his legs crossed carelessly, not bothering to offer his callers a seat, and would talk freely about anything that came to mind. Yamagata, in contrast, was formally attired and drew himself up politely, urging his visitors to be seated before the conversation began. Kikuchi heard that the Satsuma leader Saigō Tsugumichi, an especially valued friend, was the only person accorded a formal farewell when he visited Itō. Apart from him, Itō never accompanied his departing guests outside the room. In contrast, Yamagata always saw his visitors off; in the case of ordinary people like Kikuchi, despite all their remonstrations, he would always stand up and accompany them as far as the door of the room.[24]

Everyday Amenities

Above all, Itō treasured life at Sōrōkaku, though official business did not allow him to stay there all the time. In earlier years he lived in Tokyo, but sold his house in Shinagawa Yatsuyama in 1889; thereafter, except for a short period when he lived in Shiba Isarago, Itō had no regular abode in the capital. For nearly twenty years whenever government business kept him in Tokyo, he lodged at official residences, the Imperial Hotel, or rented houses. He returned to live in Tokyo in 1908 when he reconstructed Onshikan mansion at Ōimachi, on the southwest outskirts of the city. Onshikan was a gift from the emperor when a new official system for the palace was completed in January 1907. This task had been undertaken on Itō's initiative, so in gratitude the emperor presented him with one of the mansions within the Akasaka Detached Palace compound.

Itō was quite matter of fact about where he lived, often saying that however splendid your house, you had to leave it behind when you died. If a house kept out rain and frost, and if it was convenient to live in, that was enough. When rebuilding was needed, he took no interest in situation, design, materials, or construction, but simply wanted everything to be done as quickly as possible. He prided himself most on speed—the fact that the new building had taken only so many months and repairs so many days, that all was completed with dispatch. He did not select the site for Onshikan with any care but had it constructed on a plot in the middle of a barley field. Quite indifferent to garden layout, he planted hardly a single tree in the spacious grounds of this mansion. When Inoue called there in 1909, just before Itō went on his final voyage to Manchuria, and saw the miserable state of the garden, he suggested that at least a stone lantern should be installed. No, too expensive, replied Itō; if he was going to spend money, he would rather buy a good sword.

Sōrōkaku, built in 1896, was his favorite villa, and in Itō's lifetime everyone had heard of it. To contemporaries, the hastily constructed edifice looked like a rural post office or police station. The original house was so narrow that Itō added two extensions to it, making its outside appearance very ugly. Journalist Kawamoto Ujō described the house in some detail. It was situated in a field among a few plum trees, he said, with flowers and shrubs dotted here and there in a most haphazard way. In one corner stood the Four Heroes Hall, right next to a compost heap. Built on a stone foundation, in style and size the hall looked rather like a Tokyo police outpost, a very unimposing sight. The end wall was graced by a tablet inscribed "Four Heroes Hall" in the calligraphy of the crown prince, but above it the four portraits were just crude lithographs of a kind on sale everywhere. No vase or offering table funished the hall, only a single rattan chair. Yamagata, in contrast, put heart and soul into planning and building his residence and summer villa, helping to direct construction and taking infinite care to create beautiful gardens.

Itō was equally carefree about food and clothing. Both at Sōrōkaku and in Tokyo, his domestic life was very simple. He got up early in the morning, kept no fixed mealtimes, and dined on very plain food. After Itō's death, Saionji Kimmochi recalled, "I was once invited to Itō's for a meal, but the coarseness of it was most embarrassing." Saionji's summer villa Tonarisō was next door to Sōrōkaku, so he probably suffered this experience at Ōiso. Itō loved cigars, and also had a great fondness for *saké*, often drinking late into the night. But he enjoyed tippling as a pastime in itself, and he is reputed to have been a very poor judge of the quality of what he drank. When at home he did not like to trouble the servants; he went to the kitchen himself when he wanted a drink and returned to the room with a cupful or small bottle of *saké*. His way of life was always rough and ready, rather like that of a young bachelor.

[34]

Itō also had no desire to accumulate wealth and was quite inept at managing money. Now and then he spent lavishly, but those times were said to be special occasions, such as after receiving a gift from the emperor. When consulted about financial affairs, he would reply that his only care was to spend money, so people should discuss such complicated matters with his friend and colleague Inoue Kaoru. According to another story, Itō's wife once asked him for one month's housekeeping expenses. He replied that he was out of money, but if really necessary would sell Sōrōkaku and move to Onshikan. His wife laughed at such impracticality: how could he think that they needed to sell the house to raise such a modest sum! "Well, anyway," said Itō nonchalantly, "just do your best with what we have." When living in Ōiso he was said to have put money aside in a table drawer, taking out a handful of notes and stuffing it in his pocket before going out. After visiting a favorite inn, such as Shōsenkaku, he often carelessly pulled out a wad of notes and gave it to the waitresses, uncounted. During his term as resident general of Korea, on the way home from Seoul he often stayed in Nagoya at an inn called Uobun. The proprietress told journalist Matsumaru Kenzō that once after a cheerful and noisy party, Itō left without paying the bill. Two or three years later he returned with a bag full of banknotes, scooped out a generous handful and passed them over, paying no attention to whether they tallied with the long-overdue bill or not. After Itō's death, Inukai Tsuyoshi said of him, 'Saigō Takamori apart, he was the only government leader who was simple and straightforward in money matters.'[25] No unsavory rumors of financial corruption ever sullied Itō's name, and his honesty was widely acknowledged.

Tastes

In 1908, a well-known magazine published some recollections by an elderly man who had been employed in the official residence at Kōjimachi Nagatachō during the terms of several prime ministers. He remembered Itō as the most careless of them all, quite oblivious of the furnishings of the reception or other rooms, and indifferent to good pictures or hanging scrolls. Even if he acquired something costly and rare, in no time at all he would give it away without a second thought. He paid no heed when the servants neglected to sweep the garden or finish their other duties, so they were overjoyed whenever Itō became prime minister. On one occasion a rare peony with red and white blossoms arrived as a year-end present. For a day or two it stood on top of a desk as a curiosity but was left unwatered, until Itō ordered it to be thrown out to a corner of the garden. A nuisance, he said. So the servants did exactly that. Whenever Itō was in office the official residence became quite slovenly.[26]

Itō did not care for antiques, *bonsai* dwarf-trees, the tea ceremony, Noh drama, or other such fashionable pursuits. But he was interested in swords, and especially in his latter years developed quite a liking for them. Itō loved books and reading. In one of his poems he wrote:

> After several days away from home,
> Deprived of my beloved books,
> I return, sit at my desk, and
> Feel as though I have rejoined
> The great men of antiquity.

Besides Japanese and Chinese books, he took pains to read foreign newspapers and magazines, sometimes visiting Maruzen, Tokyo's leading bookstore, to buy them. Even when he was very busy he enjoyed composing Chinese-style poetry.

In general, true to his penchant for harmony, Itō did not like competitive games. An exception was *go*, which he played whenever he had spare time. He was not, however, very good at it. He moved his pieces quickly; a short game with Itō took only fifteen minutes, a long one not more than thirty. He often played several games within the hour. He would fire off his plays impatiently, pushing hard until his partner got rattled and began to make mistakes. Then his whole face lit up with childish triumph; "Well, how is it? What do you make of that?" Itō would chortle, brimming with good humor. And if the game was going well for him, he liked to hum cheerful little tunes, or imitate the twanging strings of the *shamisen*. Beaming at his pained opponent and swelling with pride, he would ask, "How are you doing? Have you had enough?" It is interesting to see how Itō's character revealed itself in this game. He seemed to enjoy it when he got the better of opponents and made them suffer.

During the later years of his term as resident general of Korea, he would invite all sorts of close friends to play *go* at the Seoul official residence, keeping them there into the dead of night, and urging them on with rousing bursts of "Well, let's go to it! Let's go to it!" Just after Itō's assassination, the magazine *Manchōhō* published an article entitled "Itō and His Good Friend, the High Official's Wife." This lady recounted that her husband held a post in the resident general's office and Itō came almost every day to her house. On arrival, he always went to change into a simple cotton robe; barefooted, he would then proceed to a tiny upstairs room to play *go* with her husband and a neighbor, Lieutenant General Murata. If Itō lost, he would go on tirelessly playing game after game well into the night. In many ways the contrast was startling between this man and the Itō who bore himself so proudly in his splendid uniform beneath the flag of the resident general of Korea.

Itō said of himself, "By nature, I am content with little and give absolutely no thought to saving money. . . . I have no wish to live in a splendid house and so have no urge to heap up wealth. What I like best is a geisha companion to entertain me after work." Itō's favorite pastime was womanizing. When he died, the newspapers were full of reminiscences by people who had known him well. Many of them were female managers of restaurants and red-light establishments. Itō enjoyed himself with great glee, full of mirth and clatter like a young boy. When drunk he liked to sing the ditty: "When eager lovers get together like this—a simple four-mat room, no noise except the kettle boiling—they seesaw like two pine needles in the wind!" In her reminiscences, the famous head geisha O-Koi offers a glimpse of Itō the libertine. "Itō's conversations with geisha consisted almost entirely of improvised songs. Out they came, fast and funny, old and new. He seemed to have an unending supply of abusive ditties that just tripped off his tongue, one after another. . . . If there was a geisha he particularly liked, he would contrive for her companions to be sent home early. One way of suggesting this was to come out several times in succession with a favorite ditty such as 'Oh, what a boor and a nuisance you are!' Getting

[37]

the point, the other geisha would say, 'Oh, am I? Sorry!' and hastily leave the room."

Ozaki Yukio believed that a weakness for women was Itō's greatest fault. But they never dominated him. Like someone who buys flowers at a festival, admires them for a while, and throws them away, he would take up with women, enjoy himself, and then forget all about them. The same tended to be true of his trusted protégés. Itō would discover a talent in a person and use it to the full, but when no longer needed, its possessor would be allowed to depart without further thought for his future career. Yamagata, according to his follower Kiyoura Keigo, was completely different. He never paid much attention to the cleverness or ability of the people he employed. As long as an employee had no great faults, Yamagata would never abandon him or fail to provide support. People employed by Yamagata repaid him by intense devotion. Kiyoura goes on to say that Itō's behavior toward women was in keeping with much else he did. He was on amorous terms with numerous geisha and young waitresses, but he dismissed them from mind as soon as his appetite was sated. He would often assist other men to win the favors of women he had previously been intimate with.

Itō's frank and artless character appears clearly enough in this delight in attractive women, but his debauched life was notorious enough to earn him an unsavory reputation. After his assassination in 1909, an imperial order was issued for a state funeral to be held for him. The education ministry notified all schools in the nation that on the appointed day respect should be shown by giving appropriate moral lectures with Itō as the subject.

Shortly afterward, the *Tokyo Asahi* newspaper, in an article entitled "A Trial for Teachers," reported as follows: When the notification arrived, schoolteachers hurriedly got together biographies and newspaper articles about Itō. But Itō "had certain faults to which great men in East Asia are prone," as was well known to most young people. How to make Itō the subject of moral instruction was therefore quite a headache. A middle school teacher and a primary school headmaster confessed to a journalist that they had never been so troubled as by this notification from the education ministry. It was easy to recount Itō's services to the nation, but when speaking of the man himself, it was hard to handle certain faults that young pupils would necessarily associate with him.

At a certain Akasaka primary school, for example, a second-year pupil, having just heard the required lecture on Itō, said that his father told him Itō was a man of abandoned conduct and not to be imitated. Was this in fact true? The perplexed teacher was reduced to the lame reply that such criticism might perhaps be mistaken. The headmistress of a girl's high school found herself praising Itō as a benefactor to women, at which the girls tugged each other's sleeves and finally all burst out laughing. The headmistress was left standing sheepishly on the platform, without a word to say.

It was clearly necessary, continued the teachers, to make careful "preparations" for the Itō lectures. Any person selected as a moral example had to have suitable qualifications, but in Itō's case "these were largely lacking." The education ministry must have known that famous political leaders were often poor models for moral instruction. The recent notification was outrageous. But orders were orders, so the schools would just have to do their best, pointing out Itō's merits and defects and telling pupils to adopt the former and avoid the latter.

In 1895, at the time of his second cabinet, Itō hosted a dance party at the prime minister's residence. Scandalous rumors about his behavior circulated afterward, and he was lambasted in the newspapers. When someone urged him to order the suppression of these hostile articles, Itō just laughed them off—if public morality was at stake he would naturally have to take notice, but there was no need to do so when sporadic attacks were made on the reputation of individuals.[27] Such a distinction between public and private life was perfectly natural to Itō. "Drunk, my head pillowed on a beauty's lap; awake and sober, grasping power to govern the nation." This pre-Restoration popular ditty, often sung by young, pro-emperor loyalists steeped in debauchery and political intrigue, never lost its appeal for Itō as an ideal way of life.

Even in everyday matters, Itō was careful to draw a clear line between public and private. He traveled constantly between Ōiso and Tokyo and always took great care to pay his train fare. The other genrō living in Ōiso are said to have traveled on the train free, by "face," not deigning to buy a ticket. Itō was very critical of such behavior—it was only normal when traveling by train to pay the fare, he told others. Again, when resident general of Korea, he had three maidservants to attend to his personal needs, but never employed them on any occasion connected with official business. When wearing his uniform and attending to his duties, he always used the residency servants to make tea or light the tobacco. As many examples illustrate, Itō's behavior as a public official was vastly different from that of the private man, and the distinction he drew between these two capacities was basic to his character.

His Death and Its Significance

Itō resigned as resident general of Korea in June 1909. Later that year he set out on a tour of Manchuria, his chief purpose being to meet the Russian Finance Minister V. N. Kokovtsov at Harbin for discussions on Japan's East Asia policy, in which Korea had a pivotal place. On the night of 14 October, setting out from Sōrōkaku, Itō wrote this poem aboard the westward-bound train:

> Leaving home for afar on an autumn evening
> When chatting at the carriage window ended,
> I still seem to hear the plaintive humming
>   of insects.
> Tomorrow morning, the mountainous waves
>   of Chili Gulf,
> On this journey to mourn Japan's loyal dead.

Next morning, Itō sailed from Moji to Dairen. Arriving in South Manchuria, he paid his first visit to Hill 203 at Lushun, a battlefield fiercely contested in the Russo-Japanese War. A surge of feeling overwhelmed him. Afterward, he wrote:

> Hill 203, so long in my thoughts,
> The mountain grave of 18,000 soldiers.
> I went up to see it today and was profoundly moved,
> Gazing uselessly as white clouds circled the peak.

[40]

Leaving Lushun, Itō passed through Changchun, and on the morning of 26 October his train arrived at Harbin. The day was dark and gloomy. A cold northwind blew fiercely, the sky threatening snow. Winter was about to descend on Manchuria. Itō wore a heavy greatcoat over his formal attire and a hard bowler hat on his head as he stepped down to the platform. Finance Minister Kokovtsov ordered a guard of soldiers to stand to attention, and Itō shook the hands of the consuls from various nations. Then, as he turned to meet the Japanese contingent waiting to greet him, pistol shots rang out from behind the Russian guard, and Itō collapsed. The assassin was a young Korean, An Chung-gun, a member of the Korean independence movement. Seized by the Russian military police, he gave three shouts of "Long live Korea!" The dying Itō was carried back into his train carriage. He asked who had attacked him; Murota Yoshifumi, one of his entourage, told him that it was a Korean and that he had been taken into custody. Itō murmured, "What a fool!" Those were his last words. He was sixty-nine years old.

The assassin was tried for murder in February 1910 at the Lushun regional court. An Chung-gun's defense was that the emperor of Japan, when declaring war on Russia in 1904, had announced that the object was to maintain peace in East Asia and guarantee the independence of Korea. At that time the Korean people were delighted, and many of them had worked for Japan during the war. When hostilities ended, the Korean people joined with the Japanese soldiers in victory celebrations, confident that their own nation had won too, and that their independence was now firmly assured. But soon afterward, Itō arrived as resident general, whereupon conventions were signed making Korea a protectorate of Japan, which subsequently tightened its control. This clearly went against the wishes of the emperor of Japan as announced in the declaration of war. Consequently, the people of Korea regarded Itō as an enemy. Convinced that Itō's existence was a major obstacle to the achievement of Korean independence, An Chung-gun had resorted to this violent act. He was sentenced to death and executed.

In a short biography of Itō written in 1912, Uematsu Takaaki observed that several of the great leaders of the Meiji era had been killed or wounded by assassins, often because they were

[41]

"warlike" in character and behavior, provoking violence against themselves. But according to Uematsu, Itō was not that kind of man; he knew how "we must heed the portents by which divine providence gives warning to man."[28] So what does Itō's death tell us about this mysterious force? The diplomacy of Meiji Japan was very cautious toward the Western Powers, and mostly co-operative and submissive in tone. But in relations with Korea, it veered sharply to threats and aggression. How reminiscent of Itō himself—timid against strong resistance and overbearing toward weak. When one considers the role of Itō in Japan-Korea relations, both before and after his appointment as resident general, he can truly be called the very personification of the two-sided diplomacy just described. His conduct of relations with Korea was completely consistent with his character. The policy he adopted toward it was, in Uematsu's words, "warlike," and as a result he did indeed provoke violence against himself.

How does Itō's death at Harbin look from the calmer historical perspective of today? The young assassin who killed him was backed by the bitter anger of the Korean people, robbed of their independence. Preserving Japan's independence had been a major motivation behind the Meiji Restoration. After 1868, while carefully guarding its own autonomy, Japan adopted a policy of imperialism, expanding its power on the Asian mainland and joining in the colonizing thrust of the Western Powers. Leaders of national independence movements in other parts of Asia acclaimed Japan's victory over Russia in 1905 as a bright light for the future of a darkened continent. But such hopes were betrayed by Japan's subsequent actions. The sharp crack of the pistol shots at Harbin station symbolized the anger of fellow Asians against Japan. But Japan's leaders failed to hear them as a warning bell, though in view of subsequent history they clearly should have done.

Already well over half a century has passed since Itō's death under the dark, wintry sky of Harbin. Circumstances in East Asia are vastly different today: the empire of the Russian tsars is no more, the sway of the Ch'ing dynasty over China has long ended. By what path of destiny has Korea arrived at the present day? Or Japan? The East Asia of Itō's lifetime, even in part, has left no living vestiges. Mindful of this transformation, and thinking about our times, we are told in a poem of Itō's later years:

[42]

ITŌ HIROBUMI

Nothing changes in the universe;
Past and present are as one.
Fish frolic in deep waters;
Seagulls soar across the sky.

ŌKUMA SHIGENOBU

Champion of Democracy

1838–1922

It was 17 January 1922. On this day, under a cloudy winter sky, an icy wind relentlessly harried the snow lingering on the frozen ground. But Hibiya Park in the heart of Tokyo was alive, surging with people mindless of the cold. They had come to attend Ōkuma Shigenobu's funeral. After considering past precedents, the authorities ruled that he did not qualify for a state ceremony, and so the people were honoring Ōkuma Shigenobu in a tribute of their own that the government could hardly have equaled.

Early that morning Ōkuma's relatives held a farewell meeting at his Waseda residence; then the funeral carriage and its guard of honor passed slowly through the streets, followed by a large number of automobiles. All along the way houses flew black flags at half-mast, and under this mournful canopy the teachers and students of Waseda University moved in a thick, unbroken column along the road to Hibiya Park. There the coffin was carried onto the athletic field, securely placed on the funeral platform, and buried beneath a mountain of floral wreaths. At the entrance to the funeral enclosure a veritable forest of black flags fluttered in the breeze. A brief formal ceremony was conducted, and beginning at noon all those who wished could enter and pay their last respects. The site immediately filled as more and more people crowded inside. Without any special directions to do so, the throng of mourners carefully took off their hats and overcoats, and filed quietly past the coffin to pay their last respects. The swelling human tide seemed to surge on endlessly. When one person cast some small change as a token of condolence, others would follow, until coins were showered on the coffin like rain.

[45]

At three o'clock the main gate of the park was closed to further entry. Already 300,000 mourners had entered and the line of people outside the gates waiting to pay their respects was said to have continued for about two kilometers all the way to downtown Kandabashi. This indeed was a people's funeral, mustering crowds rarely seen before or since. After the public ceremony, a burial service was performed at Otowa Gokokuji temple. On that day, the number of people lining the roads to Waseda, Hibiya, and Gokokuji totalled 1,500,000, said to be the largest concourse of people since the funeral of Emperor Meiji in 1912. The newspapers reported that for about a month afterward 3,000 people a day still went to visit the tomb.

What, then, were the history, achievements, and character of Ōkuma Shigenobu, that his death should inspire such an overwhelming response from the people?

Destined for Greatness

Ōkuma got off to a very good start in life. He was born in 1838 at Saga, castle town of the strategically important Hizen domain in Kyūshū. His father's status was upper-ranking samurai. Ōkuma studied classics at Kyōdōkan, the domain academy, then took up Dutch studies at its Foreign Learning Institute. He completed his education at nearby Nagasaki, studying English in addition to gunnery, fortifications, and other military matters. Early on in his student years he supported the "Honor the Emperor, Expel the Barbarians" movement, but after the experience of Dutch learning and travel to Nagasaki to study Western military systems, he came to advocate opening up Japan to foreign trade and knowledge.

Brimming with vigor and enthusiasm, the young Ōkuma was also impatient to move the Hizen domain into the forefront of the bewildering and violent politics of the pre-Restoration years. But Nabeshima Naomasa, the feudal lord of Hizen, cautiously refused to make any positive moves throughout those years. His policy was to work toward harmony between the imperial court and the Bakufu. To Ōkuma's frustration, Hizen played no part in the movement that led to the Meiji Restoration. The main thrust in that advance was spearheaded by Satsuma and Chōshū,

[46]

culminating in the return of governing power to the emperor.

Early in 1868, Ōkuma was made a junior councillor and an executive official of the foreign ministry, with official duties at Nagasaki, an important center for diplomatic affairs. His career in the Meiji government had begun. Next, he was commissioned to go to Kyoto as negotiator with the ministers of the Western Powers, who were protesting the harsh government measures against a clandestine community of Japanese Christians in Urakami, a suburb of Nagasaki. The young Ōkuma, then just over thirty years old, found himself facing the angry remonstrations of Sir Harry Parkes, the feisty and seasoned British minister, but he refused to back down and deeply impressed government leaders by his wide-ranging abilities and sturdy determination. But for this, his future might not have been very bright. As the main driving force behind the Restoration and victors in the brief civil war that followed, the Satsuma and Chōshū leaders now dominated the Meiji government, enjoying a feast of power and prosperity. As a man from Hizen, which had played a passive role in Restoration politics, Ōkuma could well have been remained just a minor official. Yet from this first success as negotiator over the Urakami issue his "star of destiny" began to shine.

At the end of 1868, Ōkuma was appointed vice-minister of foreign affairs and began talks with the ministers of the Western Powers over the contentious problem of counterfeit currency, which was having a disruptive effect on overseas trade. Because this was closely connected with economic policy, he took on the additional post of vice-minister of finance. His involvement in fiscal affairs began from this time. Ōkuma recalled in later years that he was a pure layman in the field at first, but because of the diplomatic implications he quickly to become a master of it. With his ability to frame plans on the spur of the moment, to make decisions and resolutely carry them through, Ōkuma was soon planning the fundamentals of government finance. His negotiations with the Western Powers were also successful; he promised speedy reforms to combat counterfeiting and quickly resolved the dispute. Early in 1869, he gave up his post in the foreign ministry to devote himself full-time to his duties as vice-minister of finance.

In 1870, Ōkuma was promoted to councillor of a smaller and

more effective Council of State in addition to his executive post. At this time, his colleagues were Ōkubo Toshimichi of Satsuma, Kido Takayoshi and Hirosawa Saneomi of Chōshū, and Sasaki Takayuki and Saitō Toshiyuki of Tosa. Thus Ōkuma was the only councillor from a domain that had played no active part in the Restoration movement. Why such exceptionally rapid promotion? The foreign and finance ministries were the two most important departments in the government and demanded special skills and knowledge that were often lacking among the activists of the previous "Honor the Emperor, Expel the Barbarians" movement. In these ministries, Ōkuma's resourcefulness and fighting spirit could be applied to difficult problems, and his flexibility and powers of rapid decision given full play. At the time, Kido Takayoshi likened Ōkuma's ability to that of the great medieval swordsmiths Yoshihiro and Muramasa, creators of blades famous for their resilience, sharpness, and strength.[1]

In 1871, Ōkuma was relieved of his executive post as vice-minister of finance but remained a councillor. His successor was Inoue Kaoru, who resigned in 1873 when challenged by other department ministers over budget allotments. Councillor Ōkuma was given a temporary post as director of the finance ministry. His adept handling of a pressing and difficult task—to draw up the first comprehensive budget of the Meiji government—won him general acclaim. Later that year Saigō Takamori and several other high officials pressing for a war with Korea resigned from government. In the ensuing reshuffle of key posts, Ōkuma replaced Ōkubo as finance minister. Thereafter, Ōkubo as councillor and home minister became the central pillar of the government. His two most important colleagues were Ōkuma and Itō Hirobumi, councillor and minister of public works. Ōkuma had quickly made his mark in the Meiji government. But even so, under the nominal leadership of Council of State Presidents Sanjō Sanetomi and Iwakura Tomomi, the Satsuma and Chōshū men continued to hold the real power. Consequently, as Mutsu Munemitsu later pointed out in a critical review of Ōkuma's career, in all the really important actions of the new government, such as the replacement of domains by prefectures in 1871, the defeat of the advocates of war with Korea in 1873, and the Osaka Conference held in 1875 to discuss

[48]

structural reforms, he either played a muted role or else kept completely out of things.

When Saigō Takamori and his allies launched the Satsuma Rebellion in 1877, suppressing it put a heavy strain on government resources. Ōkuma as finance minister raised the necessary funds by the bold expedient of issuing inconvertible paper currency, and he earned much praise for this. Kido Takayoshi died in the year of the rebellion, and in 1878 Ōkubo Toshimichi was assassinated. These untimely deaths greatly enlarged Ōkuma's prospects. No longer subject to control from above by these two powerful superiors, he was now the most senior of the councillors. Ōkuma, forty-one years old, stood on a par with Itō as the key leader in government.

What kind of a person was Ōkuma around this time? A friendly letter written to him in January 1872 by Godai Tomoatsu, a Satsuma businessman with strong government connections, advised him to pay attention to five points, listed as follows: 1) When you feel opinions or arguments are stupid, please be patient and listen. You are brilliant, but this tends to make you impatient, feeling you know everything after hearing only one-tenth of it. 2) When a subordinate has much the same opinion as yourself, take pains to praise him and agree with his views. Unless you do this, you will fail to grow in popularity. 3) Be careful to avoid anger and heated words. Your subordinates know they are no match for you, so to behave in this way is simply to lose your influence and popularity profitlessly. 4) When you make decisions on important matters, wait until the time is ripe. 5) People you dislike will probably dislike you in return. So try to get on well with everybody.[2] These five points of advice provide a vivid image of Ōkuma as his contemporaries saw him. With his driving vigor, towering aloofness, and curt taciturnity, Councillor Ōkuma seemed disdainful of what others said and indifferent to what they thought. Even so, people noted that he was quite skilled and stimulating in private conversation.[3]

Breakdown

It was a most unusual thing in Meiji politics for someone outside Satsuma or Chōshū to wield the influence Ōkuma did after the

Satsuma Rebellion of 1877. He became very self-assured, perhaps all the more so because his influence derived from ability alone. Yet precisely because he lacked the powerful backing that the Satsuma and Chōshū leaders drew from former domain connections, both that influence itself and the base on which it stood were highly insecure.

In February 1879, as the Freedom and People's Rights movement swept across the nation and demands for the opening of an elected national assembly became ever more vociferous, the emperor requested all the councillors to submit their opinions on constitutional government. For some time, Ōkuma had given serious thought to this question. According to his reminiscences, before the Restoration he had read books about the Dutch Constitution and had also studied the American Declaration of Independence. Thereafter, he was increasingly attracted to constitutional government.[4] Initially, Ōkuma requested permission to convey his opinion directly to the emperor in an audience. That was not allowed, and so after some delay he submitted a written report advocating the promulgation of a constitution modeled on the British parliamentary system, to be followed by the opening of an elected national assembly in 1883. These proposals were very radical compared with the views of the other councillors. He entrusted his report to Imperial Prince Arisugawa Taruhito, recently appointed a third president of the Council of State, asking him not to show it to fellow presidents Sanjō and Iwakura or to the other councillors before presenting it to the emperor. That took place in March 1881. Ōkuma had previously discussed the constitution issue on many occasions with Itō Hirobumi and Inoue Kaoru, whose opinions on the subject were rather more progressive than those of the other councillors. Yet Ōkuma did not consult them when he prepared his report to the emperor. The other councillors soon learned what Ōkuma had proposed. The Satsuma leaders in particular were irate, but so were Itō and Inoue. It seemed to them that in advocating such rapid progress Ōkuma was aiming to destroy Sat-Chō influence at a single, bold stroke.

Ōkuma and his fellow councillors managed to reach a temporary accommodation over this incident, but almost immediately afterward he was again at odds with them over the Hokkaidō

Colonization Office scandal. In mid-1881, it became known that the government proposed to sell off valuable enterprises, at what seemed to be very low prices, to a group of merchants with strong Sat-Chō connections. Public opinion and the press seized upon the sale as clear proof of the venality of clique government. As attacks on the sale mounted, the mood of the nation swiftly turned hostile. Freedom and People's Rights supporters all over Japan united in criticizing the government and clamoring for an end to the despotic regime of the Sat-Chō clique. Ōkuma made no direct pronouncement on the proposed sale, but was reputed to be critical of it and earned public acclaim for this. Faced by a torrent of criticism coming up from every quarter, the Sat-Chō leaders became more convinced than ever that Ōkuma had plotted with the Freedom and People's Rights group to whip up public opposition to the sale. Their immediate goal became to oust Ōkuma from government. In October 1881, when his colleagues combined to exclude him from council meetings and demanded his resignation on pain of their own, Ōkuma had no alternative but to resign. At the same time, in order to appease public indignation, the Sat-Chō leaders persuaded the emperor to issue an edict promising that a national assembly would be opened by 1890.

Ōkuma might have avoided this humiliating reverse if the Sat-Chō leaders had not been so inordinately mistrustful of him. That their suspicions were in fact unfounded is recognized today. However, Ōkuma himself touched off the crisis by presenting his report on constitutional government in such a furtive way. He might well have hoped that his political horizons would expand under a new constitutional regime in which he and his followers could expect to play leading roles. However, in submitting such a radical report without first consulting Itō and Inoue, he grossly overestimated his real influence in the government and was much too precipitate in attempting to achieve his aims. Despite his high position, he was very insecure, and he forgot that. Ōkuma's failure was largely due to lack of careful planning.

Shifting Fortunes

Ōkuma now entered a period of adversity. In an attempt to

restore his own political fortunes and provide a future for the young followers who had left office with him, he embarked on a number of projects, notably the establishment of Tokyo Semmon Gakkō, the forerunner of Waseda University, and the acquisition of the *Yūbin Hōchi* newspaper. During this period, he also founded the Kaishintō party, which joined in the Freedom and People's Rights movement. The Kaishintō was set up in March 1882, about six months after Itagaki Taisuke's Jiyūtō. Having been driven from office as a renegade, Ōkuma was thereafter subjected to various kinds of devious pressures and threats by his Sat-Chō opponents. But he tolerated it all with cheerful disdain, buoyed up by his natural energy and forcefulness.

When the Kaishintō dissolved in 1884, hamstrung by government restrictions on political activity, Ōkuma resigned from its presidency but remained the de facto leader. Founding a political party and keeping up his connections with it provided the springboard for his official comeback in February 1888. Just before this, certain concessions to the Western Powers in the treaty revision proposals of Foreign Minister Inoue Kaoru were widely viewed as weak and insulting. The Freedom and People's Rights supporters raised a storm of protest, and the cabinet ran into difficulties. The talks were suspended, and Inoue resigned. Prime Minister Itō then proposed Ōkuma as Inoue's successor. Itō valued Ōkuma's skill in diplomacy, but perhaps he also hoped to gain Kaishintō support for the cabinet if Ōkuma joined it. This promised to shear off one section of the Freedom and People's Rights movement, and enable the cabinet to regain control of the situation.

Six and a half years after his expulsion, Ōkuma was again in office as foreign minister. Invigorated by the new possibilities the appointment offered and burning with ambition, he plunged right in to resume negotiations for treaty revision, quite undaunted by Inoue's failure. Ōkuma was now fifty years of age and anxious to make his mark in history. Accounts of the time describe him as full of energy, unable to keep still for long, and constantly pacing his office, puffing away on cigarettes. Treaty revision was a major national issue, and he wanted to settle it on his own. This, he believed, was the chance to open up a brilliant political future for himself—a possibility that roused all his combative instincts.

Not long afterward, Itō became president of the Privy Council and was succeeded as prime minister by the Satsuma leader Kuroda Kiyotaka. Ōkuma continued to serve as foreign minister under Kuroda and pressed on with the back-breaking task of treaty revision. But he was up against a near impossible challenge: the negotiation of revisions acceptable to the Western Powers while satisfying public opinion in Japan. Sure enough, when Ōkuma completed a draft and it leaked out, angry critics immediately castigated it as weak and subservient. Opinion within official circles was deeply divided on the issue, and the cabinet soon found itself attacked from both inside and outside the government. Yet Ōkuma refused to back down. No matter what the obstacles, he was determined to bring treaty revision to a conclusion. Just as opposition to his proposals reached its peak, he was injured by a bomb thrown into his carriage while on his way to the foreign ministry. His attacker was an outraged critic of the Ōkuma draft. With Ōkuma severely wounded and with opposition mounting, the Kuroda cabinet called off the treaty revision talks and resigned in October 1889. Ōkuma was once more out of office.

He surprised visitors during his convalescence by telling them, "I am glad I was injured by a progressive Western invention and not a sword or some such old-fashioned device." He expressed sympathy for the late Satsuma leader and education minister Mori Arinori, who had been stabbed to death earlier in the year as he set out to attend the constitution promulgation ceremonies. After surgery, Ōkuma was left with only one leg. Ozaki Yukio relates that on regaining consciousness from the anaesthetic Ōkuma remarked to the doctor that the loss of his right leg would improve his health, since all the blood that had previously gone there would now go to other parts of his body. Whether this story is true or not, it makes an interesting anecdote about Ōkuma's character. His refusal to flinch at the formidable challenge of the treaty revision negotiations and his cheerful disdain for the grisly reality of losing a leg in a bomb attack created a favorable impression of Ōkuma as a spirited and courageous leader, whatever people might have thought of him as a person.

Nevertheless, certain notable defects in Ōkuma's character

had again served him ill. That the so-called Ōkuma draft gave rise to such a deep cleavage of opinion within the government itself should have warned him of the need for accommodation and caution. His failure to keep in close touch with other government leaders seems like the rash action of a man impatient for success, overconfident in his own ability, and determined to achieve treaty revision by a single, masterful effort. As in the case of his previous failure, he showed a conspicuous lack of prudence and caution.

Ōkuma spent the next seven years out of office. When Matsukata Masayoshi formed his second cabinet in 1896, he sought support from the Shimpotō, a new party formed after the Kaishintō had been joined by other groups. Ōkuma was offered a cabinet post as foreign minister, so once again his party connections proved advantageous. Before accepting office, Ōkuma presented a list of conditions: (1) Men in good repute with the people be appointed cabinet ministers. (2) Freedom of speech, assembly, and publication. (3) Capable men from the ordinary citizenry be allowed access to official posts. When Matsukata agreed, Ōkuma took office, though not for very long. About a year later he quarreled with Matsukata and resigned.

Six months after that, Ōkuma awoke to the day when he took charge of the government himself, as prime minister. In June 1898, the Shimpotō and Jiyūtō had merged to form the Kenseitō, with the avowed purpose of overthrowing the Sat-Chō clique regime. Itō's third cabinet was in office at the time, and promptly resigned. None of the Satsuma and Chōshū veteran statesmen, now known as the genrō, were prepared to form a cabinet in confrontation with this powerful new people's party. Instead, they advised the emperor to request Ōkuma and Itagaki, the joint leaders of the Kenseitō, to form a cabinet. With Ōkuma as prime minister, Itagaki as home minister, and all the other ministers except those of the army and navy appointed from the ranks of the Kenseitō, Japan's first party cabinet made its appearance. But the Kenseitō was an uneasy alliance between two previous parties with a long history of mutual rivalry and disputes; soon internal feuding got out of control and the newborn Kenseitō split. Its former Jiyūtō component continued to call itself the Kenseitō, but the Shimpotō group broke away to form the Kenseihontō. Thereupon, the Ōkuma cabinet collapsed after only four months, without conducting a single Diet session. Once again, in becoming prime minister, if even for so short a time, Ōkuma owed a great deal to his party connections.

Ousted from Party Leadership

The Kenseitō dissolved in 1900 and merged with Itō Hirobumi's Seiyūkai. Both in its earlier Jiyūtō period and after joining the Seiyūkai, the Kenseitō played a pro-government role and kept close to the power center. In contrast, even during its Kaishintō and Shimpotō era, with the exception of the brief second Matsukata cabinet, the Kenseihontō had never supported the government and continued in opposition when Ōkuma was officially made party president in December 1900. But this separation from power irritated one faction in the party. In time, they began to make moves to oust Ōkuma, whose unpopularity with the genrō "cabinet makers" made him more of a hindrance than an asset. The opponents of Ōkuma's leadership wanted to appoint a president who would forge closer ties with the genrō and bring the party nearer to the government. These demands of the so-called reform faction were opposed by an anti-reform faction determined to stick to the policy of no compromise with the genrō. As this factional dispute grew more bitter, Ōkuma found himself in an intolerable position, and he finally resigned from the Kenseihontō presidency at the party rally in January 1907.

Ōkuma's farewell speech expressed regret that during the seven years since his appointment as president the party had not flourished. Nevertheless, he was overjoyed to see that the members as a whole were determined to increase party strength, draw up new regulations, and do everything they could to make it an effective, unified political force. While happy to take his leave of them, this did not mean that he was tired of politics or worn out by problems. "I am old, but I shall fight on. Out of respect for our nation and the emperor, I shall stay in politics until I die. Politics is my life. You can oust me from the party, but not from my vocation, which embraces all Japan." Active involvement in politics, continued Ōkuma, was his "chief duty to the nation. It is my right under the constitution. . . . While I shall obey the

[55]

emperor and the law, no power on earth can limit my freedom of action as an individual." He felt no resentment personally but hoped that in future the party members would act "with a little more sense of responsibility." His own actions as a free individual would assist the party's development. Hard work or difficulties would not deter him. "If problems arise, I shall fight all the harder. Problems are my friends. They don't upset me." He thanked the membership for giving him his freedom. Relinquishing the Kenseihontō presidency by no means implied abandoning the party, Ōkuma concluded, nor did he intend to give up active politics.

Since the early 1880s, Itagaki Taisuke and Ōkuma Shigenobu as the respective presidents of the Jiyūtō and Kaishintō had emerged as the two great leaders of the Freedom and People's Rights movement. But in 1900, as Itō Hirobumi prepared to launch the Seiyūkai, the thirst for political power drove the Kenseitō to dissolve and join Itō's camp. At that point, Itagaki Taisuke, their former president, was abandoned by his party comrades after many years of shared successes and hardships, and he retired from politics. A little more than six years later, Ōkuma suffered the same humiliating fate.

Ōkuma was still in robust health. The vigor of his farewell speech when resigning from the Kenseihontō presidency was true to form—clearly he had lost none of his famous forcefulness. Even so, he was now seventy years of age, and his long political career seemed to have reached its twilight.

Strengths and Weaknesses

To a large extent, Ōkuma's political career in itself provides an accurate portrait of the man. Naturally energetic, determined, and confident, the obstacles he faced as a native of Hizen in carving out a career for himself after the Restoration served only to reinforce these qualities. The undaunted spirit in which he took on difficult problems, such as the Urakami Christians, the counterfeit currency issue, and the budget dispute, came out even more strongly during his bout while foreign minister with the treaty revision negotiations. He often boasted that his wounds were all gained in front-line combat. Ōkuma was very extrovert, optimistic, and quick to show off his merits, qualities quite consistent with his strong urge for domination and power. As part of the price he paid for such a character, he had virtually no inclination toward inner reflection and seemed quite unconcerned about giving his life any kind of deeper fulfillment. Insensitive, shallow, and prosaic, Ōkuma was never able to take stock of himself or even to form an accurate estimate of his own limitations.

In the long run, some of these personal traits hindered Ōkuma's effectiveness as a political leader. First, and most obvious, in his impatience to vaunt his merits he was often insolent or condescending, seeking to overawe people with his expansive, didactic harangues. Second, overconfidence in his own ability encouraged an optimistic outlook toward almost any situation, and as a result his response tended to be makeshift. Both his great strengths and weaknesses as a high official and political leader seem to have stemmed from that opportunism; his actions succeeded or failed depending on whether the situation he faced could be controlled or restored, quite apart from self-confidence or intuitive ability. When the circumstances favored his talents, Ōkuma's actions were brilliant. In the hectic and confused period after the Restoration, many matters demanded ad hoc and speedy decisions. Ōkuma worked well in such circumstances, as his early achievements demonstrate. But it is hard to say that his political career as a whole was aided by such opportunism. Because he gave little, if any, prior thought to circumstances and conditions, his actions were often rash and thoughtless, leading to frustration and failure.

Mutsu Munemitsu said of Ōkuma that "his brilliant ideas were often impractical"; he was "a man of talk rather than action," always "hoping for quick fame," and negligent in "thorough and detailed planning."[5] These are pointed words. In official and political life, Mutsu was hostile to Ōkuma, but his stinging comments seem to ring true. Ozaki Yukio, a close associate of Ōkuma since the founding of the Kaishintō, corroborates Mutsu's criticism. He wrote that although Okuma's self-confidence was an asset, his thinking was too random, too offhand, so that his response to a situation often miscarried, and he brought on his own failure for trivial reasons.[6] In Ōkuma's latter years, an anonymous critic observed acidly that he was "brash, without

[57]

strategic finesse; trusting in his strength, he was negligent in planning"; he was a "blustering political leader. . . . Although not at his best in combat, he enjoyed a good fight above all. In reality, he was a clumsy muddler."[7]

Third, the egotism of proud, extroverted, self-aggrandizing Ōkuma aroused strong antipathy. He often came across as shallow and coarse. He talked on and on, not only about politics and economics, but virtually about any subject at all, proud to show off his command of such extensive knowledge. This superficiality provoked mocking criticism of him as a man of "secondhand opinions," or as lacking "deep mastery of the truth." After Ōkuma's death, Kume Kunitake, a close friend since childhood, described him as an "extemporiser, with no permanent or consistent views."[8] Against such evidence, Ōkuma can hardly be acclaimed as a political leader of deep principles or firm convictions.

In October 1907, the Tokyo Semmon Gakkō commemorated its twenty-fifth anniversary by a ceremony held at Waseda University, into which it had developed. A statue of Ōkuma had been erected in the university garden, but before the unveiling ceremony took place, journalist Fukumoto Nichinan published an article entitled "The Bronze Statue of Ōkuma" that contained some sharp barbs. Fukumoto acknowledged that Ōkuma had performed a great service in founding the university. He became its chancellor and was a "true exemplar of the citizen's university." Waseda had made an appropriate gesture in setting up a statue of him. But he had heard, Fukumoto went on, that "the bronze statue of Ōkuma showed him in formal court dress with ceremonial sword, evoking the prime minister, political leader, and nobleman, just like a latter-day feudal lord." Scandalous, exclaimed Fukumoto. Whether it was someone else's idea or Ōkuma's own, the statue was highly improper—"Was it erected in gratitude for Ōkuma's role as university chancellor or as previous Kenseihontō president or as present patron of the party? Or did it acclaim him as Senior Second Court Rank, Order of Merit First Class, and Count? If the statue honors Ōkuma as chancellor, then the thirty thousand students of Waseda— intelligent young men of today aspiring to distinguished leadership in the future—will be thoroughly disillusioned." In conversation, Fukumoto continued, Ōkuma constantly harps on his admiration for democracy, but underneath he is really enthralled by a kind of shoddy nobility. If such a statue was to be erected at the university, "Why couldn't it portray Ōkuma in the ordinary dress he normally wears? Informal Japanese clothes suggest gentleness and peace. If they are regarded as too homely, then he should have been shown in the more formal *hakama*."[9]

Others shared Fukumoto's irritation. As if constrained to apologize for the statue, on the day of the unveiling Ōkuma stood before it and in his speech of thanks made several vague and cumbrous allusions to such criticisms: In himself, he was a "country samurai"; at the time of the Restoration, he had simply followed the lead of superiors and had actually done very little. But for some reason, he had received the gracious favor of the emperor, and at times he wore court dress. The statue showed him dressed that way, Ōkuma continued, and then declared: "I am one who loves democracy. Of course, I am staunchly opposed to certain forms of it like the Socialist party. And I do not like wearing court dress. I do so only out of grateful respect for the emperor." Sometimes circumstances oblige one to dress formally, behave in a dignified manner, and maintain an attitude proper to the occasion. That expressed the "samurai spirit," continued Ōkuma, "but on the other hand, normally I tend to behave like an ordinary citizen. I think that real, comprehensive progress in society requires a harmonious blend of both these elements. You have kindly erected a bronze statue of me in formal court dress. It does not represent my outward appearance very well, but can be said to express the inner discipline of the samurai spirit."[10]

Inept Leadership

After he set up the Kaishintō in 1882 and established party connections, Ōkuma's approach to people changed. Whereas previously he had often given the impression of being coldly aloof, the same Ōkuma began to treat his guests with affability, and he enjoyed talking with them. Writing in 1897, Mutsu observed that when Ōkuma was at home entertaining guests, he rarely opposed or questioned what they said, but rather agreed with them, putting them at ease.[11] The inclination to avoid ruffling the feelings of others remained strong to the end of his life. In speeches, too, he was clever and tactful to a fault. On occasion, this allowed his critics to trip him up. For example, one day, he advocated temperance to an audience in Sanuki province, and then extolled the medicinal values of *saké* in a speech at Nada, a well-known brewing center, the very same afternoon. Such flexibility made Ōkuma an ineffective party leader. Even after he resigned from the Kenseihontō presidency, the fierce disputes between the reform and anti-reform factions of the party continued unabated, and both sides called on Ōkuma separately to seek his support. Each time Ōkuma echoed the views of the faction present and expressed sympathy; as a result both believed that he was on their side, so the internal feuding became even worse.[12]

Ōkuma's boundless self-confidence had other damaging repercussions. When he employed people, he did so out of necessity, with no commitment to their futures when he no longer needed their services. Fearing no enemy, he never bothered to build up a strong following that would provide a base for support. Politician Uchigasaki Sakusaburō remarked that "the two Meiji political leaders who never acted like a boss toward their followers were Itō and Ōkuma." In this, Ōkuma and Itō resembled each other as much as they differed from Yamagata Aritomo and Hara Takashi.

Whatever the reasons why no clique developed around Ōkuma, he was certainly hampered by not being able to attract talented, dedicated men to his service. In Ozaki Yukio's opinion, this was due, among other things, to his overbearing self-confidence, which prevented him from really listening to others. To a certain extent, Itō suffered from the same defect, but in his case the unaffected simplicity of another side to his character attracted loyalty and affection. Ōkuma's extroverted, brash, and earthy manner, in contrast, made it hard for people to like him or develop close relationship with him. Consequently, he was unable to attract good advisers. Yamada Ichirō, a journalist and former Kaishintō member, wrote a criticial article in 1896 entitled "Ōkuma— Unsuited to Party Leadership." People praise Ōkuma as great and strong but nobody loves him, Yamada observed. Ōkuma was very clever in social conversation, but when he sought to impress local leaders with his proud, unyielding, and lofty view of the world, they often suspected that he was just pulling the wool over their eyes. Itō and Ōkuma were regarded as the two great champions in politics. But intelligent people, after contrasting Itō's gentle warmth with Ōkuma's fiery temperament, concluded that "Itō is loveable, like the winter sun. Ōkuma is unpleasant, like a hot summer day."[13] This comparison between Ōkuma and Itō at the summit of their careers has an authentic ring. Given his dubious integrity in public life, it is easier to understand why so few people remained in Ōkuma's service for long; without doubt, most of his followers were out to exploit rather than to help him. Such was the general quality of Ōkuma's leadership as a party president.

Speeches and Conversations

After setting up the Kaishintō in 1882 and becoming its president, Ōkuma appealed to the people for support in opposing the Sat-Chō clique and challenging it to do battle. This campaign to rouse the nation soon became second nature to him. Appealing to the people and holding them in thrall satisfied Ōkuma's thirst for dominance, and he came to relish that role. After being driven from the Kenseihontō presidency in 1907 and withdrawing from active politics, he was left with no reasonable hope of regaining high office. These appeals to the nation became the only way for Ōkuma to gratify his fierce cravings for power, and he continued to stage grand public appearances to the day of his death. Nothing gave him more satisfaction than the vigorous roar of welcome and thunderous applause of a large crowd at his speeches, or the delight and admiration beamed upon him by throngs of guests crowding the reception room of his Waseda residence.

Speeches and conversations were essential tools in Ōkuma's appeals to the nation, but it took him some time to develop his technique. He had little skill as a public speaker when he became president of the Kaishintō in 1882. Kamata Eikichi, in his later years president of Keiō University, recalls that in those days Ōkuma "would stand up and say two or three words, go red in

[61]

the face, and just sit down again." At first much more awkward an orator than Itagaki Taisuke, Ōkuma grew progressively more commanding, until his eloquence finally became a matter of wide renown.

As an orator, he often shared the platform with others and so there are several good accounts of his speech-making style. When he mounted the platform, his clean-shaven face was always set in a firm expression, his broad mouth arched downward in a forceful curve. Even on his first leisurely glance at the packed crowd, the intensity of his bearing already dominated the hall. Ōkuma's voice was not clear or sharp, but rich in resonance; effortlessly parading his extensive knowledge as he unfolded his deft and original arguments, he captivated large audiences by the sheer dynamism of his performance. Adroit in timing and intonation, when he rose to the climax of his peroration he would gesticulate vigorously or pose for a moment with both hands held out above the heads of the audience. Sometimes he thrust out his right hand suddenly like a flash of lightning to emphasize a point or brandished a clenched fist here and there as a sign of his determination.

Ōkuma's speeches were an inseparable part of his personality. Resounding with vigor, the spirit of challenge, and self-confidence, they made a forceful and commanding impression. He was most noticeably in his element when attacking political enemies, although on such occasions his overbearing and menacing tone was repellent to some people in the audience. On first impact, many of his statements seemed very bold and majestic, but intelligent listeners often found them shallow and irresponsible. For example, when talking about Japan's diplomacy at the Paris Peace Conference, Ōkuma dismissed the problem by suggesting that if the delegates first loudly exclaimed, "We'll go along with anything you like!" thus disarming the antagonism of the others, it would be easy work; after all, that was precisely what Wilson and Clemenceau did, and the Japanese delegates should do so too.[14] Unlike the careful Itō, Ōkuma paid insufficient heed to how his listeners might interpret his words. As a result, especially in his political speeches, he rashly committed himself to promises that he had no intention of keeping.

Even as a young student, Ōkuma set out with great energy to

[62]

amass the encyclopedic knowledge he was so proud of later in life. When Ōkuma was studying English at Nagasaki, his teacher, G. F. Verbeck, is said to have admired his application and to have predicted that he would grow up to be a man of formidably wide erudition. In his later years, Ōkuma indeed had knowledge in rich store. He is said to have become noted for his extensive knowledge after being ousted from office in 1881. He was an avid reader and attentive listener, while also gifted with an unusually sharp memory. Unlike Itō, he rarely read foreign books in the original; he relied on translations, especially those of recent Western works published by the Bummei Kyōkai, a publishing company he founded himself. He was always eager to learn anything he could from informed people in meetings and conversations. History, religion, philosophy, fine arts—almost all subjects were food for Ōkuma's hungry appetite for knowledge. But his ability to discourse fluently on such diverse topics depended greatly on his memory, which was quite extraordinary in its retentive power. Ozaki Yukio relates that, just before his first trip to China in 1885, he paid a farewell visit to Ōkuma, who proceeded to tell him in great detail about the country. In Shanghai there was this place, that hotel; Ōkuma knew just as much about London or Paris. Although he had never been overseas himself, Ōkuma knew all the details. His memory remained keen well into old age, when he continued to impress people with his instant recall of facts and figures.

One of Ōkuma's personal quirks throughout his life was his great aversion to putting anything down in his own handwriting. The reason for this, so the story goes, is that when he was studying at the Hizen domain school a younger boy ranked first in the class at calligraphy; Ōkuma worked hard to improve his brush writing but finally realized that he could not top this rival. Piqued at being outmatched, he petulantly refused to study calligraphy any further. Be that as it may, Ōkuma's own explanation of why he wrote so little was that he could retain so much knowledge in his head. But other reasons may be surmised for Ōkuma's acquisition of such extensive knowledge. It certainly enabled him to give an instant opinion on virtually any subject and thus to satisfy his urge to show himself off to advantage. Impressing people and playing on their emotions enabled Ōkuma to dominate them. In a way, he used knowledge as a weapon, and this does much to account for his unflagging pursuit of it.

Ōkuma's speeches were aimed at the national audience, but he was equally renowned as a conversational host. He welcomed people to his house on an "open door" principle, and there was always a large crowd of guests at his Waseda residence. Among the many groups he received at set times in his spacious drawing room journalists were always well represented. This room became a window on the world, where the gregarious, voluble Ōkuma reveled in the kind of conversation he most enjoyed. Here he was the undisputed authority, with a ready supply of answers to the wide-ranging questions posed by his guests. As he grew more stimulated, his replies began to resemble speeches, complete with the clenched fist and other characteristic gestures. Even after his harangue rose to a climax, he talked on ecstatically, heedless of the yellow Egyptian tobacco in his pipe that was turning to white ash. In his final years, he gave up tobacco for health reasons; the pipe was missing, but his animation never diminished, nor did his skill in displaying his extensive knowledge. Always eager to explain, interpret, or give an opinion on diverse topics, he won the delighted admiration of many of his visitors.

Mutsu Munemitsu observed in 1897 that, like Itō, Ōkuma conversed with people in the style of a "professional storyteller or teacher," but that he did not share Itō's habit of barely allowing his partners to open their mouths; rather, he took pains to let them speak too. But as the years passed, Ōkuma's tendency to lecture grew stronger, and he became much less inclined to permit conversational gaps where others might interject their comments. Even when he did, he rarely allowed them time to finish. His conversations became more and more like solo performances. Mutsu also commented on Ōkuma's need to impress his listeners with his prowess and dignity to the point that self-assurance often degenerated into ostentatious bragging. This did not change as Ōkuma grew older, but he mellowed somewhat later on. Waseda Professor Tsubouchi Shōyō recalled that Ōkuma's conversation, for most of his life, tended to have an overpowering vigor and blustering vanity, but after the age of seventy he became much more moderate, charming people with his good humor. Certainly, Ōkuma's conversations were among his dearest pleasures. When it rained and only a few visitors came, he would complain, like a disappointed actor, "Not many people today!"

Unabashed by his bombastic words, Ōkuma made no attempt to veil his pride. As a youth, he had a rather common personal name, Hachitarō. He maintained that its first component "hachi," although written with the calligraphic sign for "eight," could be understood in its Japanese readings as a term for important places and deities, and as "all," "numerous," or "leader." The chevron-like shape of the sign also suggested a wide opening, and hence signified expansion. So Hachitarō, claimed Ōkuma, was a very appropriate name for himself. Recounting to his friend Ichijima Kenkichi the history of beards, Ōkuma told him that they were fashionable in the Warring Domains era of the 1500s, but that Tokugawa Ieyasu banned them after he had established his rule over the whole nation in 1615. That was supposedly because warlike trappings such as beards no longer had any use. "So," continued Ōkuma, "my clean-shaven face is a symbol of peace."

Ōkuma also had a famous 125-year-lifespan theory that he enjoyed explaining. According to physiologists, he maintained, the life expectancy of an animal is five times the period it takes to reach maturity. If humans reach maturity at twenty-five years, then they should live to be five times that age. "Going by physiological principles, lifespan can be deduced mathematically. To die at 100 or even 110, isn't that the unnatural destruction of a life span before its proper time for expiry?"

When G. E. Morrison, the world-famous authority on China, called on Ōkuma at his Waseda residence in 1909, he unwittingly provided his host another chance for self-congratulation. Ōkuma said that he knew of Morrison's reputation as a China expert but asked to what extent had he really studied that country? For thirty years, replied Morrison. Ōkuma gleefully exclaimed that his own studies of China had extended for fifty years.

As Ōkuma grew older, he became renowned for making dogmatic statements on all kinds of diverse topics. He criticized birth control, for example, as the product of "hedonistic thought. . . . If women decide they dislike bearing children, it will ruin the nation. . . . Demands for birth control herald the end of Western enlightenment. Humans must bear many children in profusion,

[65]

the more the better. Children are born to challenge the world of nature. After conquering the earth, they will master the sky and sea. Oceans cover two-thirds of the earth but their wealth has not yet been exploited. If human skill is applied, the sea can support a great deal of human life.''

In another such statement, Ōkuma summed up his views on recent history, after the scientist Dr. Hata Saburō had suggested that Kropotkin's theory of mutualism owed its inspiration to something an eighteenth-century French physiologist had written. Ōkuma replied, ''I always thought as much. Kropotkin and Marx are getting a lot of attention these days. Marx is certainly a great man. He is Jewish, of course, and coming from a people that has been persecuted for two thousand years, his resentment is very deep. When a person is so filled with bitterness and discontent, his ideas reflect his feelings; these ideas are then taken up by a strong leader in order to create a despotic regime. Germany seems somehow or other to have escaped from Marxist despotism, but Russia has succumbed. We probably had to expect as much, since the Russian people have been under the thumb of a strong leader for much of their history. Anyway, Marxist thought is a crude simplification. And it is embraced by people of a crude, simple mentality.''

Lordly Tastes

Ōkuma's interests and tastes, like his speeches and conversations, clearly portray his character. Renowned for his lordly way of life, Ōkuma loved ''magnificence'' in all things, as might be expected of such a shallow, showy, and domineering type of personality. A story passed down in the family of Ōkuma's mother related that when he was studying English at Nagasaki in pre-Restoration days, he went every night to the Maruyama red-light district. On such visits his dress and swords were of the most expensive kind, giving him the aura of a high-ranking military retainer or feudal lord. Once, when the proprietor of the establishment he was visiting asked him what he planned for himself in future, Ōkuma surprised everyone by replying that he aimed to become the greatest lord in the land. Thereafter he often repeated the remark. He may have meant it to be taken in jest, but not wholly; the young Ōkuma seems already to have set his sights very high.

A fire in 1901 destroyed the Waseda residence he had lived in since 1884. It was rebuilt the following year with a separate annex in the Western style, but the main building was an imposing structure resembling a feudal lord's mansion. The large Western-style garden was among the most famous in Tokyo. In these spacious and elegant surroundings, Ōkuma could freely indulge his love for entertaining visitors and giving banquets. Around 1902, it was estimated that on average dinners were served to 800 guests at the Ōkuma residence every month. Exaggerated or not, Ōkuma's close friend Ichijima Kenkichi recalled that the kitchens at Ōkuma's residence were always hard at work and the dining room packed with guests, like a restaurant. Ōkuma also used the spacious garden as a meeting place for his numerous friends and acquaintances. The chrysanthemum-viewing parties in the autumn were famous, going on for several days and attended by members of the imperial family, diplomats, and other prominent people. Such occasions gave him a welcome opportunity to lecture his guests on chrysanthemums, yet another subject on which he could proudly display his extensive knowledge. This flower, with its magnificent blooms, had a special appeal for Ōkuma. Starting from 1886, Ōkuma's garden parties at the Waseda residence became a regular annual event until 1910, when financial problems compelled him to cut down on lavish entertaining.

True to form, Ōkuma also traveled in the style of a latter-day feudal lord. Losing a leg was an inconvenience, but that did not prevent him from journeying happily all over the country. Wherever he went, he attracted attention and comment. Including the friends he always urged to come along, his entourage often numbered as many as twenty to fifty people, and invariably others would join him on the way. He often hired two or three entire railway carriages to hold them all. Traveling with a large crowd of people was most enjoyable, he always declared with pride. Everywhere they stopped, he gave generous tips at inns, large gifts of money to shrines and temples, and handsome fees to geisha at banquets. When the train drew in to a station, there he was by the window even in the dead of night, ready to greet the eager throng coming to pay their respects. On arrival at large

[67]

cities, he was only too happy to meet the journalists who crowded around him, delighting them with his vivacious and animated talk.

Local worthies were at pains to think up pleasing ways to welcome him when he stopped in their districts. As a friend of Ōkuma for many years, Ichijima Kenkichi knew his tastes very well. Since he usually helped plan and manage Ōkuma's journeys, people often consulted him about organizing a reception for Ōkuma at places on his itinerary. For example, Ichijima later recalled a journey Ōkuma made one summer to Echigo province in northern Japan. The inn at Nagaoka city where Ōkuma decided to stay was brand new, the building just completed. The garden was still under way, however, and upon hearing that Ōkuma was due to stay, the manager made plans to work non-stop, day and night, in a frantic attempt to finish it. Knowing Ōkuma's tastes, Ichijima was well aware that no matter how splendid the garden he would probably take little pleasure in it. So he suggested to the manager that on the day of Ōkuma's arrival people should get together a lot of snow and heap it into a large pile; a white pyramid beneath the summer sky would certainly be an impressive sight for Ōkuma. Besides, even in summer, snow was plentiful in Echigo, so the expense would not be great. All was done as Ichijima had suggested.

Another of Ichijima's revealing stories goes as follows: Shimomura, owner of Daimaru, a Kyoto drapery store, invited Ōkuma to visit him. Ichijima told Shimomura that he need not spend a large sum of money on Ōkuma's reception; it would be better to think up something unique but simple, tailored to suit his tastes. For example, if Shimomura had one hundred pairs of gilt folding-screens lined up on both sides of the path from the gate to the front entrance and then along the corridors leading to the main reception room, about one hundred meters in all, what a dazzling sight this would make! Shimomura seized upon the idea. When Ōkuma and his wife arrived, a light rain was falling. White-uniformed servants held large umbrellas over the couple as they escorted them from the gate to the front entrance. Ōkuma gaped in astonishment at the majestic array of gilt screens glowing with color in the dim drizzle. As he entered the house the first thing he saw hanging before his eyes was a curtain of purple silk crepe emblazoned with the Ōkuma family crest, and beyond that a continuous line of gilt screens on both sides of the corridor all the way through to the reception room. "Splendid!" exclaimed Ōkuma. Ichijima concludes, "Many times Ōkuma remained totally unimpressed even after lavish sums had been spent; it was this kind of thing that he really liked the best."

There was a definite *nouveau riche* caste to Ōkuma's high-blown tastes. While he always styled himself a champion of democracy, Ōkuma was enthralled by cheap magnificence and a rather questionable lordly style. How utterly different from Itō Hirobumi, who in his capacity as a high official loved solemn dignity and behaved like an aristocrat, but cast these feelings completely aside on returning home, where he acted with the carefree simplicity of a young bachelor and was quite content to be treated as an ordinary citizen.

In all probability, Ōkuma's wife, Ayako, had a great deal to do with his lordly tastes. Her family had been *hatamoto*, high-ranking Bakufu retainers. She shared Ōkuma's taste for gaudy magnificence, and she also had a very strong character. Not at all the ordinary housewife content with her domestic role, she exerted strong influence over her husband, who is reputed to have once said that only three people awed him: god, the emperor, and his wife. Ayako had strong likes and aversions and could be critical and opinionated; people she disliked found it very uncomfortable to visit their house.[15]

Contemporaries often asked themselves how Ōkuma, a political leader almost continually out of office, could sustain such a rich and ostentatious lifestyle. Some simply said he lived in an enchanted palace and asked no further. Even today, this is still something of a mystery. He is thought to have depended heavily on the Nabeshima family, former feudal lords of the Hizen domain, for whom he acted as financial adviser after the Restoration. The Iwasaki family, founders of the Mitsubishi shipping and industrial combine, also seem to have supported him financially. In 1874, Ōkuma, head of the Taiwan Affairs Bureau, set up to direct a punitive expedition against aborigines who had murdered Japanese castaways. The Mitsubishi Company provided the ships for this expedition and thereafter received handsome government subsidies. Even after leaving office in 1881, Ōkuma's ties with the Iwasaki family remained close.

[69]

He made handsome profits from land sales, too. After Ōkuma's death, historian Kume Kunitake suggested that he was not in fact very wealthy, and that he probably sold half of his land at Waseda to the Nabeshima family. Kume thought that the Waseda residence itself was a gift from the Iwasaki family and that Ōkuma's coastal villa at Kofutsu southwest of Tokyo was built for him by Muroto Seiroku, a wealthy businessman. His other villa at Karuizawa in the mountains of Nagano prefecture was a gift from Nezu Kaichirō, a speculator who calculated that the value of his landholdings there would be much enhanced by the fashionable presence of Ōkuma. Apparently, even in his student days at Nagasaki, Ōkuma liked urging others to make money. He did not need to do so himself, he said, because people who owed their success to his encouragement would show their gratitude by giving him a share of their wealth. Ōkuma is reputed to have prodded Muroto Seiroku into making his large fortune.[16]

In artistic and cultural matters, Ōkuma's tastes were what one might expect of such an insensitive, commonplace, and mundane man. Ōkuma impressed people by discoursing at length on almost any subject, and superficially at least seemed to have wide interests. But while he liked to describe himself as a patron of the arts, he had no real appreciation for pictures and antiques. During his travels he was often shown paintings and other family treasures by his hosts, but he simply gave them a cursory glance and made no comments.

Ōkuma himself had a story he liked to tell about his artistic visions. "Once, an artist from Chikugo province called Kawabe was asked to do a painting, and I was to choose the subject. I settled on something very difficult. First, I like anything majestic. At the time, relations between Japan and Russia had suddenly grown stormy and people were anxious. Japan really seemed to have become part of the world, so a subject like the 'Three Views of Japan' sounded trite to me. Why not 'Three Views of the World'? People speak admiringly of the evening glow on the White Nile—though of course I have never seen this myself—the great river flowing languidly like a wide sea, the pyramids and the Sphinx on one side, and on the other the vast, boundless desert scorched by the blazing sun, a desolate landscape never

[70]

viewed by man. This, I thought, must be a magnificent sight. One hears praises of the dawn colors on snow-clad mountains. The peaks of the Himalayas, soaring almost 30,000 feet between India and Tibet, glittering and sparkling in the morning sun, capped by virgin snow unsullied since the dawn of time. What an awesome sight this must be! Or the autumn moon over the Great Wall of China. Stretching for 20,000 miles all the way from Lingtao to Liaotung, the crumbling ramparts of the Great Wall under a full, mottled moon high above in lonely suspension, the mountains and rivers on both the Chinese and Mongolian sides sharing its ghostly light—the purity and grandeur of such a landscape must surely be spectacular. So I asked Kawabe to paint these three things. At first, Kawabe was very troubled because on top of being most demanding subjects for a painting, all three were sights he had not seen himself. But I described them to him with care and enthusiasm, and I also got together lots of photographs. But he remained quite daunted by the task, and then, unfortunately, just when he was about to begin, he fell ill, and it all came to nothing." This self-congratulatory tale by a person who had never been overseas provides a revealing glimpse of Ōkuma both as a person and as a patron of the arts.

His appreciation for antiques was hardly more refined. When Ōtani Kōzui, a famous scholar of religion, returned from India, he brought Ōkuma the gift of a fine antique porcelain from Cochin. Ōkuma thought the surface looked dirty and he ordered his servants to give it a good wash, to the disappointed astonishment of people present. On another occasion, a certain Diet member presented him with an antique porcelain packaged in a wooden box whose dusty, weathered appearance conveyed age and elegance. Ōkuma, it is said, threw out this box and had a new one made.

Ōkuma did not compose Chinese or Japanese poetry and had no interest in elegant calligraphy. Traditional musical and dramatic forms such as Noh and Bunraku were distasteful to him. When he hired performers to entertain at banquets, he asked them to stick to popular narrative songs and storytelling. Outside the main gate of his Waseda residence a monumental statue of the two Deva kings towered imposingly, commanding the attention

[71]

of passers-by. When walking in his garden, he was often accompanied by a pet dog. Ōkuma's attitude toward this faithful animal seemed rather overbearing. He addressed it brusquely as, "Dog! Dog!"

From 1876 to 1884, Ōkuma's main residence was at Kijibashi in central Tokyo; he then moved to the Waseda residence in the northern outskirts of the city. During the years in Kijibashi he developed an interest in plants and flowers. He often said, "All people who love flowers are good. So I am not a bad person." But he took no pleasure in wielding the tools or trimming the shrubbery himself. He employed gardeners and explained their achievements with pride, lecturing his guests on the finer points. Gardening was in fact a "sociable" pastime that provided indulgence in display. Ōkuma also liked reading, but one suspects that his pleasure in literature was shallow, nothing like the love of books Itō celebrates in his poems and which was so important a part of his life.

Ōkuma and Itō were alike in their enjoyment of the game of *go*—and their lack of skill in it. After Ōkuma's death, Ozaki Yukio made a very interesting comparison between them as *go* players. "Even though he was unskilled, Itō put quite a great deal of thought into his first moves, and they were fairly good. As for Ōkuma, if at the start a critical formation emerged that could determine the outcome, he refused to concentrate or take things seriously. Instead, he would slap down his pieces in rapid succession, with careless abandon. When he got into trouble on one section of the board, or if it looked as though he might lose the game, for the first time he would stay his hand and think. When he concentrated, he could make very interesting moves, some way or other shoring up his weak position and worming his way out of what had looked like certain defeat. Just to be able to recoup some strength after such an amateurish start was an impressive achievement. But in overall strategy, Ōkuma always seemed to wait until a critical situation arose and only then would he begin to think and skillfully escape from it—by then it was too late to save a virtually lost game. If he had shown the same degree of thought and skill at the start, he could have won the advantage as the game progressed. Whenever he played *go* he did the same thing, moving carelessly through the first plays and beginning to think only after he ran into trouble. Ōkuma acted this way not only in the game of *go* but in many other matters. He had such brilliant talents, yet he so rarely achieved his aims. I think that was because he failed to make full use of his great natural talents and wisdom at the outset, but only after falling into difficulties."[17]

By and large, Ōkuma's tastes were pedestrian, his interests shallow. At times he himself spoke apologetically of his prosaic life or admitted that refined things were beyond him, a mere country samurai. The critic Yokoyama Kendō ventured that Ōkuma could justly be described as a coarse glutton at the dinner table, since he was a strong man with a very large appetite for food. But one could also say that his oratory had the same coarse and gluttonous character.

In his younger days, Ōkuma was a great libertine and tippler, but later on rumors of his flings with women died away and he drank sparingly. His daily life was carefully regulated and he paid great attention to his health. In many ways, this was quite in keeping with his character, but it might also have had something to do with his 125-year-lifespan theory. He could not possibly have really believed in such a thing, but when a journalist friend Kuga Katsunan died in 1907, Ōkuma asked reproachfully, "Why was Kuga so faint-hearted? Did he have to die?" as Miyake Setsurei records.[18] These revealing words suggest that Ōkuma's theory of longevity was rooted in an urge for individual self-assertion against nothing less than nature itself. Being scrupulously careful about his health—and thereby prolonging his life—may have been Ōkuma's way of declaring his challenge to the natural order of things.

Ōkuma and Itagaki

After relinquishing the Kenseihontō presidency in 1907, Ōkuma spent much of his time in pompous talk before large numbers of visitors at his Waseda residence. His conversations were often reported in the newspapers. He seized every opportunity to make speeches, transporting his audience with rushing torrents of rhetoric that won him hearty applause. He also spoke at each stop on his lordly travels around the country, and became a very

[73]

familiar and popular celebrity. In 1915, the year after Ōkuma formed his second cabinet, Yokoyama Kendō published a book about contemporary politics in which he made some telling points. "A political leader," he argued, "must keep in the spotlight at all times. A surpassing skill in self-display is vital for him. . . . When his name is very familiar through newspapers and magazines, then people will feel his presence even if they do not see him. To achieve this, the political leader must, as an urgent priority, work to keep himself regularly and constantly on display, especially if he is out of office. . . . He must not allow the people to put him out of their minds for even a day; he must always remain a celebrity, the center of talk. . . . Politicians in power have frequent opportunities to meet many people. Meeting people is meeting the world. But when out of office they must strive hard to create such opportunities. After stepping down as prime minister, Ōkuma astutely understood this and has worked strenuously at it. Today he is carefully cultivating the habit of meeting people."19

Ōkuma made great efforts to keep himself in the public gaze even after he withdrew from active political leadership. In contrast, Itagaki Taisuke quickly faded from view. He had served as a councillor together with Ōkuma in the early days of the Meiji government and later shared with him the credit for leading the Freedom and People's Rights movement. In some ways, Itagaki was very intellectual; in others, fiercely emotional. Combining conviction with passion, he naturally played a leading role as a progressive political leader. But in time these qualities worked against him. His fondness for abstract speculation weakened his powers of practical statesmanship. He was often too touchy, too liable to get carried away by his feelings, and as a result became intolerant. These were grave defects in a party leader when the opening of the Diet in 1890 began a new era of pragmatic, self-seeking politics. Deserted in 1900 by comrades who had shared his creed for so many years, Itagaki gave up politics completely and spent his days in humble seclusion.

Two years later, Toyabe Shuntei called on Itagaki at his home. He wrote afterward: "The man who was once the incarnation of the spirit of liberty, the veteran hero of the noble struggle to

[74]

overcome the wicked Sat-Chō devil and build the heaven of constitutional government, Itagaki has now given up the fight against ogres and is at peace. As an old man, he consoles himself in soft-hearted philanthropic endeavors such as moral progress, improving Japanese music, worker protection, education for the blind, and care for infants of women convicts. Now in the twilight of a life that continues to serve society, he is sustained and supported in this work by the compassion and help of old ladies." Talking with Toyabe that day in his thick Tosa accent, the white-haired Itagaki was wearing Japanese dress, while seated on a rattan chair, puffing away at cheap cigarettes. Politics, said Itagaki, had become an arena of contention for the spoils of success—power, honor, profit, and rank. Social work provided no gratification of such worldly desires, and for that reason he was glad to be involved in it after retiring from politics. He went on to say that to make constitutional government a reality, public morals must advance to a higher level. Then he spoke on about the need for social progress, especially in such matters as worker protection, but above all in providing care for the infants of women convicts. His eyes moist and his voice trembling, he described the pitiful condition of these innocent babes. As he recalled all that had been done so far to care for them, a warm smile lit up Itagaki's face. Then his mood changed abruptly, and in very emphatic tones he declared that crime was not the result of a depraved character; it could only be eliminated by a national effort to provide better education and welfare for the poor. He gave Toyabe a copy of a covenant for a child welfare association, and somewhat gloomily lamented that people with deep compassion for others were usually not wealthy, while the rich were rarely charitable. That was not right, he said.[20]

Itagaki thus spent his old age in lonely dedication to welfare work, living impecuniously in his modest house near Shiba Park. The public completely forgot about him once he left the political limelight. Itagaki was an active supporter of *sumo* wrestling, but the white-haired old man who regularly watched on from the gallery at the Kokugikan arena appeared to be a living fossil from the distant past. Itagaki's way of life in his final years was thus poles apart from Ōkuma's.

Sudden Triumph

As the year 1913 opened, Ōkuma was vigorous as ever in his old age. The third Katsura cabinet was in trouble, having provoked widespread opposition and a powerful Movement to Protect Constitutional Government. That January, Katsura announced his intention to form a new political party of his own as a device to help him out of his difficulties, but this news only aggravated the current political agitation and disorder.

It happened at this time that the Kōyūkai, the alumni association of Waseda University, met at Seiyōken restaurant near Ueno Park. At the meeting, Ōkuma made a speech to over 500 members, telling them that when the university was founded thirty years before, the Sat-Chō regime had refused to recognize independent, privately funded education based on progressive ideals. At about the same time, a number of political parties had been formed; the government refused to recognize them also, proclaiming the transcendence principle. Later, out of the Sat-Chō clique itself there emerged a sharp-witted fellow who realized that political parties were a fact to be faced and set out to lead one himself. Others in the clique reviled him as a "traitor"; his party had a majority in the House of Representatives, but the House of Peers was still committed to the transcendence principle and opposed to this hastily contrived notion of party supremacy. That is how the sharp-witted politician— Itō Hirobumi—found himself chained down by the very transcendence principle he himself had formulated.

All that had transpired ten years ago, but what of the situation today? "With his titles and decorations of Supreme Order of the Chrysanthemum, prince, and Imperial Military Order of the Golden Kite Third Class, Katsura Tarō was to all appearances an even greater leader than Itō," declared Ōkuma, but "now he has been forced to publicly affirm the principle of party government." It seemed that the old fogies in the Privy Council and House of Peers had recognized the same thing.

Henceforth, Katsura would have to reject the transcendence principle and openly take steps to foster liberal ideas in education. As prime minister, Katsura was grasping at political power and attempting to construct an instant party right before the eyes of the Diet. This was like planting an apple seed the night before guests arrived in order to feed them with fruit. A farcical effort, Ōkuma concluded—organizing a political party in the same way that plutocrats set up companies, vaunting their profits to push up share values.

Journalists reported the gist of the speech, commenting that recently Ōkuma's tone of voice and commanding expression were designed to give the impression that he himself, after many years of patient instruction, had inspired the Movement to Protect Constitutional Government now sweeping the nation.[21] Around the time of this speech, Ōkuma's magazine *Shin Nippon* published an article entitled "The Center of Power Must Move to the Diet." It argued that the Sat-Chō clique and the genrō had now lost their raison d'être; if the will of the people as concentrated in the Diet was only determined enough, it would be easy to supplant them. Very few of those who had participated in the Restoration were still alive, the article went on, and the remaining veteran statesmen "daily and hourly face the prospect of death. They find it hard enough just to keep alive and are tired out by the effort to exist." They could not carry the burden of important national affairs. Yamagata, for example, is actually "thin-faced and gasping for breath when one meets him face to face . . . a man close to the grave," and is not, as was generally rumored, a man of strong political aims and deep stratagems. Neither the Satsuma genrō Ōyama Iwao nor Inoue Kaoru have any such ambitions.[22]

In the end, the Katsura cabinet could not resolve the difficulties confronting it and resigned in February 1913. The genrō recommended Admiral Yamamoto Gonnohyōe, a leading member of the Satsuma clique, to form the next cabinet. But a year later, in February 1914, Yamamoto came under attack when high-ranking naval officers were court-martialed for taking bribes from the Siemens Company in return for lucrative contracts. Once again, the political world was thrown into turmoil. This time, *Shin Nippon* published Ōkuma's article, "Sat-Chō Drama Becomes People's Drama." The Sat-Chō clique, wrote Ōkuma, had maintained its power for over forty years, but when Katsura's cabinet collapsed the Chōshū clique arrived at its final hour. Now the situation of the Yamamoto cabinet made it apparent

[77]

that the Satsuma clique was equally doomed. Satsuma and Chōshū had held onto political power ever since the Restoration, even though the implementation of constitutional government in 1890 had promised to bring this to an end. The people at large, however, still had only a shallow understanding of what constitutional government entailed and, aided by inertia, the Sat-Chō clique had retained its power. As a result, Ōkuma continued, for nearly fifty years government leaders had been Satsuma and Chōshū men, or their close followers. "In terms of the theater, until now only Sat-Chō actors have appeared on the stage. But their long run has now come to an end and must henceforth give way to a drama starring the people."[23] Soon after Ōkuma's article came out, an odd and unexpected quirk of history put him back into power. In April 1914, after recommendation by the genrō, he became prime minister for the second time.

As a result of the Siemens scandal, the Yamamoto cabinet was fiercely attacked both inside and outside the Diet, and had resigned when its budget failed to be approved. That made the formation of a successor cabinet very difficult. The potential impasse was skirted when Inoue Kaoru proposed Ōkuma as the next prime minister and the other genrō agreed to recommend him to the emperor. The choice of Ōkuma was to some extent a repercussion of rivalry within the Sat-Chō clique. After Katsura's third cabinet was overthrown by the Movement to Protect Constitutional Government, the Seiyūkai continued in its pro-government role by supporting the cabinet that succeeded it, despite the fact that Yamamoto was a Satsuma leader. Inoue Kaoru of Chōshū was infuriated by this opportunistic desertion, and when the Yamamoto cabinet collapsed he began to see that Ōkuma might provide a means for revenge. Ōkuma had a deep-rooted hatred of the Seiyūkai, as a legacy from the distant days of strife between the Jiyūtō and Kaishintō. If appointed prime minister, he could be counted on to strike the Seiyūkai a heavy blow. Yamagata and the other genrō agreed. The Sat-Chō genrō had never trusted Ōkuma, who as a leader of the Freedom and People's Rights movement had kept up his steady, vocal support for constitutional government, coupled with repeated fierce attacks on the genrō and the Sat-Chō clique.

Before recommending his appointment to the emperor, the

[78]

genrō summoned Ōkuma to inform him of the policies they expected his cabinet to adopt. Having convinced themselves that Ōkuma had agreed, they put him forward as prime minister. Ōkuma then received the imperial mandate, and in April 1914 formed his second cabinet. He was supported by the Dōshikai presided over by Katō Takaaki, a distinguished ex-official and relative of the Iwasaki family, and by the Chūseikai, of which Ozaki Yukio was a prominent member. The Dōshikai was the new party planned by Katsura and set up after his death. The reform faction of the Kokumintō, successor to the Kenseihontō, had broken away to join it. Between them, the parties supporting Ōkuma held about one-third of the seats in the House of Representatives when he first took office.

Staging the People's Drama

The welcome awaiting Ōkuma's return to politics, after sixteen years out of office, was auspicious. There was, in today's jargon, a huge "Ōkuma boom." Not surprisingly, for Ōkuma had spent years carefully nurturing a good image of himself. Above all, he had worked hard to cultivate friendly relations with journalists. He took great delight in talking with them and always lavished them with charm. With his friendly welcome and forceful views, Ōkuma had long been a hero with the pressmen. When the Siemens scandal escalated into a public outcry, the newspapers castigated the Yamamoto cabinet, stirring up public opinion so effectively that the newly formed All Japan Journalists Alliance came forward to demand Ōkuma's appointment as prime minister. The Ōkuma boom indeed owed a great deal to the contemporary press. But the sources of his popularity went deeper. His constant efforts to keep himself well in the forefront of the people's consciousness had made him a national favorite. He never let the masses forget how vigorously he had supported people's rights, how greatly the Sat-Chō leaders mistrusted him, and how his own ungrateful colleagues had pushed him out of active politics. The general public as well as the press tended to sympathize and to admire how splendidly unperturbed he remained in spite of his political reverses. Ōkuma was as vigorous and spirited as ever in his latter years, constantly attacking the genrō and the Sat-Chō clique. All this gave him enormous popular appeal.

The fact remained, however, that Ōkuma owed this opportunity to become prime minister to the genrō, for whom he was simply a weapon against the Seiyūkai. After long years in confrontation with the Sat-Chō clique, Ōkuma had gained power as the tool and prisoner of his sworn enemies. Nevertheless, the nation now welcomed its new prime minister with all the festive enthusiasm of a crowd viewing cherry blossoms in early spring. In a somewhat Euripidean reversal, the fickle goddess who had smiled so warmly on the young Ōkuma now mocked him with sardonic laughter in his old age. Ōkuma himself could hardly have failed to appreciate the pathetic irony of his situation. But the lust for power still burning in his old body overcame all scruples and enticed him into a humiliating compromise with the genrō.

He was euphoric. On the evening before the palace ceremony to formalize his appointment, Ōkuma appeared before a large audience of reporters at his Waseda residence, telling them: "Gentlemen, trust me! My cabinet will fully satisfy your expectations. There are no weak soldiers under a brave general. Don't forget that the new cabinet is an Ōkuma cabinet! Just see what statesmanship it exercises and what ability it displays!" In the past, continued Ōkuma, the parties and government officials had conspired with each other, and this had given rise to great evils. However, "My mission is to rid the bureaucracy and the parties of abuses. Gentlemen, trust me! And do not begrudge me your words of friendly advice. I will gladly listen. Just let me prove myself. Could I possibly do anything that would betray your expectations? I am not one to change my standpoint, and I am always ready to leave office if I disappoint you. Right now, my task is to remedy the difficulties that beset our nation. With numerous problems facing me in the autumn, I shall strive with might and main to achieve my original aims, supported by all of you who share my concerns." While full of his customary bombast, Ōkuma wooed his audience with suave skill. He also told reporters who called on him a few weeks after forming his cabinet, "I have a cold and my leg hurts, but my spirits are high. I apply an anaesthetic to the painful area, then

I enter the official residence and start the morning's work. Human beings need this kind of gumption." To Ōkuma as he approached his eightieth year the fruits of power were very sweet and alluring.

The official actions of the second Ōkuma cabinet in the two-and-a-half years following April 1914 can be charted fairly concisely. Its first major step was in diplomacy. About four months after the cabinet was installed, approval was received from the genrō for Japan to join the Allies in the First World War. Then, in January 1915, Japan took advantage of its status as a belligerent to present China with the Twenty-One Demands. This harsh ultimatum demanding a wide range of new privileges and concessions produced an anguished protest from the Chinese. Nevertheless, after protracted and bitter bargaining, the president of China was forced to capitulate in May 1915, accepting a modified version of the demands, while public outrage took revenge in a widespread boycott of Japanese goods. This act of brutal diplomacy brought about a profoundly negative change to relations between the two nations, and Ōkuma's cabinet must be held responsible.

In domestic policy, Ōkuma took constant care to keep in touch with the genrō, especially with Yamagata, the most powerful of them, and to win their approval. In December 1915, he dissolved the Diet and called an election to be supervised by Home Minister Ōura Kanetake, a henchman of Yamagata. It was the most notorious rigged election in Japan's constitutional history. The Ōkuma boom had not yet subsided, but it took harsh and widespread interference to ensure a resounding defeat for the Seiyūkai. The pro-cabinet Dōshikai, Chūseikai, and Ōkuma's own support group gained an overall majority in the House of Representatives, much to the genrō's satisfaction. Then the new Diet, the 36th of May to June 1915, passed a bill for two new infantry divisions that Yamagata, the "patron deity" of the army, had been urging for some time.

After this Diet session, it came to light that Ōura had bribed Seiyūkai members to vote for the army increases bill and had been granted a stay in legal prosecution on the condition that he resigned. Ōkuma and his cabinet had to admit responsibility and tendered their resignations. The emperor consulted the genrō

[81]

on whether to accept them or not, and on their advice he ordered Ōkuma to stay in office. Thereupon, public opinion turned fiercely critical. Attacked by the opposition parties for his failure to resign in the 37th Diet of November 1915 to February 1916, Ōkuma defended himself, saying, "To be ordered by the emperor to stay in office, and yet disobey and resign on one's own volition —could anyone do such a thing? Your demand for a 'responsibility' resignation violates imperial sovereignty!"[24] After so many years of determined and eloquent exposition of the ideal of constitutional government, Ōkuma was now using the well-worn clichés of the transcendence principle, so dear to his enemies, the Sat-Chō clique. In reaction to the Ōura bribery scandal and Ōkuma's refusal to resign, the popularity of the cabinet suddenly plummeted to the depths. Even then, Ōkuma was reluctant to leave his post as prime minister. Eager for his Chōshū protégé General Terauchi Masatake to form a cabinet, Yamagata found Ōkuma's obstinacy insufferable. When Yamagata summoned him and pressed him to leave office, Ōkuma had no alternative. He and all his ministers resigned in October 1916.

After such a miserable performance, the Ōkuma boom faded quickly and vanished without trace. In later years, journalist Miyake Setsurei described the administration of this Ōkuma cabinet as so vacillating and inept as to "strike one dumb with amazement." Prime Minister Ōkuma had revealed for all to see a blatant discrepancy between word and deed, coupled with gross irresponsibility. A contrite Ōkuma later admitted, "When I look back on my past career, for the most part it is a history of failure and stumbling."[25] Doubtless, his second cabinet was uppermost in his mind when he said this.

Posthumous Judgment

Ōkuma was seventy-nine years old when he left office. Once again, he retired to his Waseda residence and resumed his former way of life. Gradually, almost inevitably, Ōkuma's previous image restored itself in the hearts of the common people. When he died in January 1922 at eighty-five, he was given a people's funeral of imposing magnificence amidst widespread public acclaim.

Two years before Ōkuma's death, Itagaki died in his modest house at the age of eighty-three. In the autumn of 1918, when confined to bed by illness, Itagaki began to dictate his views on politics, compiling what he called a final testament to the people. When the manuscript was completed, he kept it carefully by his pillow, showing it to no one. He sent it for publication on the day before his death. Itagaki had been raised to the third grade of nobility in 1884, and one of the three clauses in his will stated that because he had always maintained that peerages should last for one generation only, his eldest grandson, Morimasa, was not to inherit the title of count. On hearing of his death, five men representing the blind asked to keep a funeral vigil over him. Itagaki had campaigned for shampooing and massaging to be restricted as occupations for the blind, and they were very grateful. On the day of the funeral, his coffin bearers were *sumo* wrestlers who had enjoyed his warm patronage. Newspaper articles reporting Itagaki's death were brief, indicating the social obscurity that had befallen him. Even so, some 3,000 people attended his funeral at Shiba Seishōji temple. It was a cold winter day, but the setting sun shone bright and clear.

Itagaki's manuscript was published after his death under the title *Rikkoku no Taihon* (Great Principles on Which Japan Is Founded). The book reads as though it had been written in the 1870s on behalf of the Freedom and People's Rights cause. That was quite in character: he stuck firmly to his convictions all his life, arguing for them in terms of abstract principles and never swerving from them.

Today when we think of Ōkuma Shigenobu and we recall his political career, some people may find it tragic. But it had its lighter, even comic elements. Toward the end of his life, Ōkuma once said, "For many years I have been an 'open door' person; I have friends even among farmers and townsfolk. When I discuss matters with the servants, we talk heart to heart. I don't puff myself up like a high official. I have always championed democracy." In his later years, he was often acclaimed as a "democratic" political leader. But after Ōkuma's death, critic Chiba Kameo observed that "Ōkuma was raised in the peerage to count, and then to marquis; when I think of Ōkuma's way of life at his Waseda residence, I cannot feel any affection for him. Perhaps there was never a possibility that he could be called a 'commoner' noble. Marquis Ōkuma as an aristocrat tried hard to be liked by ordinary people, and I suppose that some of those who still felt a nostalgic respect for the nobility were grateful. But he did not really understand the common peoples' heart."

Ōkuma was a leader of the Freedom and People's Rights movement, and later as a champion of constitutional government he pressed for the overthrow of Sat-Chō rule. His attacks on the impropriety of genrō dominance were matched by his harsh criticism of corruption in the pro-government Seiyūkai. Even so, in view of his disastrous second cabinet, to acclaim him as a democratic political leader is perhaps too generous. Keeping up a barrage of appeals to the nation through speeches, newspapers, and magazines, he loved the limelight and kept himself talked about. He cast himself in the role of the people's champion, and they responded with warm feelings for him. The fact that Ōkuma was acclaimed as "democratic" probably says as much about the public as about him. It suggests that the common people, so little esteemed by most prominent men of the time, yearned for a leader who, as one of themselves, would truly represent their feelings and aspirations. If this is what they expected of Ōkuma, the accolade "democratic" given him can truly be called a tragedy for the people.

When political freedom was restored and greatly extended in Japan after the Second World War, Itagaki, who had died poor and lonely, neglected by the public, was elevated to a higher place in common estimation than Ōkuma, for all his spendid people's funeral. More significant now than any comparison between the merits of Ōkuma and Itagaki is the fact that time appears to be in the course of ranking these two political leaders in their just order. As a general rule, the judgment of history seems to require the calm and quietness of a later era before it can deliver its verdict.

HARA TAKASHI

The "Commoner" Prime Minister

1856–1921

Throughout his varied career, Hara Takashi retained a sense of being different from his colleagues, and that stemmed from the time and place of his birth. The word "commoner" is often used when speaking of Prime Minister Hara, but his grandfather Hara Naoki Masamoto was a senior retainer of the powerful Morioka domain in northeast Japan. Hara was therefore a member of the samurai upper class. He was born in 1856 at the family residence just outside the walls of Morioka castle, and his childhood coincided with the pre-Restoration political upheavals. When he was twelve years old, Morioka and several other northeast domains rallied to the defense of the Bakufu against the newly declared Meiji government. Together with its allies, Morioka was branded an imperial enemy and suffered a bitter defeat in the brief civil war of 1868; its lord and leading families were disgraced and suffered a sharp reduction in stipends.

Meanwhile, the Satsuma and Chōshū victors enjoyed all the delights of power and prosperity. Mutsu Munemitsu, himself a former samurai of the relatively unfavored Kishū domain, acidly observed, "In the twelfth century when the Taira clan flourished in politics, people said that if you were not one of them, you were less than fully human. Today it seems that the men of Satsuma and Chōshū enjoy a comparable superiority." Many talented men from other domains were brushed aside under the Sat-Chō regime and withered away in obscurity. Those from defeated domains like Morioka fared even worse; they were mocked and insulted by the Satsuma and Chōshū victors as a "mountainous heap of worthless northerners."

Wounded Feelings

In such circumstances, young Hara Takashi's future did not look bright. Energetic, competitive, and full of determination, Hara was by nature inclined to draw a sharp distinction between friend and foe; in these early years he suffered numerous humiliations that pierced him to the marrow of his bones, and he never forgot them for the rest of his life. For example, when he took the pen names "one mountain" and "excellent mountain," in conscious allusion to the "northerners'" insult, that was not in self-ridicule. It embodied a proud and determined spirit of resistance. Much later, in 1914, when Hara was home minister in the Yamamoto cabinet, he held an additional post as chief commissioner for the enthronement ceremony of Emperor Taishō. On 6 February he wrote in his diary: "Afternoon. When I attended the commissioners' conference and we discussed a number of matters, I was annoyed to see that certain banners to be displayed at the enthronement ceremony bore titles such as 'Used in the suppression of the northeast at the time of the Restoration,' or 'Designed after an imperial standard entrusted to the commander-in-chief during the subjugation of Ōu province.' It was agreed that today, when we are all grateful subjects of the emperor, expressions usually used to describe foreign conquest were improper, and I had them removed."[1]

Again, the year 1917 marked the fiftieth anniversary of the Restoration war. At that time, Hara was president of the Seiyūkai. Public ceremonies were held by many former domains to commemorate their war dead. Leading men of the former Morioka domain also made several attempts to prepare for such ceremonies but could not manage to raise sufficient funds. When Hara heard about it, he immediately donated money and asked the Morioka city authorities to go ahead with their plans. His support enabled a memorial service to be held at the local Hōonji temple in honor of the Morioka domain samurai who had died fifty years before in the Restoration war. Hara attended the service and read out an address he had written himself: "We have come together today to commemorate Lord Nambu's samurai who died in 1868. When we look back, how could any Japanese subject of olden days, any more than now, draw his bow against the emperor? The Restoration was simply a conflict of political views. At the time, there was a popular song, "Winners—the imperial army; losers—rebels." That accurately describes the situation in 1868. But now all subjects share in the radiance of the emperor's gracious favor, as is clear to all. So be at rest! I chanced to be visiting our province and am honored to participate in this ceremony. With utmost sincerity, I address you on this day, 8 September 1917. A man from the former domain, Hara Takashi." He included the text of this address in his diary, adding, "I don't know what others will think, but it clearly expressed my innermost feelings."[2] A verse he wrote just after the ceremony tersely summed up his sad reflections: "The smoke of incense harried by the wind; a mood of autumn."

The Winding Stair

On a visit to his home province, after several terms as a cabinet minister, Hara replied to a question asked him one day by some villagers: "To tell you how I resolved to conduct myself throughout life, I left home fully determined to overcome whatever hardships lay ahead, and I have kept this resolve ever since." In 1871, aged sixteen, Hara set out for Tokyo, keenly aware that his future would be hard and filled with obstacles. His father had died when Hara was still very young, and the family finances were now in difficult straits. When he returned after making a name for himself in politics, he always said the same thing whenever he was asked to speak at places such as a village school, "It is no use relying on parents, brothers, relatives, or friends in this life. Success or failure depends entirely on one's own efforts." Repeated again and again to the young people of his home province, these words were no doubt accompanied by bitter memories of those distant days when he lived far from home, relying only on his own isolated and earnest efforts.

After a year in Tokyo, too poor to embark on a regular course of study, Hara entered a theological school founded by a French Catholic missionary. In 1873, he was baptized. Early Meiji officialdom was so dominated by the men of Satsuma and Chōshū that outsiders seemed "less than fully human." Business, also, was largely controlled by government-connected merchants.

[87]

Many young students such as Hara abandoned all hope of advancement and dedicated their lives to preaching the gospel. For the next few years, full of pessimism about his future, Hara remained in service with his missionary teachers. However, in 1876, he was fortuitously accepted as a pupil of the Justice Ministry Law School. His classmates found him stubborn and fond of argument; but he was always neatly dressed, well behaved, and free from all taint of rustic boorishness. Two years later, Hara and some fellow students became involved in a dispute with the school principal, and he was expelled before he had acquired any formal qualifications.

So Hara changed course again, turning to journalism, perhaps his last resort as a talented outsider. He joined the *Yūbin Hōchi* newspaper in 1878, on the sponsorship of Abe Hiroshi, two years his senior and previously a fellow student at the Morioka domain academy. When expelled from the government after the Political Crisis of 1881, Ōkuma Shigenobu became proprietor of the *Yūbin Hōchi* and appointed as editor Yano Fumio, a young protégé who had followed him out of office. Other colleagues of Yano soon joined the newspaper, notably Inukai Tsuyoshi and Ozaki Yukio. Hara felt swamped by this influx of talented young rivals and began to talk of giving up his job. Yano Fumio, seething with anger against the government, was well aware that Hara held moderate political views and was friendly with Watanabe Hiromoto and other prominent officials, so he made no attempt to dissuade him. Nevertheless, Hara found Yano's attitude very annoying and despised him for many years afterward.

Hara then moved to Osaka as chief editor of the *Taitō Nippō*, a newspaper recently founded by the Chōshū leaders Itō Hirobumi, Inoue Kaoru, and Yamada Akiyoshi. As the organ of a new pro-government party, the Teiseitō, this newspaper adopted a moderate line in politics, and on taking up his post Hara announced that its principles were exactly in accord with his own. Hara's six months with the *Taitō Nippō* provided him with the opportunity to become friendly with Inoue Kaoru. At length, a new path with exciting prospects had opened up for Hara. He was establishing close ties with the leaders of the Sat-Chō clique. That was not an unusual course for outsiders in search of a future career, but in Hara's case his choice by no means implied an unconditional surrender to his patrons. He simply adopted a compliant posture in the hope of gaining sufficient power to challenge them in the future.

When the *Taitō Nippō* folded for lack of funds in 1882, Hara returned to Tokyo and was appointed a secretary in the foreign ministry. His appointment was allegedly made with the backing of a middle-ranking Satsuma official, Nakai Hiroshi. But at the time, Inoue was foreign minister and he and Nakai were on close terms. They were relatives of a sort, and the year after Hara joined the foreign ministry he married Nakai's daughter by a second wife. Many years before, in an amicable arrangement, Nakai's first wife had divorced him and married Inoue. Thereafter, the two men had remained friends, and Inoue is said to have gone to great lengths to arrange Hara's marriage. After that, a patron-protégé relationship between Inoue and Hara was thoroughly cemented. Under Inoue's backing, Hara rose steadily in the foreign ministry, serving as consul at Tientsin and then as secretary to the Japanese legation in Paris. In 1888, he transferred to councillor in the agriculture and commerce ministry. As before, his patron was Inoue, the minister at that time.

A Close Friendship

When Mutsu Munemitsu replaced Inoue as agriculture and commerce minister in 1890, Hara stayed on as his private secretary and councillor. Hara had always been stubborn and fond of argument, often tending to create friction. Even toward the intelligent and energetic Mutsu, then at the peak of his career, Hara often stuck to his views and refused to budge from them. He once said, "If the minister orders, I shall obey. But I will not submit to mere quibbles." So thereafter, the story goes, Mutsu always told him, "That is an order!" Nevertheless, Mutsu was deeply impressed by Hara's vigor and ability, while Hara repaid Mutsu with admiring devotion. Coming from the Kishū domain, which had played a passive role in Restoration politics, Mutsu was not a member of the Sat-Chō clique. During the Satsuma Rebellion of 1877, he had plotted a coup to overthrow the government with some young militants of the Tosa Risshisha party. The conspiracy came to light, and Mutsu was imprisoned. On his

[89]

release in 1882, he seemingly changed his allegiances, throwing in his lot with the Sat-Chō leaders. His underlying intention was to earn their trust and have his talents recognized and then to overthrow the Sat-Chō clique from the inside. Mutsu and Hara in character and choice of career were very much alike. Hara's devotion to Mutsu therefore comes as no surprise, and for the next few years he followed his mentor in and out of office.

When Mutsu resigned as agriculture and commerce minister in March 1892, Hara resigned as well. A little later, Mutsu became foreign minister in the second Itō cabinet, and Hara joined the ministry as a bureau head, eventually rising to the post of vice-minister in 1895 and minister to Korea a year later. In 1897, a year after Mutsu had left government service for reasons of health, Hara became editor of the *Osaka Mainichi*. Long afterward, Saionji Kimmochi attributed that appointment to Inoue's sponsorship. Hara had already discussed the matter with Mutsu and obtained his approval. When everything was settled, Hara visited Mutsu in hospital and sat at his bedside to report. This was to be their last meeting.

According to Hara's diary, Mutsu raised his emaciated body from the bed to listen and declared that he was greatly relieved to hear that all had gone well. "Mutsu then said he would like to eat; ordinarily he continued his interesting talk at mealtime; but sensing that this would be our last conversation together, he found it hard to keep up a pretense of normality. He was also very tired and in pain, and to see him struggling to hold a conversation was agony for me. So I said that for years we had conferred on almost everything, and I knew what his opinion would be on this occasion, even if he did not state it. I could not bear to tire him more and intensify the sadness with a useless, lengthy conversation. But I promised to come often until I left Tokyo at the beginning of the year. With that, I said farewell and left the room. As I was about to go downstairs, Mutsu called me and I went back. He asked me again about my strategy when I went to Osaka. I replied that I had to go there first and take a look, but then I would come back to ask his opinion. I would also call at the beginning of next month whenever I had time. Mutsu looked as if he wanted to talk further. His face showed how unhappy he was to part with me. Despite myself, I was moved to

[90]

silent tears. A family member in that situation might understandably break down, lose control of his emotions, and be unable to keep calm and rational. But someone that close would also not want to hold a long conversation, I thought, so I braced myself and took my leave."[3] A little over a week later, Mutsu died.

Hara's diary contains innumerable entries describing the very close bond between him and Mutsu. But nowhere else in these voluminous pages does Hara describe his emotions in such a detailed and passionate way. With the death of Mutsu, he had lost a true friend. It is open to speculation whether Mutsu would have joined the Jiyūtō had he lived longer. If so, his devoted follower Hara might perhaps have taken a different path as a political leader.

The Seiyūkai

Hara's term as editor of the *Osaka Mainichi* was brief. At the urging of Itō and Inoue, he resigned in 1900 to join Itō's new party, the Seiyūkai. Itō had known Hara for many years. When Itō went to China in 1885 as special envoy to sign the Treaty of Tientsin, Hara was there as consul, which gave them many opportunities to meet. Inoue and Hara had a personal, family relationship going back even farther. Inoue provided much advice and assistance from behind the scenes when his longtime friend Itō set up the Seiyūkai, and he was also involved in getting Hara to accept posts as a member of the party's board of directors and as its secretary general. When journalist Ishikawa Hanzan enquired what kind of man this secretary general was, Itō praised Hara enthusiastically: "In future he will become a pillar of the state. He is a capable man, whom young people like yourself should get to know."[4] Itō clearly held Hara in very high esteem. If Hara was now firmly committed to ties with the Sat-Chō ruling clique, even more striking was the defection of so many members of the Kenseitō, successor to the Jiyūtō, who dissolved their party and joined Itō's Seiyūkai despite long years of dedication to the Freedom and People's Rights movement and strident clamors for the overthrow of the Sat-Chō clique. Clearly, a fresh wind was blowing in politics, and Hara took it at full sail.

Soon after launching the Seiyūkai, Itō formed his fourth

cabinet. With the exception of the foreign, army, and navy ministers, all the others were members of the new party, and in effect it was a Seiyūkai cabinet. Hara soon took office in it. When Communications Minister Hoshi Tōru was forced to resign in December 1900 after involvement in a bribery scandal, Itō appointed Hara his successor. So Hara suddenly found himself the first cabinet minister to hail from a defeated domain. The "worthless northerner" was now well on the way to political success.

The fourth Itō cabinet was shortlived, in office for barely six months. Just after the cabinet resigned in May 1901, Hoshi Tōru, a veteran politician acknowledged as the de facto leader of the Seiyūkai, was stabbed to death by an outraged opponent of his corrupt manipulations in Tokyo city government. His death opened the way for Hara to increase his influence in the party until his only rival was Matsuda Masahisa, who had studied law in Paris during the early 1870s at the same time as Saionji, and had then gone on to a distinguished career as a journalist and Jiyūtō leader. Hara was talented and able, but he remained as stubborn and argumentative as ever, so his relations with other party members tended to be thorny. Popularity in the party went rather to Matsuda, whose vague and all-embracing powers of accommodation made him a good coordinator.

Hara was often intensely dissatisfied with Itō's leadership. Itō had set up the Seiyūkai chiefly as a means to realize his own political aims and publicly admitted that his commitment to the party was far from total. In addition to maintaining long-standing ties with the veteran Sat-Chō leaders, Itō seemed to compromise too much in other areas, as well. He was not a fighter but skilled in creating harmony. These qualities naturally came to the fore in his leadership as Seiyūkai president. Hara, with his inclination to see people either as friend or foe and his compulsive urge to win, regarded Itō's presidency as weak-kneed. In June 1903, for example, Itō summoned Hara and Matsuda to tell them that the Katsura cabinet was in trouble over finance and diplomacy and would probably collapse soon. At this juncture the Seiyūkai should not rush; the transfer of power from Katsura should be smooth. Burning with ambition and fighting spirit, Hara found this suggestion most objectionable. He retorted that it was all

[92]

very well for Itō, who had many achievements to his credit and little further ambitions, to talk in this way. However, Hara continued, he and the other party members were in quite a different position. Itō was now growing old and if he did not speedily appoint a successor the party faced imminent collapse.[5] These sharp words are a good indication of Hara's feelings at the time.

Disappointment with Saionji

When Itō was appointed president of the Privy Council in July 1903, Saionji succeeded him as Seiyūkai leader. Saionji regarded the party presidency as a burdensome chore he had taken over as a duty to the aging Itō; he had no particular desire to form a cabinet. He took very little interest in the job and left the running of party business entirely to Hara and Matsuda.

Hara soon showed his talent for political strategy. In 1905, while the war against Russia was still in progress, he held secret negotiations with Prime Minister Katsura that committed both to an elaborate trade-off. If the Seiyūkai supported his cabinet, Katsura was prepared to hand the government over to Saionji as soon as the war ended and agreed to ask his patron Yamagata for help. In return, Hara intimated to Katsura that when Saionji formed a cabinet, the Seiyūkai would not ally with the Kensei-hontō but would remain friendly toward Yamagata, Katsura, and their following. While promising to gain Yamagata's approval for a transfer of government and to assist the new Saionji cabinet in maintaining good relations with the other genrō and the House of Peers, Katsura also requested that Saionji should not form a party cabinet. Hara and Katsura thus made a compact, but its success relied heavily on Yamagata's "assistance," "approval," and so on, words that came up again and again in the negotiations. The fact was that Yamagata's opinion was vital in selecting the next prime minister. Thus in December 1905, the Katsura cabinet resigned and Saionji formed its successor. The fact that the transfer was so smooth owed a great deal to Hara's planning and negotiating skills.

Hara took the key post of home minister in the new Saionji cabinet. But his position as a party man was not strong. The Seiyūkai's real power had diminished considerably since Saionji

[93]

took over as president. As a political leader, he was of distinctly less caliber than his predecessor. In fact, Katsura even intervened in the choice of ministers to serve in Saionji's cabinet, and as a result far fewer posts were held by party members than in the fourth Itō cabinet. The only party members with cabinet posts were Hara and Matsuda, who had to accept as their colleagues several henchmen of Yamagata. By this time, a huge clique network centered on Yamagata had spread throughout the political world. Again and again it operated to check the actions of the Saionji cabinet, even to administer hostile shocks from time to time. And there was Hara, hemmed in on all sides, not least by cabinet colleagues of Yamagata's following, right in the thick of the political fray.

Home Minister Hara carefully cultivated ties with the genrō, especially Yamagata, all the while scheming to weaken the clique regime at its roots by expanding Seiyūkai influence at the level of local administration. For example, he tried to pass a bill for the abolition of rural divisions, which were often headed by ex-officials or pro-government local worthies, but he could not get it passed by the House of Peers. He also engineered a massive shake-up of prefectural governors, who had constituted an important base for Yamagata's following. Claiming to be weeding out old and useless incumbents, Hara appointed many young and capable university graduates to replace them. He was equally active in attempts to create an opening for the Seiyūkai in the House of Peers. For example, he secured cabinet posts for Senke Takatomi and Hotta Masayoshi, respective leaders of the powerful Mokuyōkai and Kenkyūkai factions. But despite all his stratagems and strivings on the Seiyūkai's behalf, Hara made little real headway, while making himself the chief target for Yamagata's followers in their attacks on the Saionji cabinet.

That made Saionji's apathetic party leadership all the harder to tolerate. Hara vented some of his anger and discontent in his diary: "I have helped Saionji for quite some time, but as Mutsu once observed, he is much too languid and careless. I have labored tirelessly for him, and I am astounded that he has never once thanked me for my great efforts on his behalf. Saionji must surely know that his popularity in the party and his chance to form a cabinet owe much to my great influence."[6] Another entry states:

[94]

"Perhaps because Saionji wants to appear frank in matters of politics, he tends to confide in people that he will probably not last long in office. To speak so imprudently worries me, and I have asked him to stop; there is always the danger that Katsura or followers of Yamagata will exploit such statements."[7]

Impatience

The collapse of the Saionji cabinet in July 1908 gave Hara an opportunity to visit Europe and America for about six months. He had recently remarried, having divorced his first wife three years before. When he returned to Japan at the beginning of 1909, the second Katsura cabinet, which had succeeded Saionji's, had not yet been in office a full year. Hara at once began to bargain with Katsura over the next change of government. Arguing that under the present circumstances only Katsura and Saionji were of sufficient stature to be prime ministers, Hara suggested to Katsura that the nation would benefit if the two leaders took it in turn to govern without too much deadlock. He reassured Katsura that he did not want a cabinet change for the time being, and Katsura seemed to understand what he had in mind. Katsura himself attached great importance to Hara's opinions and tended to heed his suggestions, realizing that Hara had commanding influence over the actions of both the Seiyūkai and its president, Saionji.[8] At the end of the following year, Hara conferred with Katsura to reaffirm their previous understanding. This time he went one step further and asked when, roughly, Katsura thought his cabinet would resign. From Katsura's answer, Hara surmised that it would be after treaty revision finally became operative, whereupon the cabinet could rest on its laurels.

Meanwhile, the Kokumintō, successor to the Kenseihontō, had approached the Seiyūkai with plans for an alliance to push the Katsura cabinet out. But having already made an agreement with Katsura, Hara rejected these overtures. Soon thereafter, in January 1911, under the slogan of "mutual understanding," the Seiyūkai formed a coalition with the Katsura cabinet. Hara explained in his diary that to join the Kokumintō in moves to overthrow the Sat-Chō clique would be to "stir up calm waters; it would not only fail to arouse any sympathy among the public, but

[95]

would also force our party into a long period of adversity." The
political situation was not as simple as the Kokumintō members
thought.[9] As always, Hara opted to avoid an out-and-out clash
with the Sat-Chō leaders and Yamagata's followers, but rather
to compromise with them, thereby increasing the Seiyūkai's
influence and prospects of power.

Desperate to get the Seiyūkai into office a second time, Hara
found Saionji's ambivalence toward the second Katsura cabinet
more and more infuriating. In spring 1910, for example, Hara
and Matsuda visited Saionji to discuss strategy. They urged Saionji to reject any suggestion by Katsura that General Terauchi
Masatake, a Chōshū protégé of Yamagata, should form the next
cabinet. If Katsura made even the most casual offer to hand over
the cabinet to him, Saionji should definitely accept. Saionji
replied that both in body and mind, he was too weak to take
office, even if Katsura made the offer. To be frank, the position
of Seiyūkai president was really too much for him. Hara warned
that if Saionji did not take office, the Seiyūkai faced collapse,
and plans to avoid this must be made straightaway. Surely there
must be some good plan or other, suggested Saionji lamely. Hara
shook his head. How could any plan possibly be good in this desperate situation? Despite Saionji's pleas, he was not a sick man,
and to refuse to form a cabinet while president of the Seiyūkai was
quite incredible. Surely respect for Itō's departed spirit made it
imperative to save the Seiyūkai from ruin. If Katsura offered a
transfer of government, Saionji should take office for as long as
his strength allowed, if but for six months or a year. After that,
if he was too ill, a contingency plan would have to be made.
Pressured by Hara, with Matsuda in support, Saionji finally
gave in. But his heart was not in it. He continued to speak as if
becoming prime minister would be an irritating burden.[10]

Hara's constant worry was that Katsura would exploit Saionji's
complete apathy toward political power in order to monopolize
government leadership. But in June 1911, Katsura told Hara
that he wanted Saionji to take over the cabinet in August, and
that Yamagata had approved the transfer. Hara immediately
began preparations for a second Saionji cabinet. He impressed
upon Saionji that this time the cabinet must be firm and durable.
Once more, Saionji demurred: he was a sick man, he said; he

could not take office for very long and wanted that to be understood in advance. Much better that someone else take the job.
Beside himself with anger, Hara retorted that if becoming prime
minister was so distasteful to Saionji he should, of course, refuse.
But in that case, the Seiyūkai would collapse and everything it
had achieved over the years with such resolution and effort would
be in vain. If Saionji was ill, he could limit his tenure and step
down after choosing a suitable person to succeed him as prime
minister and Seiyūkai president. But it would be the height of
irresponsibility to resign suddenly before such matters had been
settled. Hara argued the same points again and again, until
finally Saionji was convinced.[11] When speaking so vehemently
about the need to select a future prime minister and Seiyūkai
president, Hara gives one a strong impression that inwardly he
was casting himself in these roles.

A Devious Situation

The process was tortuous, but Saionji's second cabinet was finally
installed in August 1911 after Katsura resigned, and Hara again
took the post of home minister. He was careful to warn Saionji
not to inform Katsura about the allocation of cabinet posts until
after the event, in order to prevent interference. The same policy
would help ensure unity and solidarity in the new cabinet. Yet,
once again making allowances for the Yamagata camp and their
distrust of the parties, Saionji appointed only three Seiyūkai
members to cabinet posts: Hara, Matsuda, and Haseba Sumitaka.
If Hara had hoped for strong leadership this time round, he was
swiftly disappointed. Saionji's performance both as party president
and prime minister seemed so flabby that Hara even threatened
to resign. Petulantly, he wrote in his diary: "I have assisted Saionji for many years; most of his seeming success is entirely due to
my plans. Both Saionji cabinets were also the results of my efforts.
But he never gives me a moment's thought. I do not, of course,
seek wealth or fame. I do not care a whit for such things. My
assistance to Saionji has not elevated me a single grade in court
rank or class in the Order of Merit. Yet after all my work on his
behalf, both openly and behind the scenes, he still has no concern whatsoever for my troubles. When I think about going on

like this—helping such an ungrateful person in the demanding world of politics—the risk of failure and disgrace seems too big, and it depresses me. I think I should leave the cabinet at once and make a new start at something else." Hara confronted Saionji with these complaints and exchanged bitter words with him. But Saionji finally persuaded him to stay in office.[12]

In his second term as home minister, Hara pressed ahead with his drive to expand Seiyūkai influence. Accordingly, in the 28th Diet of December 1911 to March 1912, he put up a bill for revisions to the electoral law. Hara wanted a return to the small, single-seat constituencies of pre-1902. Under the present system, the rural divisions of each prefecture were grouped into large, multiseat constituencies; Seiyūkai candidates were often forced to compete with each other and found it harder to build strong electoral bases.

Before the Diet opened, Hara approached Yamagata and sought his approval for the bill. Single-seat constituencies were desirable, he told Yamagata, for a reason that could not be stated publicly: the multiseat system offered a greater chance for candidates to seek election by putting forward extremist views. Socialist-type speech and behavior were on the increase, Hara continued, and the single-seat constituency was the best way to keep subversive ideas in check. While seeming to agree with Hara, Yamagata changed the subject to observe that if proposals for manhood suffrage succeeded, this would wreck the nation. Hara agreed that extending the franchise was still premature. Without Seiyūkai backing, a manhood suffrage law could not be passed, but the Kokumintō and other parties were pushing for an extension of voting rights. That, concluded Hara, was another reason why the single-seat constituency was the best policy at the present time.[13] In short, Hara set out to exploit Yamagata's deep distrust and fear of democracy in order to gain advantageous revisions in the electoral law.

When Hara's bill came before the Diet in March 1912, it was easily passed by the House of Representatives where the Seiyūkai had an absolute majority; but in the House of Peers it ran into opposition led by Yamagata's followers and was rejected by an overwhelming majority. This defeat in the House of Peers was in some measure a reflection of Yamagata's belief that the triangular balance between the Seiyūkai, Kokumintō, and lesser groups that had emerged under the multiseat constituency system provided a good way to control the parties.

In December 1912, after less than a year and a half in office, the second Saionji cabinet collapsed when it was unable to resolve an imbroglio with the military over the issue of forming two new infantry divisions. Having relinquished his post as Lord Keeper of the Privy Seal in August, Katsura now came forward to set up his third cabinet. But within a few weeks the Movement to Protect Constitutional Government was launched under slogans to "Defend the Constitution" and "Overthrow the Sat-Chō Clique." In the midst of great national upheaval, the cabinet resigned in February 1913 after barely two months in office. Katsura was succeeded by Admiral Yamamoto Gonnohyōe. Yamamoto pressed Hara and Matsuda to join the cabinet and support him, saying that if they did not do so he would not take office. For their part, Hara and Matsuda both feared that if Yamamoto declined the appointment, the next cabinet would be headed by a follower of Yamagata. So after negotiations, Hara, Matsuda, and Motoda Hajime of the Seiyūkai took cabinet posts and the Seiyūkai put its support behind Yamamoto. To many, this represented a betrayal, for having joined the Movement to Protect Constitutional Government, the Seiyūkai now blatantly reversed its position. Such a self-seeking compromise with Yamamoto, an acknowledged leader of the Satsuma clique, outraged the public.

Having failed to achieve much advantage for the Seiyūkai under the second Saionji cabinet, Hara did better this time. Soon after taking office, the Yamamoto cabinet revised the official regulations of the army and navy ministries. Until then, ministers of the army and navy were required to hold the rank of lieutenant-general, vice-admiral, or above; under the new regulations those on the reserve or retired list also became eligible. The Civil Service Appointment Act was revised to open up a wider range of free and special appointments to people outside the regular bureaucracy. These were valuable political concessions gained by the Seiyūkai.

Shortly afterward, during the 31st Diet session of December 1913 to March 1914, the cabinet was rocked by revelations of corruption among senior naval officers, the Siemens scandal. It was rumored that Yamamoto, too, the so-called father of the navy, was involved. The popularity of the cabinet plummeted and violent demonstrations erupted as huge crowds mobbed the Diet compound to demand its resignation. With public contempt for the Yamamoto cabinet running so high, Hara feared that the Seiyūkai would suffer by association and find it hard to recover. Seiyūkai support for the cabinet seemed too risky, so when the 1914 budget bill failed to pass the Diet, Hara used the occasion to force a cabinet resignation in April 1913.

Party President

When the Yamamoto cabinet collapsed, Inoue Kaoru proposed Ōkuma Shigenobu as the next prime minister. Inoue was incensed by the treacherous opportunism of the Seiyūkai, which had joined the Movement to Protect Constitutional Government in order to overthrow the cabinet of fellow Chōshū leader Katsura, but had then switched to an alliance with Yamamoto of the Satsuma clique. Ōkuma's intense dislike of the Seiyūkai and its many former Jiyūtō members had roots going back to the days of the Freedom and People's Rights movement. Inoue could be confident that as prime minister Ōkuma would be a willing tool in putting down the Seiyūkai, and the other genrō agreed with him. So Ōkuma formed his second cabinet with the support of the Dōshikai and other anti-Seiyūkai groups.

It was in these troubling circumstances that Hara was appointed Seiyūkai president. The fortunes of the Seiyūkai had declined perceptibly under Saionji's inept leadership. His last positive act as party president had taken place in February 1913, during the last days of the third Katsura cabinet. When the Seiyūkai and Kokumintō agreed to propose a vote of no confidence in the cabinet, the emperor sent a message to Saionji encouraging him to do his best to resolve the confrontation. When Saionji failed to persuade the Seiyūkai Diet members to change their attitude, Katsura was left with no alternative but to resign with all his cabinet. Simultaneously, Saionji announced his intention to give up the Seiyūkai presidency and from then on refused to attend to party business. So Hara and Matsuda together handled matters for him. But during the last days of the Yamamoto cabi-

net, in March 1914, Matsuda died. Hara and Matsuda had been
the actual leaders of the Seiyūkai under Saionji's presidency.
Hara's resourcefulness and ability as a fund raiser gradually gave
him the most weight, and in the two Saionji cabinets he had become the true leader of the party. After Matsuda died, Hara was
appointed party president on Saionji's recommendation, which
came as no great surprise. At first, when Saionji urged him to
assume the post, Hara was very hesitant. As he wrote in his diary,
if he became president, "Suppose I am assassinated . . . the party
would suffer a terrible blow." Also, faced with the emergence of
a cabinet headed by his arch-enemy Ōkuma, the future of the
Seiyūkai looked bleak. But he changed his mind about accepting
the presidency. "Leaving aside how I would respond if things
were going well, right now the party faces hard times. Precisely
because the party is not thriving, I feel I must accept against my
will and do my best."[14] Hara's abundant conceit and rugged
determination come through vividly in this diary entry.

As the new Seiyūkai president, Hara brooded anxiously about
how to extricate the party from its current difficulties. In discussions with Hirata Tōsuke, Kiyoura Keigo, and others in the
Yamagata camp, he observed that the genrō, the cabinet, and
rival political parties alike were all bent on destroying Seiyūkai
influence. But, he pointed out, despite many errors in the past,
the Seiyūkai had contributed much to the nation. The party
could not just sit back and await destruction. If the genrō and
other influential men gave the Seiyūkai no credit for its construc-
tive stand up to the present and plotted its demise, the party would
have no alternative but to adopt radical positions on reducing
taxes, liberalizing the press, extending the franchise, and so on.
Once that happened, it would not be easy to turn back. Whether
events went that way or not would be determined in the next two
or three years. Hara asked Kiyoura to convey this opinion to
Yamagata.[15] That is to say, by hinting that the Seiyūkai, if forced
to do so, might decide to join up with the masses, Hara sought
to threaten Yamagata and his followers and compel them to stop
attacking the Seiyūkai.

But on the other hand, Hara tried hard to reach a friendly
understanding with Yamagata. So far, there had been only very
few opportunities for amicable discussions with him, but after

[101]

Hara became party president, he called frequently on the genrō. Aware of Yamagata's long-standing desire for the formation of two new infantry divisions, Hara hinted to him if one of the genrō formed a cabinet at the present juncture, the Seiyūkai would approve a bill for army expansion. His basic aim was to force Ōkuma out, but that strategy was preempted when Ōkuma's cabinet itself presented a bill for army expansion to the 35th Diet of December 1914. The bill was voted down by the Seiyūkai and Kokumintō, whereupon Ōkuma dissolved the Diet. In the general election of March 1915, the odds were against the Seiyūkai. For one thing, the nation was in the grip of an Ōkuma boom, but other factors including electoral interference and lack of funds all worked against the party. Whereas the Seiyūkai lost its absolute majority, the rival Dōshikai and allied groups together gained enough seats to keep the cabinet firmly in power. Ōkuma had dealt a heavy blow to the Seiyūkai, amply satisfying the expectations of its enemies.

Having lost a lot of ground, Hara racked his brains even harder for ways to win over the genrō. He warned Seiyūkai members not to attack them, especially Yamagata, for he feared that any confrontation would simply add another enemy to the existing one— Ōkuma. At length, Yamagata, Matsukata, and the other genrō grew tired of the Ōkuma cabinet; Yamagata finally forced its resignation. In October 1916, General Terauchi Masatake of Chōshū became the next prime minister.

Success at Last

Hara foresaw that an alliance between the new Terauchi cabinet and the rival Dōshikai would keep the Seiyūkai pinned down. As soon as Terauchi took office, therefore, Hara began urging him to form a transcendence cabinet. When Terauchi did indeed form a non-party cabinet, Hara's next plan was to have him dissolve the Diet and then in the ensuing election to recoup the damage done to the Seiyūkai under the Ōkuma cabinet. Hara's first move was to solicit Yamagata's approval for a dissolution, explaining that if an election were held now, it would produce the triangular party balance Yamagata favored. When the Terauchi cabinet faced its first Diet in December 1916, the

Kenseikai (successor to the Dōshikai) joined with the Kokumintō to put up a no-confidence motion, but the Seiyūkai backed the cabinet. Thereupon Terauchi, prodded by Hara, came out with a vigorous indictment of the previous Ōkuma cabinet and dissolved the Diet. In the general election that followed, the Seiyūkai gained a great victory, and with 160 out of 381 seats once more became the leading party.

Hara was now burning to form his own cabinet, but he waited patiently, hoping the Terauchi cabinet would pave the way by destroying itself. In the long effort to win over Yamagata, he had exhausted his tactics. When winding up one of their frequent discussions, Yamagata once told Hara that on matters of government policy their views were in complete accord, except on a single point—Yamagata could never agree with Hara's belief in the necessity for party government. Hara never forgot that last remark.[16] As the most influential cabinet nominator, Yamagata had begun to consider Hara as a candidate for prime minister sometime in the future. But because of disagreement on this single point, Hara could by no means be sure that Yamagata would ever recommend him.

Hara's patience with Yamagata was now wearing thin and continued subservience seemed to promise few benefits. Hitherto he had carefully avoided a direct clash with Yamagata and his followers; far from bringing the Seiyūkai closer to government, this, Hara felt, would produce quite an opposite result. However, Hara now resolved that if a Yamagata-line cabinet emerged after Terauchi's collapsed, he would not hesitate to ally with the rival Kenseikai in order to overthrow it.

"When the next cabinet comes up," Hara wrote in his diary, "Yamagata will do everything he can to keep the Seiyūkai out of office. He will not, in any case, recommend me until all other alternatives are exhausted, so I need not worry too much about Terauchi's successor. Some kind of cabinet will emerge; if it is headed by a bureaucrat, I will use all the strength at my disposal to oust it, even joining forces with the Kenseikai. If things come to that, I think we should sweep the bureaucrats out of politics and set things on a new path. I do not, however, think such a policy will necessarily be the best for the nation, and I hope that politics can be improved without such harsh remedies. But if the bureau-

[103]

crats cannot see the need for change, there is no other way to save the nation.''[17]

Hara did not have to wait long before the Terauchi cabinet fell into difficulties. In July and August 1918, over 700,000 persons in 36 cities and hundreds of towns and villages rioted uncontrollably for nearly two weeks in protest against the high price of rice. After calling in troops to suppress these so-called Rice Riots, Prime Minister Terauchi resigned in September 1918 on the pretext of poor health, and his cabinet followed suit.

Meanwhile, Yamagata had been quietly brooding over who should succeed Terauchi. He could find no satisfactory candidate among his own followers and kept coming back to Hara. Even so, his antipathy to party government was as strong as ever, and Yamagata hesitated. He was finally persuaded to act by some of his own followers, who had gradually come to share the view that there was no one but Hara capable of serving as the next prime minister. When the genrō met after the resignation of the Terauchi cabinet, Saionji recommended Hara to the post. Yamagata made it clear that he was still opposed to party government, but he finally agreed. Thus, in September 1918, Hara received the imperial mandate to form a cabinet.

Party Leader

Eighteen years after joining the Seiyūkai and four years after becoming its head, Hara now took over the reins of government, as party president and prime minister. The road behind him was steep and winding, and coming this far had brought about a noticeable change in his character and conduct. So let us first take a look at Hara's qualities as a party leader.

When Hara first joined the Seiyūkai, he always stuck fast to his views and never let an argument pass. He was constantly at odds with people. But gradually a great change took place, especially after becoming party president. He seemed a different person. He began to show tolerance and listen to others, his friendly face brimming with smiles. This often surprised people who had known him in his youth and remembered the fractious young man always ready to ride roughshod over opposition. Self-discipline may partly account for the change, but it was also a result of his rise in the Seiyūkai. As his power in the party grew and the challenge of enemies and rivals within it faded, Hara identified increasingly with the Seiyūkai. It became an extension of himself, something he regarded with affection, and whose members he treated like close companions. That was the generosity of a victor. Inherently prone to make sharp distinctions between friend and foe, Hara saw anyone opposed to the Seiyūkai as an enemy, but the party itself, as a whole, was his friend.

Especially after he became Seiyūkai president, shouldering responsibility both in word and deed and making titanic efforts for party expansion, Hara developed a great affection for its members. In particular, he lavished money on them without hesitation or regret. Ozaki Yukio heard from Seiyūkai members close to Hara that during general elections, the president would always give more campaign money to candidates than they requested, if he thought their status or ability justified it. Someone asking for ¥10,000 would get ¥15,000; those asking for ¥20,000 would get ¥30,000, and so on. Seiyūkai politician Uchida Nobuya described the never-ending stream of people coming to Hara with requests for money. Standing before the busy president, these suitors first declaimed on the realm or the nation; then, with a "by the way," they came to the point and asked for money. While they orated, Hara listened silently with folded arms. Uchida, unable to endure wasting time on such foolishness, once said to Hara, "They want money, so why not just hand it over and let them go away?" Hara replied, "These people are pitiful. Simply to give them the money and send them away would be too heartless. I couldn't bear to do that, so I just pretend to listen."

Hara took great pains to be home in his Tokyo house at the year's end. About this, Mochizuki Keisuke, a Seiyūkai leader, told the following story. On the last day of 1920, an urgent matter arose that needed to be resolved by the party president. But Mochizuki and his colleagues feared that Hara would probably be busy on New Year's Eve, no matter what the problem. They decided to enquire how things were and request him to hold discussions as soon as possible in January. When Mochizuki telephoned, Hara said, "I'll be at home; just come on round." Mochizuki went to Hara's house a little reluctantly, knowing that

Hara reserved this time of year for meetings with party members. He did not want to disturb Hara with problems. Hara was waiting at home, expecting visitors, not knowing who would call or what they would talk about. "Today is the last day of the year," he told Mochizuki. "But nobody has called. Perhaps they all think I am busy. No matter who it involves, I do not think current business should be put off until next year. I have been here all day, but everybody has been too considerate and no one has come to see me. So please stay for as long as you like." Mochizuki was moved beyond words to see Hara so solitary and dedicated. He knew that business at the year's end consisted almost entirely of callers who came to ask for money, and that Hara always welcomed these pathetic people and treated them with sympathy.[18]

Ozaki observed that Hara was unsparing in his efforts to support the rights and interests of party members. Kataoka Naoharu, who belonged to a different party but was friendly with Hara, recalled him as "an unselfish man of strict probity. As Seiyūkai president he had to be aggressive in fund raising; but the money was not for himself, but to give to others." When Hara was home minister in the second Saionji cabinet, Kataoka visited him frequently and the conversation often touched on this matter. With a gentle smile, Hara once said, "If you don't provide honors or money, you cannot influence people. At the very least, you must put them in the way of financial benefits." Kataoka went on to observe that "the reason why the whole party was so grateful to Hara, why it supported him as party president, and why Seiyūkai strength grew so much under his leadership was in truth located here."[19]

The following anecdote was told about Hara's relationship with party members. One evening, a younger politician visited Hara's house to discuss current issues. When a heated argument arose, the angry visitor took his leave and stamped out of the house. As he was about to go through the gate, Hara called out from behind, "Take care on your way home! There is a big hole outside the gate! Be careful not to fall into it!" Regardless of the harsh words exchanged just a moment ago, Hara's warning was full of kind concern. Workmen had dug a hole in the road that was dangerous in the darkness. The younger politician was

[106]

reportedly so impressed by Hara's thoughtfulness that thereafter he responded with faithful deference.

Uchida Nobuya recalled that when subordinates visited Hara's home, however angrily he reproved them for something, he always saw them off, right up to the front gate. On wintry days, he never forgot to say kind things like, "Don't catch cold, will you." Such simple words completely moved the hearer. Uchida also related that a hanging scroll purporting to be the work of the famous artist Shibata Zeshin was displayed in the reception room at Hara's house. It was clearly an imitation and so Uchida asked, "Why should the party president have to be content with this?" and made as if to take it down. But Hara said, "No! The man who gave it to me probably thought it was genuine. I want to honor his good will."

While he was so generous toward Seiyūkai members, Hara was sparing in his own needs. He lived in an old, dark, narrow house near Shiba Park. He bought the small dwelling with his retirement gratuity when he left his post as private secretary to the minister of agriculture and commerce in 1892. Thereafter, he simply added extensions to it. The land on which it stood was leased from Tokyo city. The garden was minute, and everything inside the house was plain and simple. Next to the main entrance a small six-mat room facing north was used to receive guests; the cushions for seating were dotted with patches from careful mending. "Most people would have acquired a new house in the course of rising from private secretary to prime minister," Ozaki Yukio observed, adding, "Of course, originally it was a large residence for him, but to stay in such a small house all his life, even in the time of great prosperity as prime minister, is proof that Hara was not ostentatious or mercenary."[20]

Although Hara lavished money on party members and had easy access to financial benefits, he was very frugal in his private life. Journalist Baba Tsunego was a frequent visitor at Prime Minister Hara's home. He enjoyed their talks, and once Hara said to him, "It is good to argue together now and again, like students." After Hara was assassinated, his remains were interred at Morioka, but Baba went to the Shiba Park house and burned incense there in his honor. At the time, Baba noticed that the floor mats in the small room with the commemoration tablets were almost worn out. "To think that this man, prime minister and at the height of prosperity, lived in such a simple way—I suddenly found myself weeping," he confessed.

Once, when a group of people were visiting his small summer cottage in Koshigoe near Kamakura city, Hara sighed, "Why does everybody want money? The Seiyūkai has become a great national party, but the flaw in the jewel is that so many people are after money. It is good to remember the 'well and hedge' spirit." This last expression originated from the many cases of early Meiji politicians who tried to campaign in grand style and exhausted all their financial assets, until left owning only the unsalable well and hedge of their houses. One clause in Hara's will states: "I have never tried to make money, and so I have no great wealth." The property he bequeathed was very small for a politician of his eminence. As a party leader, Hara had given himself completely to serve the Seiyūkai. Tokutomi Sohō commented after Hara's death that no Seiyūkai president had so thoroughly established his authority over the party. More so than the first president, Itō Hirobumi, or the second, Saionji Kimmochi, their successor Hara elicited from virtually every member "the sincere respect and affection a true leader merits." One reason was that Hara "took all responsibility upon himself. 'Leave the problems and troubles to me! You can have the wealth and honors!' That was Hara's attitude to his colleagues."21

As Hara committed himself body and soul to the Seiyūkai, his attitude to its members grew ever more gentle and affectionate. That did not mean he had lost his appetite for dispute or determination to keep the upper hand. He continued to draw a sharp distinction between friend and foe, but now it was his political enemies, especially members of rival parties, who learned how merciless he could be.

Correctly attired, calm, and composed, Hara mounted the Diet stand to face his critics, looking sharply toward the opposition benches. He talked rapidly in a metallic, thin, but penetrating voice. When rival partymen asked probing questions, he was quick to catch them out on a slip of the tongue, or strike back in fierce counterattack. People noticed that when Hara came to the crucial point in an argument he often took out a white handkerchief and vigorously rubbed his nose and mouth with it. At such times, his thin voice gradually became harder to hear, and from the opposition benches jeering cries of "Raise your voice!" rang out. Pursing his lips, Hara would reply, "My voice is naturally faint!" with a look of bitter contempt. When he pursed his lips in this way, it was a sign that he was bristling and ready for a good fight. Anyone who had seen him in the Diet knew that expression. Yokoyama Kendō maintained that it betokened a very strong man; Ōkuma had it, and so did Hara.[22] Hara's pugnacious attitude toward opponents did not change after he became prime minister. While some were critical, saying that he was too childish and arrogant, no one could say he lacked spirit.

Political Principles

As prime minister, Hara adopted the motto "Wipe the slate clean." That meant forgetting the past, leaving the future to bring what it might, and getting on with the job in hand—a fundamental attitude toward politics that never changed. Tokutomi Sohō's appraisal of Hara continues: "He had great gifts as a politician but was very poorly endowed in statesmanship. On that point he differed widely from his mentor, Mutsu Munemitsu, who had many faults, but was a talented statesman nevertheless. Hara, unluckily, had nothing that can be called a far-sighted political creed. He was a pragmatic realist, unencumbered by ideals or concern for the past or future. Among public figures there was perhaps nobody else who thought, planned, and acted so thoroughly for the present. If he just went ahead solving problems quickly and smoothly, that was enough for him. Lacking deep or enduring convictions, he simply handled things from one situation to the next as skillfully as possible. The ordinary, run-of-the-mill politician climbing the ladder could never match him in that. . . . Hara's greatest pleasure came not from action, but from restraint. While he was a most energetic man, he never took the initiative in raising an issue. Instead, he occupied an impregnable position and waited defensively for others to attack him. His first instinct in politics was to retire and gather strength. To stir things up by new proposals was much too foolish for a calculating man like Hara. When forced to take an initiative, Hara would pick the most opportune moment and then move swiftly."[23] Tokutomi's observations seem accurate. They tally with the comments made both by Hara's supporters and by his political enemies.

In short, Hara's strength as a political leader was in his pragmatism, in the expedient and dextrous handling of immediate problems, rather than in any commitment to principles and ideals. His speeches seem to reflect this—they were terse and inelegant, delivered in a low voice that lacked resonance. Dry and uninteresting, they left no lasting impression. Hara himself often said how much he disliked making speeches. Without the principles and ideals to raise his oratory to a higher plane, it is no wonder he never became a first-class public speaker. In any case, speeches were of little importance in the practical everyday politics of the day, so perhaps that was why he paid little attention to his own. Hara was at his best in impromptu verbal exchanges, where he could outdo his opponents by quick rejoinders. In committees as well as Diet sessions, he is said to have taken most pleasure in direct verbal exchanges, which exemplified what Tokutomi noticed—that he lived by and for the present. His great gifts as a manager and strategist dictated his political style, and account for his steady advancement toward becoming prime minister.

Hara the Man

Hara was above all a manager in politics, and a mundane concern for petty detail was equally apparent in his daily life. He always paid great attention to dress. Never a dandy, he dressed neatly, nevertheless, in good quality suits and coats, which he kept presentable even after he had worn them for several years. Whether at a banquet or in the Diet, nothing in his attire was out of place. Even at home, he never hunched his shoulders or lounged about negligently. His library was well-ordered; the books were arranged under subject titles, the documents kept in separate envelopes, classified by content and carefully shelved. Every morning Hara read the papers, then received visitors; afterward he refolded each page of the newspapers and put them in neat piles. He made two wills. One was marked to be opened immediately after his death and contained instructions for the funeral ceremonies. The other, to be opened after the funeral had taken place, concerned family affairs, property, et cetera. He expended the most minute care on these documents.

Hara had a deep attachment for his home province and a strong, lasting affection for his relatives and friends. As Yokoyama Kendō observed, "Hara was merciless to his enemies, but got on fairly well with people in general. Above all, he was very gentle toward his friends."[24] His dutiful care for his mother still living in Morioka was renowned. He did not neglect his divorced wife, either, sending her money and other gifts. Hara had no offspring by his own marriage, but adopted the child of a relative. He gave his adopted son, Mitsugu, as much affection as any true father would. In October 1921, while prime minister, he sent Mitsugu overseas to England for study. Maeda Renzan, a journalist on the *Jiji Shimpō* staff and a frequent visitor at the prime minister's house, relates that when he heard Mitsugu was preparing for the voyage, Hara said, "Let me do it. I'll pack for him," and handled everything himself. On the day of Mitsugu's departure, Hara saw him off at Yokohama. Standing at the edge of the pier, he stayed long after the ship sailed, until it receded from view. With his son absent, Hara often enquired about him to family members and even to his servants. "I wonder where Mitsugu is now?" he would say, or tell his wife, "When he gets back, he'll probably be a lot taller." All his life, Hara continued to pay dutiful respects to the Nambu family, lords of the former Morioka domain. Hara on many occasions extended his help to his home province and to his old acquaintances there. As a preface to a poem he composed, Hara wrote, "Upon enquiring at Kamo port in Yamagata prefecture after some friends of my youth, and hearing that their children had gone to Hokkaidō years before and that no further news had been received from them." The poem itself reads: "Sadly, we are like butterflies in autumn, powerless against the driving wind."

After becoming prime minister, Hara continued to hold Seiyūkai banquets at unpretentious restaurants such as Hanaya in Tsukiji, which specialized in Japanese cuisine, and Sanentei in Shiba for Western-style food. Hanaya was close to the agriculture and commerce ministry. When Mutsu was minister and Hara his private secretary, they often dined together there; Hara always thought of it with gratitude, and with long, happy memories. Sanentei was near Hara's house and he dined there for many

[111]

years. Uchida Nobuya recalled that Hanaya was very old-fashioned and, to his view, most disorderly: "Once when in charge of a banquet I asked for elbow-rests to be provided at least for Hara and one other guest, Major General Miura Gorō, but the restaurant could not even do that. The Western-style Sanentei, too, was notorious for its bad cuisine. I commented once on how insipid it was, and Hara replied, 'No, it isn't. You don't spend enough, and so you get poor food. If you are willing to pay, it is very good.' " Even if his favorite restaurants really were that bad, one suspects that Hara, always loyal to longtime friends and associates, would still have defended them.

Hara sometimes played *go* and *shōgi* when relaxing with friends, but he was not a player of any rank or skill. Growing older, he liked composing haiku verses. But as he always maintained, "I like politics more than my three daily meals."[25] That was his real interest.

Prime Minister

In September 1918, Hara formed a party cabinet, with Seiyūkai members occupying all posts except the army, navy, and foreign ministries. Hara was the first prime minister who did not hold a peerage at the time of his appointment, and, just as significant, he was the first to form a cabinet while both president of a political party and holder of a seat in the House of Representatives. At its inception, therefore, the Hara cabinet seemed new and fresh. Immediately following the inauguration ceremony, Hara told Maeda Renzan, "I am very thankful to be given such a warm welcome, but people will be let down if they expect too much of me. Had I become prime minister ten years ago, I might have done a lot. But when you get older, things become more complicated. You get tied down in various ways—frankly, you get entangled in personal considerations. I have absolutely no freedom of movement. Don't expect too much, or you will be disappointed!"[26] Hara's reference to ten years ago recalls his frustration during the final months of the Terauchi cabinet.

Hara was sixty-three years old when he formed his cabinet. Eager to plunge straight into the business of governing, he took himself very seriously and was bored by small talk. Soon after his appointment, he attended a reunion of classmates of the former Justice Ministry Law School. Hara returned from the gathering very peeved, complaining to Kodama Hideo, president of the Board of Decorations, "Tonight's reunion was very dull . . . surely there are more interesting things to talk about. The conversation, such as it was, consisted of everyone chatting together about their grandchildren. If that was all they wanted to talk about after so many years, I told them they could just as well have visited me at home and not gone to the expense of hiring geisha."

Hara must surely have been overjoyed to attain the highest seat of government as prime minister. In a brief poem entitled "Farewell to 1918" he wrote: "The wind has died down and all is calm; temple bells ring out the old year." One can only surmise what pleasant thoughts must have passed through his mind on that New Year's Eve.

His new cabinet was up against problems on several fronts. Yamagata was over eighty, but he still wielded immense influence as a genrō and was, as ever, hard at work maintaining and extending his clique network. One after another, he continued to appoint his followers to posts in the Imperial Household Department and the Privy Council, providing them with honors and peerages to boot. Hara visited Yamagata much more frequently after forming his cabinet, explaining his policies in the most minute detail, anxious for sympathy and support. Those efforts paid off, and Yamagata was generally satisfied with Hara's conduct of affairs. To his close followers, he often praised Hara's political skills. On the other hand, as Major General Miura Gorō once told Hara, "Yamagata doesn't like people to succeed in government." Careful never to let his own power and influence slip, Yamagata at the same time kept a jealous eye on other people's achievements. To prevent him from becoming too presumptuous, Yamagata sometimes confided to members of rival parties that he was discontented with Hara's cabinet. Such talk raised the hopes of Ōkuma and the Kenseikai, who had their sights on the next cabinet and needed Yamagata's backing. Hara's attempts to reach an understanding with Yamagata always had to contend with political intricacies of a very delicate kind.

The first major step taken by the Hara cabinet was to put up a bill for electoral reform to the 41st Diet of December 1918 to

March 1919 and have it passed. The new legislation lowered the tax-paying qualification for the vote, increasing the electorate to 3 million (5 percent of total population.) And of greater advantage to the Seiyūkai, it replaced the multimember by single-member constituencies, a change long desired by Hara. Hara had continuously tried to persuade Yamagata that unless some extension was made to the franchise and single-member constituencies restored, there was a strong possibility that the movement for manhood suffrage—anathema to Yamagata—would grow too strong to be restrained. At long last, Hara's arguments proved convincing. Disturbing currents were running through society at the time as demands for democratic reforms grew more and more insistent and the labor movement suddenly acquired a new vigor. Such conditions now enabled Hara to get Yamagata's agreement for electoral reforms.

On the other hand, the rival Kenseikai and Kokumintō parties sought to capitalize on the current restlessness to increase their popularity, and presented a bill for manhood suffrage to the 42nd Diet of December 1919. Given the forces that swayed the Diet, there was no doubt that the bill would be defeated. Nevertheless, when it came up for first reading, Hara suddenly dissolved the Diet, announcing that he would seek "the impartial judgment of the people" on the bill, which, he said, embodied "subversive ideas that threatened the existing social system." In the general election of 1920, the Seiyūkai came out far ahead of the other parties, gaining 282 out of 464 seats.

Immediately after the election, Hara appointed as justice minister Ōki Enkichi, head of the Kenkyūkai, the most powerful faction in the House of Peers. Furthermore, by providing financial benefits, official posts, and honors, Hara gradually gained the allegiance of other leading members of the House of Peers. Little by little, he brought the Kenkyūkai faction over to the Seiyūkai, building up in the Diet what he called a "foot in both camps." By worming Seiyūkai influence into the House of Peers, so long the proud bastion of the Yamagata camp, Hara came to control its core. All in all, under Hara's cabinet the Seiyūkai reached a distinctly higher level of power and influence.

Of all the accomplishments of the Hara cabinet between 1918 and 1921, the reform of the electoral system was perhaps the most significant. The single-member constituencies gave the Seiyūkai a clear advantage over the other parties, especially in the rural areas. Next, his cabinet opened the posts of governor general of Korea and Taiwan to appointees other than military officers, while ruling that the governor general of Kwantung could be either a civil or military official. Third, it canceled the restrictive revisions to the Civil Service Appointment Act made by the second Ōkuma cabinet in deference to Yamagata, and allowed more posts to be held by appointees outside the regular bureaucracy. Fourth, it revised the local government system, in particular the regulations for city, town, and village assemblies. Rights to elect and to be elected were streamlined, and grades within the electorate providing more seats for the higher taxpayers were reduced or abolished altogether. Apart from these measures —mostly aimed directly or indirectly at increasing Seiyūkai influence—the Hara cabinet achieved very little else. That seems to reflect the kind of political leader Hara was: an expert at handling immediate issues with dexterity.

The "Commoner"

Every prime minister before Hara had held a peerage. He did not, which is why he is often called the commoner prime minister. To remain a commoner meant a great deal to Hara. From around 1914, when he became Seiyūkai president, Hara constantly worried that the government would award him a peerage, and he wanted to avoid that, as several entries in his diary attest. Once he had acquired great influence over the Seiyūkai, the prospect of having to move to a seat in the House of Peers became distasteful to him. The evidence on this point is quite clear. Soon after Hara joined the Seiyūkai in 1900, Itō formed his fourth cabinet. Hara was very disappointed when passed over for a cabinet post and pressed Itō to appoint him a member of the House of Peers at the earliest opportunity. That much is recorded in his diary. But as he went on to build up power within the Seiyūkai and to devote himself entirely to it, Hara became determined to lead the party through thick and thin as a member of the House of Representatives.[27] Hara's strong attachment to the Seiyūkai, and his dedication to leading it, made peerages and

[115]

other official honors unattractive. And by remaining a commoner, he advanced along the correct path for a party leader.

Does the word "commoner" have any substantive meaning when applied to Hara the political leader? Such facts as Hara's winning Yamagata's trust before forming his cabinet, Yamagata's complete accord with Hara on all political issues except on party government, and his general satisfaction with the actions of the Hara cabinet are enough to inspire doubts on this point.

So let us look a little more closely at the question of Hara's reputation as the "commoner" prime minister. First, the policy of extending the vote. As home minister in the second Saionji cabinet, Hara agreed with Yamagata that manhood suffrage would ruin the nation. Hara still believed this as prime minister— he dissolved the Diet in December 1919 over that issue. His diary records that when Ogasawara Nagayoshi and Aoki Nobumitsu, leaders of the Kenkyūkai faction in the House of Peers, voiced their fears that the opposition parties might pass a manhood suffrage bill, Hara replied, "My concern is not just with the next election. If pressure for the vote grows stronger, class boundaries will be totally confused, and the nation itself put in jeopardy. By some means or other I will stop the bill from getting to the House of Peers. Don't worry!" After the Seiyūkai gained an absolute majority in the general election of 1920, Hara once more warned Yamagata that mistakes in timing would, indeed, risk ominous consequences. "The danger of hastily implementing manhood suffrage is not in the rural divisions and villages, but in the urban areas," Hara's diary records. "From ancient times, revolutions have occurred in capital cities, and if manhood suffrage were to take place suddenly, Tokyo would be rocked by riots and disorder. This was to be feared, I said, and Yamagata completely agreed."[28] On several occasions, Hara spoke in the Diet on the manhood suffrage issue; in one speech to the House of Peers, he said that far from restraining subversive ideas, extending the vote to the propertyless classes at the present time would have an opposite effect.[29]

Next, the labor issue. When Hara took office as prime minister, intellectuals and workers had protested for many years that clause 17 in the Police Regulations of 1900 had been improperly used as a legal weapon against union organization and the holding of strikes. Faced with strong demands for its abolition, Hara countered that the clause protected both labor and capital and should remain in force. To Hara, worker demands for higher wages and the frequent labor disputes of the time amounted to disorderly conduct, and he believed that the government should exercise firm control. When prominent capitalists looked as though they would give in to workers' demands, hoping to buy a "temporizing peace," Hara recorded in his diary that "unfortunately this just cannot be allowed!"[30]

As prime minister, Hara constantly fretted about the spread of subversive ideas and the danger they seemed to pose, but he could think of no other remedy than that educators should improve ways of thinking. He was also worried about the spread of Christianity in Japan; Confucianism and Buddhism had been Japanized, but Christianity was propagated by foreign missionaries. The world war had let loose new, disturbing currents of thought. The people seemed agitated, and Hara was uneasy about the future.[31]

As head of his own party cabinet, Hara had no desire to follow the standard procedure in parliamentary government by which two large parties alternated in office; he did his best to ensure the next cabinet would not be formed by the rival Kenseikai. Hara told Yamagata's protégé, General Tanaka Giichi, currently his army minister, that if Katō Takaaki headed a cabinet it would seek the support of the masses, just as Yamagata feared. Self-defense would then force the Seiyūkai to outbid the Kenseikai in its policies, and that would probably cause a massive national upheaval.[32] He hoped, of course, that Tanaka would repeat this to Yamagata. Hara also exploited the Kenseikai's demand for a wider franchise to alienate the party from Yamagata, who so much detested this policy. For example, on meeting Yamagata in April 1921, Hara mentioned that he was thinking of making cabinet changes; Yamagata suggested that maybe he should not, since good replacements were not to be counted on. Hara's diary records the exchange that followed: "I said, 'Provided Katō keeps his head, all will go well. But he is always being forced to move under outside pressure, which is very troubling.' Yamagata gave me a firm promise that if there was any prospect of Katō getting in office and pushing manhood suffrage through, he would, even if left to do so on his own, lend his support to the Seiyūkai."[33]

As Hara was well aware, Yamagata's fear of the masses had helped him to gain office. When Hara became prime minister in September 1918, journalist Maeda Renzan said to him, "Yamagata has certainly opened his eyes, hasn't he!" Hara replied nonchalantly, "That's because of the Rice Riots. Think what would have happened if our party had joined the agitation at that time. Things would have come to a terrible pass. Even Yamagata has now come to realize that cabinets headed by bureaucrats are hopelessly ineffective."[34]

Nevertheless, there was no real likelihood that Hara would ever go into partnership with the masses. His cabinet was often obstructed by the Privy Council, a stronghold of the Yamagata camp. Journalist Baba Tsunego commented in a review that lack of support by the masses was the reason why the cabinet had so much trouble from the Privy Council. With strong popular backing, as a friend of the people it could easily overcome such obstruction. When Hara read this comment, he told Baba: "That is a frightful proposition. To talk of riding on the wave of the masses and attacking the Privy Council—that is revolution. I could never support such an action."[35] Hara had no desire to forge strong links with the masses, though quite prepared to use them as a lever to prise the Seiyūkai into office. Hara's concern above all else was to expand and strengthen Seiyūkai power. Hence, he could look after the interests of businessmen and landlords very well, but never wanted to be a servant of the people. The complete absence of social legislation under the Hara cabinet is no accident. The commoner prime minister did little for the class he supposedly belonged to.

A String of Scandals

Prime Minister Hara's program was to: strengthen national defense, develop transport and communications, improve educational facilities, and encourage industry and trade. In the course of alloting government funds for the last three of these "Four Great Policies," Hara exploited them to the full as a means to expand Seiyūkai influence. As he did so, political corruption became rife and a series of scandals ensued. Early in 1921, allegations were made in the Diet that the vice-president of the Manchurian Railway Company had manipulated prices to make large private profits; a little later, high officials of the Kwantung administration were accused of illegally trafficking in opium. Meanwhile, Tokyo city administration remained flagrantly corrupt, and as these and many other scandals came to the surface, people were shocked, then angry. As early as February 1920, Inukai Tsuyoshi of the Kokumintō had attacked the Hara cabinet for its bullish attempts to expand Seiyūkai influence by bribes and other financial inducements, saying, "Were any of the Sat-Chō cabinets in the past as corrupt as this one? Certainly not!" However, Inukai's words struck many people as simply more of the usual hackneyed rhetoric of opposition politicians.

Hara himself stood firm against all criticism. In autumn 1920, yet another scandal broke, with allegations of corrupt tendering for gravel, road, and drain construction contracts in Tokyo city. Justice Minister Ōki was naturally expected to prosecute the chief offender, but the ministry was instructed "to keep the case within responsible bounds and make no arrests." When someone questioned the propriety of these instructions, Hara's diary records his reply: "Of course, they are quite proper. In such a case, as with electoral infringements, the more thoroughly it is investigated, the more criminals are turned up. Criminals are not, of course, to be condoned; but from another angle, I cannot help feeling that such cases make a bad impression on people. In this recent case, it seems that quite a few men affiliated with the Seiyūkai are involved; because so many Seiyūkai members are men of property and reputation, the party as a whole gets implicated. While it is necessary to dispose of the case fairly and properly, to widen it excessively would, on the contrary, have negative repercussions on the public and cause opposition. That is why those instructions are quite in line."[36] When the Tokyo Gas Company became the focus of a similar scandal and a public outcry ensued, Justice Minister Ōki frankly told newspaper reporters that if wholesale arrests were made, the result would be to overturn the social system. He had therefore dropped the matter without further ado. Hara would certainly have agreed with him.

In addition to noting the large number of Seiyūkai members involved, attention was focused on the personal connections of some of the offenders. Among those suspected or convicted of crimes were people in important posts who had been close to Hara for many years. Nakanishi Seiichi, for example, accused of corruption in the Manchurian Railway scandal, had been appointed vice-president of the company on Hara's recommendation after a career as a bureaucrat friendly with the Seiyūkai. Abe Hiroshi, governor of Tokyo when scandals in the city administration became rife, was a Morioka man who had helped Hara way back in 1878 to secure a job as a journalist. Koga Renzō, head of the Kwantung Colonization Bureau when it was implicated in the opium scandal, was an old friend of Hara and a fellow student at the Justice Ministry Law School. Because of these and similar associations, Hara himself appeared increasingly culpable as one scandal succeeded another. Loyalty to the party and its members and partiality to old friends often led Hara to indulge in favoritism, thus opening himself to attack when his nominees abused their positions.

Years later, Baba Tsunego recalled, "When the scandals became chronic, I said to Hara, 'Political corruption grows out of the need for election funds. I suppose the remedy is to set up a political system that doesn't require financing.' Hara replied, 'What a stupid thing to say! Doesn't everyone want money? First create a society with no desire for money. Then you will have a political system that doesn't need funding.' "[37] Especially in the 44th Diet of December 1920 to March 1921, Hara's last, the opposition parties exploited these scandals to the hilt and launched a battering attack on the cabinet. But, backed by his absolute majority and his alliance with the Kenkyūkai faction in the House of Peers, Hara came forth in his best fighting style and arrogantly rebutted his attackers. Describing Hara's attitude, Miyake Setsurei said, "Above all, he had an air of tenacity and defiance, challenging his critics to 'do their damnedest!' "

During his term in office, Hara's efforts to win over Yamagata also ground to a complete halt. Yamagata's private secretary Irie Kenkichi later recalled that Hara took special pains to visit frequently, but Yamagata always responded the same way—while their opinions were generally in accord, "on one point we shall never agree. I have told Hara this quite clearly." Even so, he praised Hara often, saying that "there are very few political

[120]

leaders now with his ability." In March 1921, on the final day of the Diet session, Yamagata told his confidant Matsumoto Gōkichi, a frequent visitor to Kokian, his seaside villa at Odawara, "Hara's handling of the recent Diet was truly splendid. I think there is no one as competent at the moment. In autumn 1915, while in Kyoto at the time of Emperor Taishō's enthronement, I often visited Saionji and we pledged to see the nation through together. Next year when the Terauchi cabinet took office, Saionji came to Tokyo and worked hard for a while, but after that he seemed to have completely lost interest. That was a very cold-hearted way of doing things. I think Hara also knows of this coldness, so in the future if my resignation is accepted [at the time, Yamagata was involved in an acrimonious dispute at the palace and had offered to resign from the presidency of the Privy Council and declared his intention to give up all other offices and honors] and I become a simple commoner, I will add my strength to Hara's and work with him. Hara is a man with no lofty vision or noble dreams, but in character and style he is truly admirable."[38]

Assassination

In the early evening of 4 November 1921, Hara penciled a memo of the important events of the day, to be entered later in the diary he had kept without a break since 1875, when twenty years old. "4th. Cabinet meeting. Manchurian Railway interim dividend state property. Hokkaidō forests. Privy Council labor committee decision. Despatch to Hokkai of rescue unit. Fleischer called. Chinese Tung called." Then the final word: "Departure." Hara left by automobile for Tokyo station. He was due to attend a rally of the Seiyūkai's central Japan branch. As he was approaching the ticket barrier, a young man suddenly leapt out from behind a pillar and stabbed him with a short sword. Hara collapsed and died a few moments later. The assassin was a railway switchman at suburban Ōtsuka station. His motive for the crime, as later stated in court, was his mounting anger at the cabinet's spineless diplomacy—in particular, its failure to avenge several hundred Japanese massacred at Nikolaievsk by Bolshevik irregulars in 1920, and concessions at the Washington Conference of 1921–22, such as restoring Tsingtao to China and the withdrawal of Japanese troops from Siberia. At home, he was equally incensed by the failure to punish the offenders in the Manchurian Railway, Tokyo city, and opium scandals. He thought that "by sacrificing my life to kill Prime Minister Hara Takashi, I would bring down the cabinet and make a name for myself as the person who brought about reform." Hara was sixty-six years old when he met his death.

By this time, Hara and his cabinet had fallen into disrepute and the criticism was harsh. His aggressive moves to increase the power of the Seiyūkai led to political corruption on a massive scale, and his reliance on the party's absolute majority to ride roughshod over criticism only made the resentment worse. When the assassin was brought to trial, his barrister, Imamura Rikisaburō, pleaded: "Public antipathy toward Hara was surprisingly strong. To give one example, a certain provincial newspaper published an extra edition blazing with the headline 'Prime Minister Hara Punished by Death.' In many areas of western Japan, it is a fact that newspaper vendors shouted 'Hooray! Hooray!' as they went about selling such extras."

These statements can perhaps be dismissed as those of a defending lawyer, but when Hara was assassinated a spate of critical comment ensued from many other quarters. For example, the *Tokyo Asahi* newspaper observed that "Hara was not an ideal political leader. To the end, he used power to do things forcibly. The members of the party followed him not only because he had power; he was like a father to them. But as their affection and esteem for Hara grew, much to the party's benefit, quite the reverse happened with others; the opposition parties came to hate him more and more. Regrettably, that hatred was infectious; it grew stronger among the people, until Hara, who had 'lived by the sword' finally ended up 'dying by the sword.'" And as Miyake Setsurei put it bluntly, "Even though the assassin had no deep motives, people did not regard the event as purely unforeseen. More often they reacted with, 'So, it has finally happened.' They could not believe that a reckless fellow had just rushed up and done such an outrageous deed."

Hara Takashi was the first prime minister to be assassinated while in office since the cabinet system began in 1885. The commoner prime minister had come to grief. His fate cannot be dismissed simply as a spiteful joke of history. Three and a half months before his death, *Tokyo Keizai Shimpō* published an article entitled "Dreams of a Movement to Protect Constitutional Government." Some of the opposition party members, it announced, were dreaming that the 1912 Movement to Protect Constitutional Government could be revived. Yet they did not realize that the times were completely different now. In 1912, there was great faith in political progress; people believed that if only the parties could unite to overthrow the bureaucrats and get a party cabinet in power, Japan's situation could be completely transformed. That, they thought, was the only way to create a prosperous nation. So they charged headlong against the Katsura cabinet and pressed hard on the Yamamoto cabinet that followed it. But today people are totally disillusioned with political parties, the article continued. The Ōkuma and Hara cabinets had behaved so outrageously and the Diet is in such disarray that the people's faith has been betrayed. It is only too clear that the parties are "factions for the selfish exploitation of government," instead of "associations devoted to the national interest and general welfare." Today the parties no longer inspire trust or hope; however good their slogans, they will fail to stir the people's emotions on their behalf.[39] Significantly, this article was written just before Hara's death. Hara's assassination was certainly a bad omen for the future of party government, coming at a time when it was still in its infancy.

In these postwar years, whenever Hara Takashi comes up as a topic for discussion, he is often esteemed very highly. The reason is not hard to find. Compared with the postwar political leaders— pitiful figures cast up and dragged down in the turmoil of sordid faction quarrels—Hara's able and gallant leadership, and his orderly, immaculate powers of control over the Seiyūkai make him appear a paragon of competent, positive leadership. It becomes all too easy to forget the dark side of his administration that provoked his violent death. If that is so, it means that the most crucial problem in postwar politics is not framing policy, but enforcing party discipline. Certainly, the standard of postwar politics must be poor beyond words if it leads people to recall Hara Takashi with such admiring nostalgia.

[123]

INUKAI TSUYOSHI

Frustration, Triumph, and Tragedy

1855–1932

The Hara cabinet from 1918 to 1921 was a trailblazer in two respects. First, the prime minister was a commoner, and second, also without precedent, he was concurrently a party president and member of the House of Representatives. Yet all prospects for party rule came to an end only a decade later with the Inukai cabinet from 1931 to 1932. Inukai Tsuyoshi had spent most of his life in political party activity. When he became prime minister, he was one of only two men who had held seats continuously in the House of Representatives since the first Diet of 1890. The other was Ozaki Yukio. But in the end, circumstances combined to cap Inukai's life with a final irony: of all prime ministers after Hara, Inukai was the professional politician par excellence. In 1932 his party won the largest majority ever gained in a free election before or since, yet his cabinet was the last of its kind in prewar Japan.

Oriental Qualities

Inukai Tsuyoshi was born in 1855 to a family of rural samurai. They lived in the tiny Niwase domain in Bitchū province, present-day Okayama prefecture. His father and several generations of his forebears had taught the Chinese classics, and from a young age Inukai intended to make scholarship and teaching his career. Other pupils at the local schools where he studied as a youth were from samurai families of much higher status than his own, but Inukai remained undaunted by this. Naturally ambitious and competitive, he gained a reputation for hard work and brilliance in his studies, aided by a fierce determination to prove his superiority through scholarly excellence.

[125]

Perhaps because he grew up in a family of Confucian scholars, Inukai never lost his devotion to Oriental studies and tastes. He loved the Chinese classics, was an expert calligrapher, and his writing was famous for its elegance. An authority on the brush, paper, and inkstone, he wrote a famous treatise called *Bokudō Kamboku Dan* (My views on brush letter-writing). He was deeply interested in swords and had a discerning eye for them. Inukai's aesthetic tastes in all such matters were highly refined. After Inukai's death, journalist Naitō Torajirō observed that in having such wide interests he was of a very different stamp from the usual run of politicians. During speech-making tours to the provinces in his middle years, Inukai used to spend much of the time conversing with local scholars and writers; when party members wanted to talk politics, his total lack of enthusiasm irritated them.

An Oriental quality showed up in his ideas, also. In the summer of 1922, he told a discussion group that Chinese studies must be promoted in order to understand the four thousand years of civilization they spanned. But above all, study of the Confucian classics must be kept up, as they formed the basis of Oriental morality. "We need to combine Eastern and Western studies, be selective, and create a new Oriental scholarship; but the first step toward this must be the traditional Chinese classics," Inukai continued, emphasizing where his priorities lay. On one occasion, when discussing debate, he observed that the techniques of public speaking were highly developed in the West, but they tended to play on the emotions of people. That was not enough. One had to address the audience with the "calm, unflinching spirit of Buddha, coupled with the confident assertion of Confucius that to someone with a clear conscience, what can there be to regret or fear?" Anyone can acquire skills, he continued; the spirit is what matters most.[1] He worshiped the Satsuma leader Saigō Takamori, who had played such an important role in overthrowing the Bakufu and restoring governing power to the emperor. Inukai often said that he was very sparing in his praise for famous leaders of the past. Only Saigō would he acclaim as a great man. It was not Saigō's military and political achievements that he admired, but rather his "totally unbounded spirit."[2]

[126]

Student Days

The turning point in Inukai's shift away from Oriental studies as a career was quite fortuitous. One day while still living in Niwase, he happened to come across a Chinese translation of a foreign book on international law. He received a powerful shock to discover that Western knowledge was wider in scope than the Chinese classics. Greatly stimulated, he determined to expand his academic horizons. Inukai reflected later that if he had not chanced to read *Bankoku Kōhō* (Elements of International Law, by Henry Wheaton), and had stuck solely to his Chinese studies, he would probably have ended up a teacher of the classics in a high school. He felt a great debt to that book.[3] Its influence at length led him to Tokyo in 1875, at the age of twenty-one, to begin his new course of study.

Inukai's father died in 1868 just before the Restoration, when his son was fourteen. Inukai described the years that followed as a period of adversity. His family's financial situation grew steadily more precarious, and he pursued his studies in Tokyo while desperately poor. By chance he became acquainted with the *Yūbin Hōchi* newspaper's chief editor Fujita Shigekichi, who admired Inukai's training and talent in Chinese studies and encouraged him to write editorials. These were accepted by Kurimoto Joun, also on the newspaper staff. Kurimoto had held an important Bakufu post, but as a "loyal follower of a defeated master" he did not seek employment in the new Meiji government. One of Kurimoto's hallmarks was his incorruptibility. To the end of his days, Inukai praised Kurimoto as a model of integrity and scholarship. It was probably Kurimoto who suggested Inukai's pen name, Bokudō (strong simplicity).

Inukai used his income from articles published in the *Yūbin Hōchi* newspaper to enter Keiō Gijuku, a private academy run by the famous educator Fukuzawa Yukichi. His future political colleague Ozaki Yukio was a fellow Keiō student, though apparently in more comfortable circumstances than Inukai, who always had to struggle to pay his fees. Ozaki was one of a group of students who were always smartly dressed and prided themselves on their skills in debate and written composition. They often found themselves at odds with a rival group to which Inukai

[127]

belonged. Far from admiring the neat clothes and earnest ambitions of Ozaki and his fellows, Inukai's group adopted the rough demeanor and boorish speech of the old-style samurai, and prided themselves mostly on their physical strength.

When the Satsuma Rebellion broke out in 1877, Fujita gave Inukai a job as a war correspondent. Trooping along with the army and sharing all dangers, Inukai sent back a constant series of reports from the front, which were highly acclaimed by the public. After this experience of army life, Inukai decided he wanted to become a soldier himself. He approached Major General Tani Kanjō, commander of the Kumamoto garrison, and offered to enlist, but Tani told him that the war was nearly over and advised him to continue his education. After the fall of Shiroyama, the hilltop near Kagoshima city that was the last bastion of the rebels and where Saigō Takamori met his end, Inukai returned to Tokyo and resumed his studies. On his return, Fukuzawa Yukichi rebuked him as a reckless fool. But his contact with Fukuzawa after entering Keiō Gijuku made a strong, lasting impression on Inukai, who developed a lifelong admiration for his teacher. Inukai's political thinking also owed a great deal to Fukuzawa.

Injured pride led Inukai to leave Keiō Gijuku in 1880, just before he was due to graduate. When examined on the Chinese classics, the subject at which he was best, he had scored a single point below a fellow student, Yada Seki, a defeat he could not stomach. There was talk of publishing a new magazine, and soon afterward Inukai joined the *Tōkai Keizai Shimpō*, in association with a fellow Keiō student and businessman, Toyokawa Ryōhei. As chief editor, Inukai soon made his mark as an opponent of the arguments for free trade put forward by Taguchi Ukichi, editor of a rival magazine, the *Tokyo Keizai Zasshi*.

Dream of "People's Parties" Union

In July 1881, Inukai entered officialdom: he became a secretary of the Statistical Institute. Yano Fumio, a fellow student at Keiō and former journalist with the *Yūbin Hōchi* newspaper, had recommended Inukai to Councillor Ōkuma Shigenobu. At the time, Yano was the chief secretary of the institute, and both Inukai and Ozaki Yukio were appointed to positions as undersecretaries. Inukai accepted an official post because he had heard that the government planned an active campaign to recruit and promote talented men in preparation for a forthcoming constitutional regime. But in October that year, the so-called Political Crisis of 1881 came to a head; Ōkuma was forced to resign and Yano and other loyal followers, including Inukai and Ozaki, left office with him. Inukai's career as an official had ended abruptly after little more than three months.

Yano then became proprietor of the *Yūbin Hōchi* newspaper, bringing Inukai back to its staff, and Ozaki a little later. More significantly, it was at this juncture that Inukai, and Ozaki also, joined the Kaishintō established by Ōkuma in 1882, thus setting out on his long career in party politics. In the next few years, when the Freedom and People's Rights movement began to waver and weaken as a result of government suppression and internal feuding, Inukai became convinced that nothing but a union of people's parties could overthrow the Sat-Chō regime.

In 1887, with constitutional government now in the offing, Gotō Shōjirō launched a Great Merger movement, seeking to gather together members of former parties into a nationwide political union. But because of Gotō's close identification with the previous Jiyūtō, very few former Kaishintō members joined him. Yet Inukai, motivated by his vision of a union of people's parties, not only enlisted in the movement but tried hard to bring about an alliance between Gotō and Ōkuma. While a student at Keiō Gijuku, Inukai had been introduced to Gotō by Fukuzawa and often visited Gotō at home. When Gotō joined the cabinet of Satsuma leader Kuroda Kiyotaka in 1889 as communications minister, he was reproached for abandoning the merger movement. But Gotō claimed he was working to achieve the aims of the movement from inside the government, and Inukai supported his ideas. Ōkuma was Kuroda's foreign minister at the time, and Inukai is said to have hoped that Gotō's entry into the cabinet would bring the two political leaders together.

But the Great Merger movement never recovered from the loss of its central figure. It split into factions and quickly melted away. The year Gotō became communications minister, Ōkuma's treaty revision proposals came under fierce attack from the public, and the cabinet itself was also divided on the issue. As tensions mounted and rifts became deeper, Ōkuma was wounded in a bomb attack and in October 1889 the cabinet resigned.

With the opening of the Diet now close at hand, plans were renewed to organize a union of people's parties embracing the previous Jiyūtō and Kaishintō members, and Inukai again made great efforts to bring this about. But nearly a decade of suspicions and rivalries had produced a mutual animosity so intractable that it completely thwarted any prospect of unity. Inukai's union of people's parties remained an impossible dream.

"Tactician of the Day"

Japan's first general election took place in July 1890. Inukai successfully stood as a Kaishintō candidate in his native Okayama. From that year until his death in 1932—for forty-two years—he continuously held a seat in the House of Representatives.

Inukai's style as a political leader bore strong traces of his scholarly background; in all forms of expression he was concise, quick, and penetrating. He wrote fine prose when he took up the writing-brush, but he did so sparingly. The same was true of debate. His ability to put forth a powerful argument eloquently was renowned even during his student days, and throughout his life as a politician he made frequent speeches to local gatherings. But he did not really enjoy public speaking, and his addresses in the Diet were rather infrequent. On the speech platform, however, his acute understanding and superb powers of insight came through with force. When he took a matter in hand, his judgment and timing were quick and thorough. Kojima Kazuo, a close friend for many years, recalled that Inukai was once compared to "a master swordsman wielding a weapon so sharp that others dare not go near him."[4] He enjoyed idle gossip. No matter how important a matter was, he could clear it up in five minutes, he said, and he disliked long discussions on weighty issues. Inukai was diligent in writing letters, but he kept them concise, rarely exceeding two pages.

His speeches, also, never lasted over forty minutes. He had a strong distaste for dramatic delivery, gesticulations, and table-thumping, but his words were nonetheless effective for that. In his attacks on political opponents, he could seize upon their weak points with a scathing ferocity that cut to the bone. Yet rather than basking in the applause of an audience, and relishing the memory later, Inukai found much more satisfaction in mulling over shifts within the party and devising subtle plans. He enjoyed the role of expert strategist controlling the party from behind the scenes. Journalist Yokoyama Kendō suggested that "his true disposition springs from Oriental studies. Resourceful stratagems are something at which scholars of the Chinese classics excel. The scholar-politician likes nothing better than to play around with subtle ploys. In the House of Peers, Tani Kanjō is such a man; in the House of Representatives, Inukai Tsuyoshi. Of course, Tani is no match for Inukai in scholarship, but they take the same delight in stratagems, and they are both political leaders with a Chinese-studies bent."[5] That was written in early 1907. Whether Inukai's gifts as a political manipulator were in fact related to his mastery of the Chinese classics is open to question, but one possible reason why he relished the role of expert strategist was that it provided some compensation for his thorny relations with most of the people he had to deal with. Inukai was painfully conscious of his notoriety for being sarcastic and censorious toward all but a few close friends and followers.

When the Kaishintō expanded to form the Shimpotō in 1896 and then joined the Kenseitō in 1898, Ōkuma Shigenobu was always the formal or actual party head. But he tended to blunder, and was often slipshod in his words and actions. He needed a prudent and thoughtful man to shore him up, which is another reason why Inukai naturally came to function as the party's expert in strategy. It is also likely that because these three successive parties and the later Kokumintō were all perennially pitted against stronger rivals, Inukai's talent for plots and stratagems grew ever more subtle and refined in the struggle to improve his party's position.

Between 1890 and 1894, repeated and fierce collisions took place between the first Sat-Chō cabinets and the people's parties. However, after the Sino-Japanese War of 1894–95, the second Itō cabinet managed to reach an understanding with the Jiyūtō under the convenient slogan of "postwar endeavor." Thereafter, succeeding Sat-Chō cabinets took it in turns to win over either

[131]

of the two large parties and governed with their support. Accordingly, when the Satsuma leader Matsukata Masayoshi formed his second cabinet in September 1896, he did so in alliance with the Shimpotō.

This coalition with the Matsukata cabinet was very largely the work of Inukai. Ever since the Restoration, the Satsuma and Chōshū leaders, commonly lumped together as the Sat-Chō clique, had regarded each other with a fair amount of mutual antipathy and rivalry, despite their common determination to form a united front against all outsiders. The Satsuma clique, however, tended to produce fewer able leaders than Chōshū. In a somewhat parallel way, the Jiyūtō and Shimpotō, the two large people's parties dating back to the Freedom and People's Rights movement, were mutually antagonistic from the start. The Jiyūtō had kept its position as the leading party ever since the first Diet of 1890, and try as it would to dislodge its rival, the Shimpotō was always relegated to second place. Even before the Sino-Japanese War, the Jiyūtō had begun making overtures to Itō's second cabinet, and after the war those probes developed into an open alliance. In self-defense, the Shimpotō drew closer to the Satsuma clique headed by Matsukata Masayoshi and eventually allied itself with his second cabinet. It was, in effect, a partnership of the runners-up.

Having failed in his plans for a union of people's parties, Inukai now sought to develop the influence of his party by forging links with the Satsuma clique. This move was not quite the political surrender it appears to be. By joining forces with Satsuma, Inukai hoped to restrain Chōshū, the stronger partner of the two, and undermine clique government. Further, as his subsequent career shows, Inukai used the alliance with the Satsuma clique as a political ploy, calling it into play alternately with moves toward a union of people's parties, switching from one tack to the other as advantage prescribed. The fact that his party remained a minority force well into the future kept Inukai operating this switch for most of his political life. Significantly, the alliance with the Matsukata cabinet was short-lived. It ruptured after just over a year, and in 1897 the Shimpotō returned to being an opposition party.

By this time both the Jiyūtō and Shimpotō knew only too well that they were simply being exploited by the Sat-Chō clique. Finally, disillusioned with the ignominy of their situation, and aided by the eager efforts of Inukai, the two parties united, setting up the Kenseitō in June 1898. Inukai's strivings to realize his dream of a union of people's parties seemed to have paid off at last. The emergence of the new Kenseitō took place during the term of the third Itō cabinet, which promptly resigned. Ōkuma Shigenobu and Itagaki Taisuke, the joint leaders of the new party, received the imperial mandate to form the next cabinet. Ōkuma became prime minister and Itagaki home minister; with the exception of the army and navy ministries, all other cabinet posts were held by members of the Kenseitō. This was Japan's first party cabinet, though its two leaders by then held peerages and therefore did not lead the party from the House of Representatives.

Ozaki joined the new cabinet as education minister; Inukai, however, was content to remain out of office. At the time, Toyabe Shuntei wrote, "When the Kenseitō cabinet was set up, Inukai, the party general secretary, seemed to have more power and greater glory than any cabinet minister. People called him the de facto prime minister; some went so far as to say that Inukai held the real power in the cabinet, not Ōkuma."[6] As ever, Inukai preferred the role of staff officer directing the party, keeping hold on the real power while he resourcefully managed its internal and external affairs. Toyabe went on to say that the mere mention of Inukai's name immediately produced a refrain familiar to all by then—"tactician of the day." His fertile stratagems were apparently already renowned. Some time later, the *Osaka Mainichi* newspaper described Inukai as "short and thin, his pale face and high cheekbones set with glittering, compelling eyes—to all appearances, a restless and ambitious intriguer." Photographs of Inukai at that time convey just such an impression.

Inukai's stratagems notwithstanding, the 1898 Kenseitō cabinet did not last even five months. One of the first signs of trouble came in October that year. In a speech to the Imperial Education Association a few weeks earlier, Ozaki had conjectured that, although very unlikely to happen, if Japan were to become a republic, it would be headed by executives of the Mitsui or Mitsubishi companies. Taken as an insult to the emperor, his words provoked a storm of protest. Ozaki was forced to resign, and Inukai took over as education minister. After this reshuffle, the long-standing hostility between former members of the Jiyūtō and Kaishintō resurfaced with renewed ferocity, bringing the cabinet to the brink of crisis. Not long after Inukai's appointment, the Kenseitō split asunder, and the entire cabinet resigned. Inukai had been education minister for less than ten days. The former Jiyūtō members continued to call themselves the Kenseitō, but the Shimpotō breakaways set up the rival Kenseihontō. Just after the split, the Kenseihontō appointed Ōkuma party president. Inukai assumed the post of secretary general, but his dream of a union of people's parties had proved as fragile and fleeting as a desert bloom.

Inukai and Ozaki

A little later, in 1900, Itō Hirobumi set up the Seiyūkai. Presided over by Itō himself, its members were largely drawn from his followers in official circles and former members of the recently dissolved Kenseitō. Ozaki Yukio now turned away from his political colleagues and hastened to join Itō's camp, the only member of the Kenseihontō to do so. He did this, some said, in an attempt to revive his political career, so seriously damaged by the Republic Speech Incident. Inukai and Ozaki had studied together at Keiō Gijuku and later had followed the same path as newspaper journalists and party members. Now they came to a parting of the ways.

Both men were vital, active, and supremely self-confident; and they were both renowned as brilliant orators. In other ways, however, they were very different. Inukai was always in his element when he was devising stratagems and operating from behind the scenes. He made speeches and appeared publicly as required, but such activities irked him. Ozaki, on the other hand, was proud of his wit and talents; showy in speech and conduct, he was full of vanity and highly conscious of being in the public gaze. A magnificent and forceful presence on the platform, he dramatized his points with expansive gestures, as he argued on with fierce earnestness. Whereas Inukai reminded one of a village schoolmaster, versed in the Chinese classics and distinctly Oriental in his tastes,

Ozaki cultivated the carefully groomed appearance of a Western-ized man of fashion. He was well acquainted with foreign litera-ture and made frequent references to the advanced nations of the West in his discourses.

Ozaki took a major step when he joined the Seiyūkai, thus as-sociating himself with Itō Hirobumi, the leading politician of the Sat-Chō clique. Yet Ozaki did not prosper as he had hoped after joining the new party, and in two years he left it, angered by Itō's accommodating attitude toward the first Katsura cabinet. In 1903, he was elected mayor of Tokyo by the city assembly and remained in this post for the next nine years, but found he could achieve little of note. He rejoined the Seiyūkai in 1908, though not for any particular reason. Much later, Ozaki confessed: "For twenty years I sought honor in my career as a politician, but then I changed my thinking entirely and decided to put career first. When I rejoined the Seiyūkai, considerations of honor played no part in this, and I did so without imposing any conditions. I was simply stopping for a second time at an inn called the Seiyū-kai and writing my name in the guest book."

A Double-Sided Personality

Just after the first Katsura cabinet was formed in June 1901, a fierce dispute arose within the Kenseihontō, a dispute that became chronic thereafter. This was the controversy between the reform and anti-reform factions, which was born of, and perpetuated by, the perennial inability of the Kenseihontō to move into the power center. It was exasperating to watch the Seiyūkai, like its forebear the Jiyūtō, holding on with such tenacity to its preemi-nent position among the parties and continuing to cultivate its close connections with the government. The Seiyūkai truly seemed to have earned the nickname "permanent pro-government party." The Kenseihontō and its predecessors, the Kaishintō and Shim-potō, on the contrary, had played this role only once, for the brief duration of the second Matsukata cabinet of 1896–98, never managing to gain the largest number of Diet seats. So consistently thwarted, many Kenseihontō members grew steadily more hungry for political power. That set off arguments as how best to acquire it. The reform faction insisted that the policy of head-on opposition to the Sat-Chō clique had simply encouraged it to rely on the Seiyūkai. Rather, the party should pit itself squarely against the Seiyūkai and build up its own ties with the Sat-Chō clique. Only this could bring the party nearer to the power center and allow it to expand its influence. The anti-reform faction was determined not to budge from the party's traditional policy: to work toward a union of people's parties in association with the Seiyūkai and to fight the Sat-Chō clique to the bitter end.

Inukai's leadership of the anti-reform faction inevitably raised the quarrel between the two factions to a higher pitch, for he was renowned as a bitter, implacable antagonist. His inborn acuity gave added force to a self-confident, but narrow-minded and intolerant, outlook. He was strongly inclined to see people in terms of good or bad, amiable or despicable. Kojima Kazuo related that if Inukai disliked a person, he would turn away and refuse to exchange a single word, even in such neutral places as the Diet corridors. Hara Takashi had inclinations and feelings of much the same kind, but he was always outwardly cordial, even to members of rival parties. When he met opponents in places like the Diet corridors, he would nod and smile, conveying the pleasing impression that he put aside his enmity when outside the assembly chamber.

Inukai's stubbornness and Hara's flexibility can be seen in their approach toward the genrō and the Sat-Chō clique. Yamagata once told the rightist Sugiyama Shigemura that of all prominent politicians both for and against the government, only two had never visited him: Inukai Tsuyoshi and Sugiyama's patron, Tōyama Mitsuru. Until he became prime minister in 1931, Inukai never once knocked at a genrō's door. Forever cherishing his dream of overthrowing the Sat-Chō regime by a union of people's parties, Inukai regarded the genrō as outright enemies and was not prepared to compromise with them. At heart, Hara also saw the Sat-Chō clique as a hostile force, but from early on he sought to develop a future for himself and the Seiyūkai by cultivating the power holders. Hara's overbearing attitude to his political enemies had its limits, and he was quite able, when necessary, to take a gentler line. Inwardly, he hated Yamagata, for example, but he often visited him, plying him with blandishments and striving feverishly to gain his confidence.

[136]

Such tactical humility was no part of Inukai's makeup; he never attempted to conceal his enmities. He was equally consistent in his warmth toward friends, followers, and family members. After Inukai's death, Ozaki remembered him as a very kind man, adding that deeply affectionate was perhaps a better term for him. Inukai kept up close, warm friendships, especially with people he had known in his younger years, and was loyal and chivalrous to those he liked and respected.

It was quite in character for Inukai to sell his valuable collection of scroll paintings around 1915 in order to build a villa at Izu Nagaoka on the coast southwest of Tokyo and use it to provide recuperation facilities for the sick wives and children of party members too poor to care for their dependents. He made many such efforts to help others and was sympathetic and understanding when giving advice.

In his collected letters, there is one addressed to a younger friend about to divorce a wife who was suffering from hysteria. Inukai's friend had described his wife's speech and conduct in some detail; that was only to be expected, wrote Inukai, since her behavior stemmed from illness; nevertheless she was quite curable. Hysteria was a troublesome complaint, but rather a common one. If a wife fell ill with consumption, continued Inukai, then neither his friend nor he himself would probably have the heart to divorce her. Hysteria, also, is a form of illness, but unlike consumption, it could certainly be cured. "While it is tedious of me to keep saying so," Inukai continued, "I think it would be very sad to hand over your little daughter to a stepmother. However wise a stepmother may be, no one can dispute that to a little girl her long-suffering, true mother is better." It was more than excessive sympathy for the wife that led him to write in this way; his concern was above all for the child's future. Very few married people lived together harmoniously until old age; at some time or other most found themselves considering a divorce and yet somehow managed to stay together till old age. If his friend went ahead with the divorce, Inukai would not think him immoral or unfeeling. He just hoped that there might perhaps be a way to handle the matter with greater mercy and compassion.

A typical anecdote about Inukai is the one concerning a memorial service held for Tanaka Giichi, his predecessor as

Seiyūkai president. At the service, Tanaka's heir was finding it painful to remain kneeling correctly during the prayers. Noticing his plight, Inukai promptly sent him a letter the next day telling him that the discomfort could be alleviated if the leg muscles were massaged with one's thumbs.

Inukai was very kind to his family and servants and cared deeply for them. In the last year of his life, when writing a moral precept on a hanging scroll for his daughter Michiko, Inukai chose the character for "compassion," explaining: "After the death of my middle-aged father, I passed my student years in hardship; but after going out into the world and becoming a politician, things became much better. Yet because I have suffered hardship, every time I see a poor person I wonder how I would cope if in such straits. I have never been able to treat lowly people such as servants with contempt. I hope that my descendants will regard others in the same spirit. That spirit is 'compassion.' "

In the reminiscences of his later years, Ozaki noted that Inukai's capacity for verbal abuse was of "peerless renown"; especially in conversation, he was noted for his bitter sarcasm and cutting remarks. Yet there was another, very gentle side to his personality.

Bitter Feuding

The inner disputes of the Kenseihontō, already aggravated by Inukai's leadership of the anti-reform faction, flared up numerous times during the ensuing years. After the Russo-Japanese War of 1904–5, the reform faction, in collusion with Ōura Kanetake, a henchman of Yamagata, made overtures to form a merger with the Daidō Club, a newly formed organization of pro-government Diet members. The avowed aim was to compete with the Seiyūkai for a greater share of power. At the same time, the reform faction made moves to oust Ōkuma, now considered a liability because of his low standing with the genrō, and appoint a new party leader in his place. The other thorn in the side of the reform faction was Inukai, the key figure among their anti-reform opponents. In January 1907, the reform faction finally succeeded in forcing Ōkuma to resign from the party presidency. Two years later, Inukai was struck off the party register by the Kenseihontō standing committee, but this decision was then reversed at a special meeting of the party rally. Ferocious quarrels between the two factions continued to rage, and both sides were drenched in gore. However, the reform faction found that getting together an anti-Seiyūkai alliance was much more difficult than they had thought. Another damaging blow fell with the disclosure that several reform faction members were deeply implicated in a corruption scandal of 1909, when a chief executive of the Japan Sugar Company was convicted of bribing politicians in an attempt to manipulate regulations for the industry. Apparently fighting a losing battle, the reform faction finally approached their opponents for a reconciliation. The anti-reform faction also was exhausted by the long years of intra-party feuding, and they accepted the overture. For a time, the strife abated somewhat, giving the party a chance to recover its strength. At that point, in March 1910, the Kenseihontō merged with several other small Diet groups, including a section of the Boshin Club and the Yūshinkai, to form the Kokumintō.

The Japan Sugar Company scandal was one of the more notorious cases of political corruption in the Meiji era, as business interests constantly sought to gain legislative advantages by bribing Diet members and making illicit contributions to party funds. In his political career, Inukai was often hard-pressed financially and had to borrow money at high interest, but he did so in ways that enabled him to preserve his independence and self-respect. According to Kojima Kazuo, Inukai told his friends and followers that while loans at high interest were not a good idea, they were also no grounds for self reproach. "A gentleman must, above all, take care not to borrow money from powerful people in positions of authority, that is, from superiors. To default on such a loan could seriously jeopardize one's independence. But commercial borrowing at high interest has no such dangers. The lenders are merchants, who bow humbly as they hand over the money, and one does not need to feel ashamed." In politics, Inukai was adept at manipulating others by means of carefully contrived stratagems, but he took great care to preserve his own integrity and freedom of action.

[139]

"Gods of Constitutional Government"

Blocked by their anti-reform opponents, the Kenseihontō reform faction had been unable to merge with the pro-government Daidō Club, and in the end the two contending factions had come together under the umbrella of the Kokumintō. When the new party was formed, many of its members began to advocate an anti-Seiyūkai union, giving a conspicuous boost to the influence of the former reform faction, which did not share Inukai's hopes of one day winning over the Seiyūkai. Inukai had foreseen this, even at the time of reconciliation with them. Talking with a friend, Inukai observed, "It is hard to refuse the overtures of people who put aside their weapons and come in peace—the big shake-up comes later. One must realize that the really large tidal wave is yet to come." Inukai could see early on that a violent storm was brewing.

It did not take long for that storm to break. The second Saionji cabinet collapsed in December 1912, unable to resolve a confused imbroglio with the military over a proposal to raise two new army divisions, and rumors circulated that followers of Yamagata had used this proposal as an issue to force a change of government. Yamagata's closest protégé, Katsura Tarō, then came forward to form his third cabinet. Katsura's appointment was greeted by a storm of protest, and the public was further incensed to learn that he had received an imperial edict bestowing honors upon himself when he left his post as Lord Keeper of the Privy Seal a few months earlier, and that to bolster his cabinet had requested another edict ordering the navy minister of the previous cabinet, Admiral Saitō Makoto, to remain in his post. A public outcry erupted against Katsura, accusing him of exploiting the emperor to further his personal ambitions.

Leading members of both the Kokumintō and the Seiyūkai saw in this a good opportunity to overthrow the Katsura cabinet. Aided by friendly newspaper journalists, they launched a campaign to "Defend Constitutional Government" and "Destroy the Sat-Chō Clique." Burgeoning into the so-called Movement to Protect Constitutional Government, it gathered steam, with Inukai and Ozaki at the head. At the time, Ozaki had recently given up his post as mayor of Tokyo but was still a member of the

Seiyūkai. Activists in the Movement to Protect Constitutional Government gave impassioned speeches all over the country, stirring up opposition against the Katsura cabinet. The whole nation suddenly seemed to seethe in protest. Inukai and Ozaki were overnight heroes. When they appeared on the platform together at numerous local political gatherings, they were greeted with spontaneous shouts of "Hats off! Hats off!" amid storms of applause. Meeting them in the street, people bared their heads in respect. The two men were widely hailed as "gods of constitutional government."

Katsura had to act quickly and decisively. He suddenly announced that he would set up a new political party of his own. His plan was to slice away large sections of the existing parties and gather them into the new one, in a bold move to escape from his predicament. Very few members of the Seiyūkai responded, but in the Kokumintō all the members of the previous reform faction, and even some members of the anti-reform faction, broke away to join Katsura's new party. So abruptly sundered, the Kokumintō was robbed of more than half its Diet strength. In the 1912 general election held during the last days of the second Saionji cabinet, the Kokumintō had gained 89 seats, but after the great defection to Katsura's party it was reduced to a mere 43 seats. Describing this in a letter to an Okayama acquaintance, Inukai wrote: "We have now been reduced to a little over 40 men, but with another election I think we will make a fair recovery. My only worry is our lack of funds. At the moment we are like an isolated and beleaguered castle. Most of my businessman friends support Katsura's new party. Although that disturbs me deeply, I think I can deal with it. I am resolved to fight this battle desperately, giving up my house, of course, and everything else I own until I am stripped bare, if necessary. It is my responsibility to do that much for all the members, past and present, who have worked so hard for the party since its founding."[7] Inukai's predicted tidal wave had crashed, almost sweeping the Kokumintō off its feet.

While the Kokumintō tottered, crumbling, Inukai began to make plans for a union with the Seiyūkai. Early in 1913, Inukai held discussions with Seiyūkai leaders Hara Takashi, Matsuda Masahisa, and Okazaki Kunisuke. He pointed out that their

[141]

party and the Kokumintō were now firmly united in common opposition to the Katsura cabinet, but if they did nothing to ensure long-term cooperation, they would probably become estranged again, as had happened in the past. They should take the opportunity before them to form a union to overthrow the Sat-Chō clique, and to establish a permanent regime of party cabinets. There was also the lure of political reward in this: a union of the two parties would effectively dissuade the Kokumintō renegades, so impatient for power, from joining Katsura's camp.

Hara and Matsuda held the real power in the Seiyūkai at that time. Matsuda had a long record as a party man; he was the leader of the previous Jiyūtō members who had joined the Seiyūkai. He was also friendly with Inukai and was inclined to favor the proposed union. He thought that if the pugnacious Inukai joined the Seiyūkai this would be a strong advantage in the struggle to overthrow the Sat-Chō clique. Yet the Seiyūkai did not respond to Inukai's proposal, largely because Hara was opposed. For one thing, Hara wanted to get the Seiyūkai completely under his own control in the future and was wary of the potential competition Inukai might represent. During the initial discussions, the Seiyūkai side had expressed no opinion at all in response to Inukai's proposal, but there were reports that Hara had afterward casually asked Inukai how old he was. Inukai understood at once that there was no hope of a union. Having earlier feared that Matsuda would take precedence over him for the post of party president, Hara now worried that if Inukai had the advantage in years, this seniority would make him one more competitor to overcome. Just that casual comparison of age was enough to warn Inukai, one year older, that Hara would not support a Seiyūkai-Kokumintō union. Another reason for Hara's opposition can be surmised: party strategy. Hara had already decided that the best way to make the Seiyūkai into a decisive force in politics was by negotiating with the Sat-Chō leaders, winning them over by compromise and concession. Once he had been accepted as a colleague by the Seiyūkai, Inukai would no doubt continue to challenge the Sat-Chō leaders to a head-on fight, a prospect that Hara certainly disliked.

Inukai had attempted a union of people's parties before—it

was a goal to which he had long been committed. In his hopes of achieving this, he had fought a desperate battle against the reform faction of his own party, which while attacking the Seiyūkai also made friendly approaches to the Sat-Chō clique. Moreover, as majority party the Seiyūkai adhered to policies that accorded with Hara's plan to edge his party into the power center by compromise or alliance with Inukai's enemy, the Sat-Chō clique. Thus from almost any angle, Inukai seemed interminably stuck in an untenable position, thwarted whichever way he turned.

Meanwhile, Prime Minister Katsura ordered a temporary suspension of the 30th Diet, and early in 1913 set about organizing his new political party, the future Dōshikai. As it turned out, no more than 93 Diet members joined it. This was less than one quarter of the total number of seats in the House of Representatives and utterly inadequate for Katsura to break free from the current deadlock. The Seiyūkai and Kokumintō had 188 seats and 43 seats respectively, together amounting to a clear majority, and just before the Diet suspension they moved a vote of no-confidence in the cabinet. After discussions with his colleagues, Katsura issued a final order for Diet suspension.

That attempt to tough things out provided further momentum for the Movement to Protect Constitutional Government; snowballing faster and faster, it seemed ready to become a political avalanche, carrying all before it. At first, only the more active members of the Seiyūkai joined the movement; the party leaders were reluctant to participate. Certainly, they had been angry enough at Katsura's appointment as prime minister, but nevertheless they calculated that joining a movement to demand the overthrow of the Sat-Chō clique would bring the party into direct confrontation with the genrō. At the time Inukai predicted to his close friend Kojima Kazuo that the Seiyūkai "will join when the conditions are right. We don't have to worry about that, so we'll push on, full steam ahead." Sure enough, as the Movement to Protect Constitutional Government rose to a climax, public pressure finally induced the Seiyūkai members to join en masse around the time that the final Diet suspension was announced.

Frantic for some way out, Prime Minister Katsura tried one

[143]

last move to prop up his cabinet; he requested Emperor Taishō to send a message to Seiyūkai president Saionji encouraging him to get the no-confidence motion withdrawn, on the grounds that political strife was unseemly at a time when the nation was in mourning for the recently deceased Emperor Meiji. But Saionji failed to persuade the Seiyūkai members to change their tactics, so this move also failed. On the day the Diet suspension was due to go into effect, things had reached a total impasse. Anti-cabinet sentiment was rampant throughout the nation, and the people were in an angry mood. The climax came when huge crowds stormed the Diet compound, shouting for the overthrow of the Katsura cabinet, while other demonstrations erupted elsewhere in Tokyo. Now, Katsura simply had to yield. His whole cabinet resigned in February 1913. Throughout the train of events leading to the overthrow of the Katsura cabinet, Inukai, leader of the Kokumintō, played a major role, standing beside Ozaki at the head of the Movement to Protect Constitutional Government.

Declining Popularity

On 20 February 1913, Admiral Yamamoto Gonnohyōe received the imperial mandate to form a new cabinet. The Seiyūkai, apparently disregarding its call to "destroy the Sat-Chō clique" in the Movement to Protect Constitutional Government, moved swiftly to negotiate with Yamamoto, a prominent Satsuma leader. Consequently three Seiyūkai members—Hara Takashi, Matsuda Masahisa, and Motoda Hajime—joined the cabinet and the party pledged to support it. Such a move was right in line with Hara's plan to strengthen the party by drawing closer to the power center. Now the public turned its wrath on the Seiyūkai for making such a squalid compromise. Yamamoto and the Seiyūkai leaders tried to persuade Inukai to join them, but he refused, on the grounds that theirs was not a party cabinet. Recently Inukai's popularity had reached its summit amid wide acclaim as a "god of constitutional government"; joining the Yamamoto cabinet at that juncture was something he simply could not afford to do.

Even so, Inukai reacted to the new cabinet with friendly tolerance and moderation, a benign attitude that can be partly

[144]

explained by his intense hostility toward the recently formed Dōshikai. After resigning, Katsura pressed ahead with preparations for his new political party, but he died in October 1913 before it could be organized formally. When the Dōshikai was established that December, Katsura's political executor Katō Takaaki became its president. The Dōshikai included many Kokumintō defectors, so Inukai detested it to the very marrow of his bones. Kojima Kazuo records that after the Kokumintō split, Inukai put "all his strength into attacking the arch-enemy Dōshikai. They say that 'there is no hatred more bitter than in a quarrel between brothers' and such feelings governed Inukai's life."[8] That animosity was not limited to the Dōshikai but extended to its successors, the Kenseikai and Minseitō of the 1920s. During Yamamoto's term of office, Inukai therefore did his utmost to prevent the next cabinet from passing into the hands of the Dōshikai, which had close links with the Chōshū clique. It is also very likely that he did not want to quarrel with the Yamamoto cabinet, because if realizing his dream of a union of people's parties proved hopeless, he calculated that an alliance with the Satsuma clique would be the next best move.

In any case, Inukai's political position was now very weak. With the advent of Katsura's new party, the Kokumintō fell to third place behind the Seiyūkai and Dōshikai. As between these two leading parties, the Seiyūkai had far more Diet seats than the Dōshikai, and there was no scope for the Kokumintō as a third party to command the balance between them. This meant that Inukai's subtle skill as a political strategist no longer had much room for deployment.

The budget proposal that the Yamamoto cabinet presented to the 31st Diet of December 1913 to March 1914 placed priority on naval expansion, and Yamamoto, being the acknowledged chief of the navy, the proposed increases aroused considerable public protest. Then, while the budget was still before the House of Representatives, high-ranking naval officers were accused of taking bribes from the Siemens Company in return for lucrative contracts. The Dōshikai and its lesser ally, the Chūseikai, seized upon the scandal to attack the cabinet, demanding that the entire naval expansion program be cut from the budget as a gesture of no confidence. Yet Inukai took the moderate position that the

Yamamoto cabinet should not be held responsible while accusations in the Siemens scandal were still uncorroborated. He also insisted that cuts in the estimates for naval expansion should be restricted to new proposals only. Once investigations of the incident got under way, however, several high-ranking naval officers were sent for trial by court-martial. Even Inukai had to back down at that point, just to hold his party together, and so he joined the Dōshikai and Chūseikai in Diet motions of no confidence and cabinet impeachment. Yet Inukai's speeches in the assembly chamber at that time seemed to lack his usual fire and aggression, probably in a calculated effort to avoid being too hard on the Yamamoto cabinet.

The pro-cabinet Seiyūkai with 203 seats had an absolute majority in the House of Representatives, and so Yamamoto was able to ward off attacks from the opposition parties. But he lost out to the Yamagata followers who, with supremacy in the House of Peers, took advantage of heated anti-cabinet sentiment provoked by the Siemens scandal to demand major cuts in the estimates for naval expenditures; as a result, the House of Peers rejected the budget, and Yamamoto was left with no alternative but to resign, taking his whole cabinet with him.

Inukai's mild attitude toward the Yamamoto cabinet earned him much public criticism. He was also hurt by constant rumors that he was making advances to the Satsuma clique. The huge popularity he had enjoyed as a leader of the Movement to Protect Constitutional Government suddenly waned. Ozaki, the other "god of constitutional government," fared better. When he saw that Inukai was not prepared to compromise with Yamamoto, Ozaki left the Seiyūkai with 20-odd fellow Diet members to set up the Seiyū Club. Later, this and other minor Diet groups united to form the Chūseikai, which Ozaki also joined. Even after the Movement to Protect Constitutional Government had died down, he continued to press for its demands to "Defend the Constitution" and "Destroy the Sat-Chō Clique." At the time of the Siemens scandal, he gave no quarter to the Yamamoto cabinet; his impeachment speech in the Diet, punctuated by characteristic gestures, was vehement and scathing. As a result, Ozaki was acclaimed by the public as thoroughly consistent, both in word and deed.

"Disloyal" Inukai

On the collapse of the Yamamoto cabinet in April 1914, Ōkuma Shigenobu was nominated by the genrō to form his second cabinet. Inoue Kaoru, Yamagata Aritomo, and the other genrō had good reasons for this decision. Their real aim was to punish the Seiyūkai for its opportunism in supporting the Yamamoto cabinet. With his intense dislike for the Seiyūkai, many of whose members were political opponents going back to the days of the Jiyūtō, Ōkuma was just the person to do this.

As soon as he was appointed prime minister, Ōkuma sought support from Dōshikai president Katō Takaaki. At first sight, this was rather surprising, since the Dōshikai included many members of the previous Kenseihontō reform faction who had pushed Ōkuma out of the party presidency. The core of Inukai's Kokumintō, on the other hand, was made up of members of the anti-reform faction who had worked hard to defend Ōkuma and might be expected to support him now. Nevertheless, Ōkuma turned first to the Dōshikai, probably because it ranked second after the Seiyūkai, which with 203 seats was still easily the leading party. Ultimately, Ōkuma was aiming at a cabinet based on the Dōshikai (93 seats), the Kokumintō (40 seats) and the Chūseikai (36 seats), all three anti-Seiyūkai parties; thus after approaching the Dōshikai, Ōkuma then asked Inukai to join the cabinet. But he refused to do so, explaining in a letter at the time, "I will not join this cabinet because its roots are in the Chōshū clique. From the start, it has absolutely no hope. The Sat-Chō clique must be destroyed if we are ever to have constitutional government, and clique power means in fact the Chōshū leaders. The very precondition of its establishment prevents the Ōkuma cabinet from ever challenging them. The only reason why I have not said this publicly is because as a longtime colleague of Ōkuma I sympathize with him and want to save him from dishonor."[9] In addition to his total lack of faith in the Ōkuma cabinet's integrity, Inukai had other reasons for not joining it. As Kojima Kazuo later observed, Inukai deeply resented the Kokumintō's loss of so many party members to the Dōshikai; he could never forgive this and hated the prospect of having Dōshikai members as cabinet colleagues.

[147]

Inukai's popularity had plummeted as a consequence of his accommodating attitude toward the Yamamoto cabinet. It was now Ozaki's turn to suffer a similar decline, when inconsistencies in his words and actions aroused sharp criticism from the public. When Ōkuma first invited him to join the cabinet, Ozaki hoped that Inukai would accept a post, too. Inukai refused, but even so Ozaki took the post of justice minister on condition that Ōura Kanetake, a henchman of Yamagata and a political manipulator quite likely to use illegal methods, would not be appointed home minister. Just after the Ōkuma cabinet had been installed, the First World War broke out. Japan joined the Allies and the Ōkuma cabinet proposed a budget increase for two new army divisions in the 1915 estimates. This proposal was quite contrary to Ōkuma's previous insistence while out of office that increasing the national wealth must come before military expansion. Yet now he presented a bill to create two new army divisions in compliance with the wishes of Yamagata, whose support had been critical in his nomination for prime minister. Ozaki, too, had consistently opposed army expansion while out of office, but now, going along with Ōkuma, he did a complete about-face and came out in vigorous defense of the budget increase. The public was astonished, Ozaki's supporters dismayed. When the army expansion bill came before the Diet, Inukai as leader of the Kokumintō joined the Seiyūkai in fierce opposition to it. Inukai's Diet speeches hammered away on the point of finances: the nation could not afford the burden of maintaining a large number of "crack troops" in addition to the present military establishment. It would be far better, he maintained, to reduce the period of compulsory military service and guarantee defense by building up the army reserves. While the bill was under discussion, Ozaki's inconsistency came under strong attack, putting him in a very humiliating position. Finally the Seiyūkai and Kokumintō generated enough opposition to defeat the bill, and Ōkuma dissolved the Diet.

The ensuing general election brought about a bitter reverse for Inukai and the Kokumintō. At the time of this election, Ōkuma's popularity was at its peak. Furthermore, many Dōshikai members had previously served under Ōkuma for many years together with the Kokumintō members when they were both in

[148]

the Kenseihontō. During the election, these Dōshikai members denounced Inukai and the Kokumintō as "disloyal" for attacking Ōkuma's cabinet. Coming at the peak of the "Ōkuma boom," this turned public opinion against Inukai and hit him hard. Just after the Diet dissolution, Ōura Kanetake had transferred from agriculture and commerce minister to home minister; under his direction, massive electoral interference by the police and local government agencies seriously undermined the strength of the anti-cabinet parties. Despite his previous adamant objection to Ōura being appointed home minister, Ozaki remained silent when this transfer took place.

The general election of 1915 resulted in a great victory for the pro-cabinet Dōshikai and the smaller Diet groups, which in total held a clear majority. The Dōshikai itself won 150 seats. In contrast, the Seiyūkai was reduced to 104 seats, losing its previous absolute majority, a bitter defeat. The Kokumintō, which had held 32 seats before the election, was reduced to 27 seats. This was the second major setback for the Kokumintō since the split of 1913 during Katsura's third cabinet. Just after the dissolution Inukai had optimistically predicted that in the coming election the Seiyūkai would get from 150 to 160 seats, the Dōshikai 114 to 115, and the Kokumintō at least 50 seats. But those 50 Kokumintō members, he said, would become masters of the Diet, enabled by their staunch principles to restrain the two rotten parties (Seiyūkai and Dōshikai) and sweep away political corruption. In fact, the Kokumintō ended up fifth in party ranking, rudely shattering Inukai's hopes of commanding the balance between the two major parties as a third force.

The Kokumintō now faced a dismal future. Once again, Inukai considered a union with the Seiyūkai, but Matsuda Masahisa, who had earlier favored such a move, had died in March 1914, just before Ōkuma formed his cabinet. Hara Takashi was now president of the Seiyūkai; he was firmly set against a union with the Kokumintō, so Inukai's proposals made no headway. Major General Miura Gorō, for many years a sympathetic admirer of Inukai, gave a graphic description of the Kokumintō members around this time: "Each and every one of them was like a fighting-cock, battling away from morn to night. Not a bird was unscathed: some were limping around with torn combs, some had

[149]

bloody heads, others had lost a spur. These forty or so fighting-cocks even when severely wounded would continue to glare at the enemy with angry eyes. Worse still, they were starved to the bone, restless and irritable. Whenever a bird from another coop hovered into view, they flew out and cruelly spurred it."[10] After the 1915 general election, journalist Miyake Setsurei reported: "Inukai, of course, has only twenty-seven followers but they are all devoted and self-sacrificing men. For as long as they remain loyal to Inukai, they have absolutely no hopes of becoming councillors or deputy councillors, much less cabinet ministers. But even knowing they might die of hunger in the meantime, they are resolved to stick with him, come what may." All the same, the Kokumintō was like a small boat adrift on a foggy sea.

During the 36th Diet convened in May 1915, the Seiyūkai and Kokumintō united in censure motions against Home Minister Ōura, who had admitted bribing Seiyūkai Diet members to support the bill for two new army divisions during the previous Diet session. Ozaki as justice minister opted not to prosecute on condition that Ōura left office. When this scandal broke, the Ōkuma cabinet took responsibility and offered to resign. But the emperor ordered the cabinet to stay in office. Ōkuma, always eager for political power, used the imperial order to justify his continuation as prime minister, but in so doing aroused objections from inside the cabinet itself. Foreign Minister Katō Takaaki, Finance Minister Wakatsuki Reijirō, and Navy Minister Yashiro Rokurō refused to withdraw their resignations and left the cabinet. When Ōura's resignation from the home ministry had been accepted and while the future of the cabinet was still very much in doubt, Ozaki had maintained that there was no reason for the cabinet as a whole to assume responsibility for the scandal. When Ōkuma finally proposed to resign, Ozaki took the view that if he did so, all the other ministers should follow suit. Nevertheless, Ozaki suggested, Ōkuma should not offer to resign with all his cabinet, but simply ask the emperor for instructions on what to do. Many years later, in his autobiography Ozaki wrote that having said this, he signed the resignation proposal. Thereupon, Navy Minister Yashiro, determined to resign himself and critical of such ambivalence, remarked slyly, "The god of constitutional government is acting very strangely!" Ozaki retorted, "It is the proper role of such a god to make the principle of cabinet responsibility quite clear." This was the same Ozaki whose impassioned speech demanding the impeachment of Prime Minister Yamamoto at the time of the Siemens scandal made such a forceful impression. Clearly, he had compromised his reputation for political integrity.

Impatience and Backsliding

In the autumn of 1916, after just over two years in office, Ōkuma resigned with all his cabinet. He did this under pressure from Yamagata, who wanted his protégé General Terauchi Masatake to form the next cabinet. Terauchi put together a transcendence cabinet that included no party members at all. There was an immediate and hostile reaction. The Dōshikai with its 154 seats joined with about half the members of the Koyū Club, a small Diet group of 52 members, and most of the 32 members of the Chūseikai to form a new party, the Kenseikai. From the outset the Kenseikai was determined to overthrow the Terauchi cabinet. One reason for that hostility was the cabinet's bureaucratic makeup, but another was tactical. The Kenseikai had an absolute majority and its leaders believed that if it now took an anti-cabinet attitude, Terauchi would not have the courage to dissolve the Diet and face an election. As things stood, the new cabinet was bound to fail. On the other hand, the Seiyūkai, now down to 105 members, took a stance of friendly neutrality toward the Terauchi cabinet. This reflected the thinking of Hara—such a policy would offer a chance to recoup the disastrous losses suffered in the general election under the Ōkuma cabinet.

Terauchi's transcendence cabinet was very unpopular, and Inukai had no hesitation in challenging its legitimacy, thus bringing the Kenseikai and Kōseikai, a lesser Diet group, over to the side of the Kokumintō. He put up a motion of no confidence in the Terauchi cabinet as soon as it faced the Diet. Now was the time to carry out a great reform, his speech declared. This isolated and helpless, impotent and weak cabinet was quite incapable of any such thing, he continued, and it had to resign. In the same speech, he also indirectly attacked the conduct of the second

Ōkuma cabinet, and by implication criticized the Kenseikai, whose predecessor, the Dōshikai, had supported Ōkuma even though now a partner in his no-confidence motion. The Terauchi cabinet responded by dissolving the Diet in preparation for a general election.

Inukai immediately called a meeting of Kokumintō Diet members to discuss party plans and policy. He announced that the Kokumintō would break its ties with the Kenseikai and henceforth act independently. Faced with the need for major reforms in national policies to meet the crisis precipitated by the world war, the Kokumintō would ally with anyone who supported its demands, even yesterday's enemy. Opponents would be attacked and destroyed. We will not belabor the political parties for their past, he said, but concentrate all our strength on surmounting the great challenges of the present and future.

Inukai hoped that provoking an early dissolution of the Diet would undercut the power built up by the detested Kenseikai under the Ōkuma cabinet and somehow or other open up new opportunities for the Kokumintō. He was counting on the ensuing general election to give the Seiyūkai and Kenseikai about an equal number of seats, allowing the Kokumintō to hold the balance between them and "control these two useless large parties, forcing them to follow our orders," as he put it in a letter written about that time. In the general election of 1917, the Kenseikai was battered and retained only 119 seats, while the Seiyūkai took the lead again with 160 seats. The Kokumintō increased its strength to 35 seats to become the third-ranking party, but that was not enough to give it a casting vote, and Inukai's hopes were dashed once again. Apart from provoking an early dissolution, he had made no further plans. What the Kokumintō should do in its present quandary therefore posed a perplexing question.

Soon after the general election, Inukai found a new role for himself when the Terauchi cabinet set up a Foreign Policy Deliberation Committee directly presided over by the emperor. Its object was to discuss and determine the basic principles of foreign policy that Japan should adopt to cope with the global reverberations of the First World War. Prime Minister Terauchi asked Hara, Katō, and Inukai, leaders of the three major parties, to join the committee and only Katō refused. Inukai and his sympathetic friend Major General Miura Gorō had in fact planned the committee to begin with, and then persuaded Terauchi to set it up. Inukai explained his position in a letter of the time: The Kokumintō still had far too few seats to wield power. A year or two must elapse before it could hope to do so, but in view of the world situation, the party could not afford to wait that long. So for the moment Inukai wanted to shelve the issue of the cabinet's transcendence, and put all his efforts into making its diplomacy a success.[11]

Having previously put up a motion of no confidence in the Terauchi cabinet, Inukai was now making an abrupt switch. Joining the Foreign Policy Deliberation Committee was a clear departure from the principles and policies he had advocated for so many years: the destruction of the Sat-Chō regime and its replacement by genuine constitutional government. Both the public and his own supporters reacted strongly in angry, betrayed protest. Even his friend Kojima Kazuo observed, "However Inukai tries to justify himself, he cannot escape criticism for abandoning his ideals."

In the course of these events, the Kokumintō as a party grew idle and enfeebled. Inukai had now reached his sixty-third year. What could have induced him to abandon the principles he had professed for long and join a committee set up by the transcendence Terauchi cabinet? Perhaps the answer is that Inukai had never been content to remain an idealist committed to the fundamental principles of constitutional government. At heart, it seems, he was much more a realist seeking to grasp the right opportunity to achieve his personal ambitions. Furthermore, the Kokumintō continued to lag, struggling just to keep a poor third to its two large rivals. Meanwhile the onset of old age had begun to cast a shadow on its leader, urging him on impatiently. Perhaps for all these reasons, Inukai joined the Foreign Policy Deliberation Committee and for the next five years gave it his full cooperation. He attempted, furthermore—in the end unsuccessfully—to have the committee's jurisdiction widened to cover national defense and government finance.

Shortly before the 39th Diet opened in June 1917, the Kokumintō tightened its party organization, appointing Inukai president. Since the great breakaway of half its members to join

[153]

the Dōshikai during the third Katsura cabinet, Inukai had been de facto party head, but now he became its leader in name also.

Hopes for Manhood Suffrage

The Terauchi cabinet felt obliged to resign after the Rice Riots of August 1918, and Hara Takashi received the imperial mandate to form the next cabinet. He set up a party cabinet in September 1918; all posts were held by members of the Seiyūkai with the exception of the army, navy, and foreign ministries. Then, during the 42nd Diet of December 1919 to February 1920, the Kokumintō and Kenseikai put up bills for manhood suffrage. On the pretext that this made a general election necessary, Hara took the opportunity to dissolve the Diet, hoping to increase Seiyūkai strength in the ensuing election.

Demands for manhood suffrage were an important part of the Taishō Democracy movement that gathered steam toward the end of the First World War, and Inukai was quick to exploit these trends. In an election speech after the 1920 Diet dissolution, he argued that the existing political parties were not capable of running the national government. The Hara cabinet, and any other party administration, was bound to degenerate into self-interest and resort to government by bribery and favoritism. Reform was possible only through manhood suffrage. Inukai admitted that while there was no guarantee that a broader franchise in itself would produce good government, there was no alternative: "This avenue to reform, which holds great promise, is the only conceivable choice."[12] In this speech, Inukai went on to pledge his support to anyone fit to receive it. Today, he said, sweeping reforms are needed in government, politics, military affairs, and ways of thinking. "It is not important who brings them into effect. Anyone—whether a member of a political party, the Sat-Chō clique, or the military—will do. If there is any man who can govern well, responding to the needs of the new age, I shall support him."[13]

Inukai might well have thought that a wider electorate was the only hope for the Kokumintō. But even if manhood suffrage became law, he still could not predict when this would take place, or even whether it would in fact bring about favorable results for

[154]

the Kokumintō. So Inukai, the pragmatic realist who had joined Terauchi's Foreign Policy Deliberation Committee, now found himself advocating good government on a non-party basis. The downward descent from his earlier commitment to party government continued step by step.

The general election of 1920 held during the Hara cabinet resulted in a great victory for the Seiyūkai, which achieved an absolute majority of 282 seats. The Kokumintō won only 29 seats, another reduction in its strength. Any prospects, moreover, of passing a manhood suffrage law in the near future had grown dim. The Kokumintō and Kenseikai sponsored bills for manhood suffrage in each succeeding Diet after that, but they were always voted down by the Seiyūkai.

On Hara's assassination in autumn 1921, his finance minister Takahashi Korekiyo succeeded him as prime minister. But Takahashi failed in attempts to restructure the cabinet, and it collapsed a little over six months later. Admiral Katō Tomosaburō then formed a transcendence cabinet in June 1922, but even so the Seiyūkai supported it. Three months later, the Kokumintō disbanded. Joined by several uncommitted Diet groups, Inukai and the previous Kokumintō members set up the Kakushin Club, a new party holding 45 seats. Speaking at a rally to formalize the dissolution of the Kokumintō, Inukai said that although the party had been rent by internal quarrels, it had endured great hardships to defend the principles so consistently advocated ever since the days of the Kaishintō. The party had failed to grow significantly because of lack of funds, and because it had always "kept firmly to the truth and refrained from improper actions." In terms of popular sympathy and support, the Kokumintō had been in no way inferior to the other parties, Inukai assured the audience. Today, we talk about two big parties, he continued, but in fact they only "represent a small section of society. . . . They cannot hope to harmonize the wills of all the people or all the classes. Another party must do that. We must clear the slate of past actions and history and set up a new party in association with spirited leaders from the nation as a whole." To make way for such a party, the Kokumintō would sacrifice itself by going into dissolution. As colleagues in this undertaking, he exhorted them, we will close our ranks, rise up with the people, and carry out the urgent task of reform. By launching the new Kakushin Club on the current tide for democratic progress and developing it into a political force to be reckoned with in the future, Inukai hoped to achieve a real breakthrough that had eluded the defunct Kokumintō. The core of the new party was provided by Inukai's personal following, and he was generally accepted as its leading light.

Inukai launched on this new venture while the world around him was being rocked by the social and political agitation following the First World War. In Japan, as well, labor and socialist movements were surging up with new vigor. A clandestine Japan Communist Party was founded in July 1922. Only a few months earlier, in the 45th Diet of December 1921 to March 1922, the House of Peers had passed a bill for a Law to Control Radical Social Movements, but it was still being considered by the House of Representatives when the Diet session ended. A few months later, in the summer of 1922, Inukai told his friends: Recently the subversive-ideas issue has been noisily debated in our country, but we must think about it more carefully. After the Restoration, a Sat-Chō despotism arose, followed by a capitalist one in which middling property owners and below, especially the lower classes, are completely disregarded. Yet now, stimulated by currents from abroad, suddenly we face demands for equality, which have unsettled ideas and ways of thinking among the common people. We should encourage liberal studies, he said, to enable a new, healthy thinking to emerge.

Labor relations had also become a contentious issue, continued Inukai. In the past fifty years, as Japan moved from government by Sat-Chō clique to a capitalist regime, the legal system had become heavily biased toward defending the economic privileges of the upper class, so labor relations were bound to become troublesome sooner or later. Only the legislature can resolve this conflict, but as presently constituted the Diet cannot act effectively. Electing Diet members requires large sums of money, and that in turn has led to close links between political parties and capitalists. Inevitably, therefore, the legislature tends to favor the latter. Manhood suffrage was the only way to correct this evil. Again, if the nation did not provide adequately for the poor, "Lenin-style" thinking was bound to take root. That would pose a dangerous threat. "Capitalists and workers, landlords and tenants, rich and poor—all are essential elements of the nation. For them to coexist, a fair distribution of power and wealth must be made, but that cannot be done without the intervention of the state. And if that intervention is to be just," Inukai concluded, "we must have a system by which all the people participate in government."[14] That is, manhood suffrage.

The Kakushin Club was joined by a number of political strays, among them Ozaki Yukio. When the Dōshikai amalgamated with lesser Diet groups to form the Kenseikai in the autumn of 1916, Ozaki had joined it along with several of his Chūseikai colleagues. But he left the Kenseikai in 1921 together with several other old-style liberals because he did not like attempts to water down its commitment to manhood suffrage by imposing property qualifications. For some time afterward, Ozaki remained an unaffiliated Diet member. Although he joined the Kakushin Club, he had some reservations; wary about the aim of Inukai and others to develop it into a bona fide party, he hoped it would remain simply a political club. Even so, twenty-two years after leaving the Kenseihontō to join the Seiyūkai, Ozaki once more belonged to the same party as Inukai. But although these two old friends in politics were reunited, their paths had begun to diverge conspicuously. Inukai had moved toward a noticeable realism in his aims, but Ozaki—though still enmeshed in political details—had begun to play the role of detached commentator, advocating lofty ideals and denouncing the current low level of political conduct.

In June 1922, Admiral Katō had formed a transcendence cabinet supported by the Seiyūkai, but by then Inukai was prepared to judge cabinets—and all political issues—on their merits. One reason for this was his view that "if there is any man who can govern well, I shall support him." But the fact that the Katō cabinet had background support from the Satsuma clique perhaps softened Inukai's attitude toward it. It is possible, moreover, that he wanted to avoid a head-on clash with the Katō cabinet, which might trigger its collapse and lead to a transfer of government to the Kenseikai. Inukai still hated the Kenseikai, the Dōshikai's successor, with a passion undiminished with the years. However, the Kakushin Club soon found the Katō cabinet insupportable, when it became obvious that the Seiyūkai was determined to stifle all economic and political reforms. So it switched to the attack in February 1923, joining the Kenseikai and other opposition groups in no-confidence motions.

Prime Minister Katō died in office in August 1923, and Admiral Yamamoto Gonnohyōe succeeded him, forming the second Yamamoto cabinet. Yamamoto tried to get together a national-unity cabinet that included all the leading party heads. Seiyūkai President Takahashi Korekiyo and Kenseikai President Katō Takaaki both refused to join, but Inukai accepted Yamamoto's offer. In explaining his decision, Inukai maintained that he had joined the cabinet because Yamamoto seemed open-minded about manhood suffrage. On that issue, he told Inukai, he was not very well informed and would need Inukai's help, suggesting a positive attitude. Since the time of the Siemens scandal, Inukai had sympathized with Yamamoto's political misfortune. Yama-moto was a Satsuma leader, and Inukai had long-established ties with his clique. Probably all these factors disposed Inukai to join the cabinet. After his appointment as communications minister, Inukai addressed a party rally of the Kakushin Club. Beginning with the Hara cabinet, he said, the way to party government had been opened, but politics was still rife with abuses. The parties must be reconstructed, but in the intervening transition period he would give his full support to any cabinet that governed with the people as its first priority. That, he declared, was why he had joined the Yamamoto cabinet, and he concluded by once more stressing the need for good government. Despite these protesta-tions, Inukai was not off the hook, however; a critical public could not forgive him so easily for joining a cabinet headed by a prominent leader of the Satsuma clique.

The Yamamoto cabinet did indeed set up a committee to con-sider manhood suffrage, and discussions were held on the issue. But the Seiyūkai remained firmly set against all suffrage bills, which acted to dampen enthusiasm for the policy within the cabi-net. Then in December 1923, before the Yamamoto cabinet had time to achieve anything, a young radical fired a shot into the prince regent's limousine as it passed Toranomon intersection, just outside the palace. Assuming responsibility for this outrage, the whole cabinet resigned. Some ministers argued that the cabinet ought to stay in office, but Inukai was firmly in favor of an overall "responsibility" resignation. Having given up hope for further progress toward manhood suffrage, Inukai had taken stock of his position and made the Toranomon Incident the occasion to leave office.

Resurgent Dreams

Privy Council President Kiyoura Keigo was recommended by the genrō as the next prime minister, and he formed a transcendence cabinet with ministers drawn largely from leaders of House of Peers factions, especially those of the Kenkyūkai. The emergence of this anachronistic "House of Peers" cabinet in January 1924 astounded the public, which responded with a hostile outcry. The Seiyūkai and Kenseikai, divorced from all prospect of power by this new political formation, joined forces with the Kakushin Club to demand that party cabinets be firmly established, in compliance with the fundamental principle of constitutional government. Then, as anti-cabinet feeling grew wider and more intense, they rallied the masses behind them in a renewed Movement to Protect Constitutional Government. Once more Inukai, the venerable champion of party government, stood at its head. He declared that if the parties fought in earnest, neither the House of Peers nor the genrō were to be feared. Now was a splendid opportunity to attack the unfair privileges of the upper classes in government; the way was open to establish once and for all the principle that the leading parties should form cabinets in alternation. Wholeheartedly throwing himself into the movement, Inukai probably felt all the excitement of his old dream of a union of people's parties once more surging through him.

When Kiyoura took over as prime minister, a sharp difference of opinion rent the Seiyūkai. Those members opposed to attacking the cabinet finally broke away and formed the Seiyūhontō. Having basked in its supremacy for so many years, the Seiyūkai had split at last, and now the major parties were four: Seiyūkai, Kenseikai, Kakushin Club, and Seiyūhontō. Such a momentous shift in the balance of national politics must have been encouraging to Inukai. A beached vessel will float at full tide—perhaps this was the opportunity his deadlocked political future needed for break-through.

The beleaguered Kiyoura cabinet had no reliable support against the swelling Movement to Protect Constitutional Government except the Seiyūhontō, with only 149 out of a total of 464 seats. Kiyoura therefore opted to dissolve the Diet in December 1923. In the ensuing general election the Seiyūkai (101 seats), Kenseikai (150 seats), and Kakushin Club (29 seats)—the Three Parties of the Movement to Protect Constitutional Government—won a solid overall majority in the new Diet. Looking at the results by party, however, only the Kenseikai had increased its strength; it replaced the Seiyūhontō as leading party. In contrast the Kakushin Club, holding 43 seats before the dissolution, was reduced to 29, and the Seiyūkai also lost seats. The Movement to Protect Constitutional Government had done nothing to improve the prospects of the Kakushin Club; its triumphant victory brought no consolation to a deeply discouraged Inukai.

Confounded by this defeat, the Kiyoura cabinet resigned. Since the Kenseikai had become the leading party, its president, Katō Takaaki, was recommended by the genrō as next prime minister. Inukai had a rooted hatred for Katō, holding him to blame for the defection of so many Kokumintō members in 1913. Katō detested Inukai with equal intensity. Before he became prime minister, Katō had proposed to Seiyūkai leader Koizumi Sakutarō that they should form a coalition from which Inukai would be excluded. Katō reminded Koizumi that when the three leaders of the major parties had been invited to join the Yamamoto cabinet in 1913, only Inukai had eagerly accepted. Inukai, said Katō in icy distaste, was not fit to be a minister in a party cabinet.[15] Yet when forming his cabinet Katō did, after all, ask Inukai to join it and then set up a three-party cabinet. Inukai took the post of communications minister, but of the three items in the cabinet's platform—manhood suffrage, reform of the House of Peers, and administrative improvement—Inukai had scant expectations for the last two, and so he put all his efforts into realizing manhood suffrage. In 1925, after years of lobbying by Inukai and others, the 50th Diet finally passed the manhood suffrage law, increasing the electorate from 3 to 12 million (19 percent of total population).

By now Inukai and Ozaki had moved another giant step apart. When opposing the third Katsura cabinet in 1913, they had stood together as the "two gods" of the Movement to Protect Constitutional Government. But in 1924, Ozaki kept aloof from the succeeding movement, directed this time against the Kiyoura cabinet. Ozaki recalled years later that fellow Kakushin Club members Akita Kiyoshi and Kojima Kazuo pushed him to join it. But as Ozaki explained: "The proper aim of a Movement to Protect Constitutional Government should be to reform the overall system of government, striving to reduce the military to an equal footing with the other cabinet ministries, to make constitutional government a reality, to uproot the Sat-Chō clique, or other such fundamental measures. Considerations of personal advantage should play no part in it. Nevertheless, although Inukai had been a leader of the movement against the Katsura cabinet, he took the view that when Katsura resigned the campaign was over, and he deserted the movement to support the ensuing Yamamoto cabinet. That was disgraceful. I did not join the later movement because it, too, aimed at gaining political power." Sure enough, as Ozaki had foreseen, when the Kiyoura cabinet collapsed and the "three-party" cabinet replaced it, Katō became prime minister, and Takahashi and Inukai also took office.[16]

Retirement

In 1925, Inukai reached the age of seventy-one. Slender and self-possessed, relaxing with hunched shoulders and crossed legs, while puffing away at his pipe, Inukai could well be mistaken for a veteran farmer. The impression he gave people in his young days of being sharp and unapproachable had changed; over the years he had mellowed and acquired a kindly look. But his piercing eyes still brimmed with a vitality that long years of political warfare had not sapped.

Even as he grew old, the satisfaction of a secure, promising political future eluded Inukai. The Kakushin Club languished; in the House of Representatives 25 members were needed to make up a negotiating group, and the party was in danger of losing even that qualification. Furthermore, certain of its members were secretly plotting with the Kenseikai to form an anti-Seiyūkai union. The party lacked funds. Manhood suffrage had at last been made law. But as Kojima Kazuo observed at the time, the newly enfranchised masses could hardly be expected to become Kakushin Club supporters, regardless of Inukai's long struggle to gain them the right to vote.

Should he continue to flog his old body aimlessly along a stony road, vainly battling against obstacles with no bright future in sight? And should he take with him on this path his loyal followers and political friends who had shared the long years of day-to-day hardship with him? These and many other troubling thoughts must have crossed Inukai's mind.

At that gloomy juncture, Kojima Kazuo, Inukai's close friend and supporter for many years, began a series of discussions with Seiyūkai leader Koizumi Sakutarō in May 1925. They turned out to be very productive: the Seiyūkai decided to include in its party platform two policies long advocated by Inukai: "economical national defense" and "first priority on industrial development." Equally portentous, the Seiyūkai and Kakushin Club joined together in what they called the Seikaku Union.

Inukai's "economical national defense" plan stipulated cuts in military expenditure wherever possible in peacetime, while providing for adequate military strength if war ever came. Its objective was to provide some alleviation for the crippling burden of military appropriations on government finance. Inukai proposed, among other practical measures, reducing the period of compulsory military service from two years to one and providing military training to all able-bodied males, including students and schoolboys. Inukai's proposal for economical national defense dated from 1907. Kojima Kazuo observed that in substance, this idea was very ordinary, but coming from Inukai, people hailed it as brilliant and farsighted. He was in fact advocating something many people wanted but could not openly demand. The issue of military expenditure was "a hidden rock in the political sea," and politicians were wary of touching on it for fear of the military.[17]

Inukai's advocacy of first priority on industrial development began around 1921. As he explained it, warfare and territorial expansion had become anachronisms in the modern world, and henceforth industrial development must be the first priority of

[162]

the state. That also meant reducing the military establishment. These were simply Inukai's political remedies to counteract the steady expansion of the military since the 1880s; specifically, this meant cutting the heavy burden on government finance imposed by military increases and using the funds freed by this to foster capital accumulation for industry.

While the Kojima-Koizumi talks were taking place, Inukai's chief concern was with the practical repercussions of the manhood suffrage law. He told members of the Kakushin Club that henceforth this was the most important issue in politics; more and more representatives from the unpropertied classes would be elected to the Diet and their presence there would probably bring about a power shift. It might take seven to ten years for this to happen. In the transition period, the government would probably remain in the hands of the established forces. Inukai wanted to avoid alienating the newly enfranchised representatives and to make the change as smooth as possible.

Inukai's address then moved on to the issue of union with the Seiyūkai. Although he had criticized the Seiyūkai for many years, he said, it was the duty of its president to restrain the party members from misconduct. General Tanaka Giichi was the current president of the Seiyūkai; like his predecessor Takahashi Korekiyo, he "had certainly not, in my belief, acted in ways deserving of public criticism." Therefore, Inukai concluded, he was quite happy to unite with the Seiyūkai and make efforts for its improvement, sustained by the courage forged during many years of adversity.

In a sense, union with the Seiyūkai in May 1925 was the fulfillment of a long-cherished dream. It began with Inukai's proposals decades ago for a union of people's parties, and in Kokumintō days his hopes for an alliance with the Seiyūkai strong enough to overthrow the Sat-Chō clique had sometimes been rekindled. But of course nobody regarded the Seikaku Union as a true union of people's parties. Far from it. When Inukai led the Kakushin Club to unite with the Seiyūkai—a party presided over by General Tanaka Giichi, a Chōshū leader in direct line of descent from Yamagata and Katsura, and widely regarded as the epitome of political corruption—it looked to the public like surrender at the enemy's gate of an army tired by battle.

[163]

Whether pitying or abusive, the general reaction was that Inukai had stained his career with a final, disgraceful blot.

Ozaki did not join Inukai in this Seikaku Union. Instead, he collected together some dissenting Kakushin Club members and a few other political strays and for a time formed a new party with about 20 seats called the Shinsei Club. Much more the lofty critic than practical politician, however, Ozaki cast himself in the role of a prophet, lacing his grand pronouncements with words of exhortation and warning. From now on, he trod a lonely path as an orphan of the political world.

Just after the Seikaku Union took place, Inukai announced his retirement from politics and resigned from his post as communications minister. His constituents in Okayama were dumbfounded to hear of his decision. They re-elected him anyway, pleading with him to remain their representative. Overcome by these entreaties, Inukai resumed his seat. He remained a Diet member, therefore, but from then on he kept in the wings of the political stage.

A few years before, in 1922, Inukai had passed the summer at Fujimi in Nagano prefecture, northwest of Tokyo. Captivated by the majestic scenery of the Yatsugatake Sanroku highlands, he built a summer villa there in 1923 and called it Hakurinsō, an allusion to the dense copse of silver birches standing nearby. After his retirement from active politics, Inukai spent much of his time enjoying the mountain scenery surrounding his villa. Inscribed above the front door was a poem he had written:

> The gate to my humble house is simply a gap in the
> brushwood hedge,
> Allowing the fresh breezes to flow in with ease.
> Inside is a heavenly grotto,
> Free from the dross of mundane affairs.

He loved to work in his garden and bring the delights of nature to life. Wearing dungarees, secateurs in hand, he trimmed the shrubbery every day. The beauty of the Sanroku highlands inspired him to return again to his earlier delight in composing Chinese-style poetry:

A white belt of mist girdles the mountains at morning,
At evening, the peaks turn crimson in a sunset glow.
Now and again an ocean of clouds surges down,
Swiftly casting a shroud of dim drizzle over the view.
Painting and poetry—so venerated since antiquity;
Yet can they compare with the wonders of nature?

And also:

All over the mountains, autumn leaves blaze yellow and
red;
An icy stream cuts a band of blue ribbon in its downward
flow.
Returning to the nest, weary birds sing out for joy;
Ragged clouds drift over the peaks, then vanish without
trace.

Tired and scarred by many years of political warfare, the
aging politician spent quiet, leisurely days enjoying the magnificent mountain scenery. His times of hardship gradually became
a distant memory. Even so, Inukai did not abandon politics
completely. After retiring to Fujimi he still traveled around on
speech-making tours from time to time.

In the statement announcing his withdrawal from active politics, Inukai stressed that leaving the Diet did not mean that he
had lost all concern for national affairs. Henceforth, he planned
to work even harder for the nation. Personally, he was a completely free man, with no family ties, no further ambitions; he
wanted to be someone with whom the young could talk things
over. It would be pleasant to say that in his forty years of political
life the successes and failures had occurred in equal measure,
but in fact, "I have arrived at the present loaded with reverses. . . .
Having failed so often, I want to talk to young people so they do
not repeat my mistakes; I want to be what one might call a ship's
pilot."

In May 1929, he visited China, together with the veteran
rightist Tōyama Mitsuru. The Nationalist government had just
constructed a monument to Sun Yat-sen outside the Nanking city
gates as a final repository for Sun's remains, which had been

[165]

transferred there from Peking. Inukai and Tōyama, two long-standing friends of Sun Yat-sen, had been invited to attend the reburial ceremony. Inukai was welcomed by the Chinese as a national guest.

Inukai's ties with China were lengthy and deep. He had always hoped that China could carry out the reforms it desperately needed, rise out of its weakness, and as a reborn nation form an alliance with Japan. These hopes for China had prompted Inukai to help found the Far East Common Culture Association in 1898 and to work toward setting up the China Reform Alliance in 1905. He also provided a secure refuge for Chinese who had failed in the 1911 Revolution and fled to Japan as exiles; among them were not only reformists, such as K'ang Yu-wei and Liang Ch'i-ch'ao, but also revolutionaries, including Sun Yat-sen and Huang Hsing. Inukai's ties with Sun Yat-sen were of especially long duration, dating back to 1896.

When Inukai visited China in 1929, it had just been unified under Kuomintang leadership. He had now retired from active politics after a career of repeated failures, consoling himself in a life of leisure. But Sun Yat-sen, who many years before as a ruined and disappointed man often sought Inukai's help, had risen to acclaim as the father of China's revolution. As he watched on while Sun Yat-sen's remains were honored at a ceremony of imposing magnificence, Inukai must have been profoundly moved.

Inukai was well known for having supported not only the Chinese exiles but also Kim Ok-kyun and Pak Yong-hyo of the Korea Independence Party, who fled to exile in Japan after an abortive coup d'état in 1884. He also assisted independence movements in the Philippines and Annam, and sheltered the Indian independence leader Rash Behari Bose, who was a fugitive in Japan during the early 1920s.

Inukai's motives in assisting Asian independence movements were partly based on his sympathy for unfortunates, but also on feelings of pride in being a fellow Oriental. After arriving in China for Sun Yat-sen's reburial, he spoke at Shanghai of their past friendship, explaining that both had experienced political adversity and disappointment in their respective homelands, and more, both had tried to liberate Asia from oppression by the white race. Perhaps the same motives lay behind his support for other independence movements, too.

Return to Politics

In 1929, Inukai reached his seventy-fifth year. Having spent so much of his life treading a winding and tempestuous path, he now seemed at last to have settled into peaceful old age. But inscrutable destiny once more suddenly intervened on his behalf. Seiyūkai President Tanaka Giichi died unexpectedly in September 1929, and Inukai was chosen as his successor. Tanaka's reputation, both as Seiyūkai president and as prime minister, had been most unsavory. His sudden death gave the Seiyūkai a chance to recoup its public credit by choosing a successor in Inukai— a man long renowned for his honest poverty and formerly hailed as a "god of constitutional government." With his natural bent for the politics of realism, Inukai joyfully rose to the occasion. Now in the dusk of a life full of failures, he grasped at this opportunity to lead a powerful political party, the Seiyūkai, with excellent prospects for becoming a future prime minister.

As newly installed president, Inukai immediately made his principles and policies clear to the Seiyūkai. His inaugural speech at the party rally declared: "Now that the Seiyūkai is run on the ballot system, as adopted by my predecessor, the president is bound by his terms of office to put all matters before the party for discussion and to act according to its decisions; that is to say, the president is simply a representative. I have always believed that this is the way to conduct a party, so on policy issues I will wait until full discussion has taken place and then declare my stand." Having reassured the members on this point, Inukai then put forward his own cherished policies. He urged the party to press ahead toward the achievement of "economical national defense" and "first priority on industrial development." In a further point, he advocated a return to the multimember constituency system implemented between 1902 and 1920 that had given more scope to the smaller political parties, and declared his support for other changes in the suffrage law to make it easier for workers, and even people from the *burakumin* outcast communities, to be elected to the Diet.

[167]

Inukai's appointment as Seiyūkai president took place during the 1929–31 cabinet of Prime Minister Hamaguchi Osachi, president of the Minseitō, a party formed in 1927 by a union of the Kenseikai and Seiyūhontō. Diplomacy came to the forefront of politics in these years. Japan participated in the London Naval Disarmament Conference of January 1930, and two months later signed a provisional treaty for naval arms limitation. This stipulated an overall 10:10:6 ratio between Britain, the United States, and Japan, respectively, limiting the number of craft in various categories that each nation's navy could maintain. The problem was that Japan's Naval General Staff had insisted on a 10:10:7 ratio, particularly in relation to heavy cruisers.

When the treaty came up for final ratification, Hamaguchi's cabinet faced bitter protests from the Naval General Staff, who objected that Japan's maritime defense had been compromised. The Privy Council backed the Naval General Staff in a concerted attempt to force the cabinet to retract and block the passage of the treaty. At the same time, the Seiyūkai eagerly planned its own steps to break the cabinet over the naval disarmament issue; as its president, Inukai acted in accordance with party plans. Notably, in the 58th Diet of April to May 1930, when the treaty was still under review, he hammered away at the cabinet, harshly demanding to know how Prime Minister Hamaguchi and Foreign Minister Shidehara could claim that the treaty posed no danger at all to national defense, although just before the London Conference it had been agreed that the minimum acceptable ratio of auxiliary warships in relation to American strength was 70 percent. Had not the Naval General Staff clearly protested, when instructed by the cabinet to approve the treaty, that the national defense was at risk if it was signed? Later, when the treaty was being debated in the Privy Council, Inukai again savaged the Hamaguchi cabinet in a speech to the Seiyūkai party rally, claiming the cabinet had exceeded its authority—the order to the Japanese delegates in London to sign the treaty without the assent of the Naval General Staff was a clear violation of the navy's constitutional rights of supreme command.

Inukai was in fact upholding the right of the army and navy to assist the emperor in powers of command without cabinet or

Diet interference. Such a conservative and authoritarian view of the constitution diverged conspicuously from the political principles he had maintained until then. In the event, the Seiyūkai was unable to overthrow the Hamaguchi cabinet over the London treaty issue. But in November 1930, shortly after the storm had subsided, Prime Minister Hamaguchi was shot at Tokyo station by a rightist youth and severely wounded. On grounds of his injury, Hamaguchi relinquished the Minseitō presidency and a few months later his whole cabinet resigned. That was in April 1931.

Genrō Saionji nominated former prime minister Wakatsuki Reijirō, the new Minseitō president, to succeed Hamaguchi. Five months after the second Wakatsuki cabinet had taken office, news of the Manchurian Incident, as it was later called, reached Japan. On the night of 18–19 September 1931, troops of the Japanese Kwantung Army had attacked the Chinese garrison at Mukden, claiming that it acted in reprisal for a bomb explosion on the Manchurian railway. In fact, officers of the Kwantung Army had rigged the explosion themselves to provide a pretext for hostilities.

In a speech delivered shortly afterward to a general meeting of Seiyūkai Diet members, Inukai said that Japan had suddenly been plunged into a "momentous national crisis unparalleled in its long history." He went on to assert that Japan was demanding only that China honor existing treaties and take into account Manchuria's history as a separate state. The right of the Japanese people to a minimum standard of living must also be recognized. Japan's actions in Manchuria were no concern of other nations, Inukai continued, yet the Wakatsuki cabinet had nonetheless blunderingly allowed the matter to come under discussion at the League of Nations. Moreover, because the cabinet had failed to give an accurate account of the facts right away, Japan was now placed in the invidious position of a defendant before an international assembly. In consequence, other nations misunderstood the situation, and "self-defensive actions in Manchuria are mistakenly regarded as the outcome of deliberate plans made by the army on its own initiative."

Inukai's words could only be construed as most conciliatory toward the military, the driving force behind the Manchurian

[169]

Incident. Behind his vitriolic attack on the Wakatsuki cabinet there lay, of course, calculations of political advantage.

Forming a Cabinet

The Wakatsuki cabinet collapsed in December 1931 as a result of internal conflicts. After the Manchurian Incident, the cabinet lost all power to control the army. Meanwhile, the dark clouds of military fascism already loomed on the horizon of domestic politics. In March 1931, a group of army officers and rightists planned a coup d'état to overthrow the cabinet and establish a military government under General Ugaki Kazushige. A similar plot was hatched by military extremists in October, this time to install General Araki Sadao, who was expected to suppress the political parties and consolidate Japan's hold on Manchuria. Both these attempted coups failed, but the plotters were defended as sincere patriots by the army minister and only lightly reprimanded. After this, military control over politics grew apace, and elements within the parties were not slow to respond. During the Wakatsuki cabinet, sections of both the Seiyūkai and Minseitō, motivated by pro-military views, began to work for a cooperation cabinet, in which both parties would share power with the military under the slogan of national unity. The circumstances were grave. After thinking long and hard, Saionji recommended Inukai as the person who, as prime minister, could best handle the situation.

After he had received the imperial mandate to take office, Inukai told his friend Kojima Kazuo, "Well, let's collect as much clean timber as we can," and made a selection of ministers that excluded several Seiyūkai members who had been tipped for cabinet posts in the past.[18] When he took office, with a menacing situation before him, Inukai was seventy-six years old. In January 1932, a month after forming his cabinet, Inukai dissolved the Diet; in the preparations for the coming election, he did all he could to avoid raising funds from corrupt sources. In particular, Finance Minister Takahashi Korekiyo did not resort to the usual practice of reshuffling the top leadership of the government-affiliated banks. That left the party short of election funds. Nevertheless, the election resulted in an overwhelming victory for the Seiyūkai, which gained 303 out of the total of 466 seats. Since the opening of the Diet in 1890, no single political party had ever won such a commanding majority.

Yet the Inukai cabinet soon found that controlling the military was going to be difficult. Immediately after the Diet dissolution, in fact, fighting broke out in Shanghai just outside the Japanese settlement compound, following a Chinese boycott in reaction to Japan's seizure of Manchuria. As the troops of both nations battled, the situation threatened to escalate into a full-scale war between China and Japan. Saionji agonized over the way Inukai's cabinet was being dragged into difficulties by the military. The emperor himself was anxious and deeply distressed that the conduct of national affairs now depended on the whim of the military; he found it difficult to sleep at night.

For his part, Inukai concentrated on trying to settle the Manchurian problem. As soon as his cabinet was set up, he sent journalist and China expert Kayano Nagatomo to Nanking for secret negotiations with the Nationalist government. For many years Inukai and Kayano had worked together on matters concerning China in a relationship of deep mutual trust. Kayano had been a friend of the deceased Sun Yat-sen, and he also had close ties with other Nationalist leaders. On arrival at Nanking, he held discussions on Inukai's behalf with Sun Fo, head of the Executive Board. Inukai's plan was to recognize China's sovereignty over Manchuria and then set up an administrative committee to handle local issues, with China and Japan sharing an equal position in Manchurian development. On the basis of Inukai's plan, Kayano and Sun Fo reached an understanding. Inukai next prepared to. send his close friend Yamamoto Jōtarō, former president of the Manchurian Railway Company, to discuss details on the spot with Chü Cheng, head of the Legislative Board, and to draw up a formal agreement. But Yamamoto suddenly fell ill and could not be replaced.[19] In March 1932, while these negotiations were taking place, an independent state of Manchukuo was proclaimed, without cabinet authorization, on the initiative of the military. Inukai found himself in a most perplexing position.

[171]

The 15th of May

Meanwhile negotiations to settle the Shanghai Incident had stumbled on with great difficulty, but in early May 1932 China and Japan signed a cease-fire agreement and, although Shanghai lay ravaged, peace was restored. Ten days later, on the 15th of May, the sun shone brightly on a fine spring Sunday. In the afternoon Inukai was relaxing at the prime minister's residence. He wrote a letter to a craftsman, Horibe Kanzan, asking why an inkstone he had ordered was not yet ready. "I wait day after day, wondering when it will arrive. As long as the quality is good, any stone will do, and I truly hope it will be ready soon." He gave the letter to a servant for delivery. Then he wrote to another craftsman, Kusunose Hitoshi, ordering a seal and had that letter posted. Inukai had invited a friend, Orita Seiichi, who shared his artistic tastes, to dinner that evening, and looked forward to good conversation about old inkstones, paper, writing brushes, and their other interests. That conversation never took place. Late in the afternoon his plans were abruptly, tragically cut short. What happened is fairly clear from the records of the court-martial proceedings and other materials.[20]

At 5:30 P.M., nine uniformed army and navy officers rode up to the official residence in taxi cabs. They divided into two groups and burst through the front and rear entrances, using their pistols either to overawe or shoot down the police guards. Inukai was in the corridor outside the dining hall. After an unusual commotion, a police guard came running toward him, calling out, "Prime Minister! Something terrible is going on! Violent ruffians have broken in. Please get away quickly!" Inukai's son Takeru and daughter-in-law were with him at the time and begged him to escape. "No!" said Inukai, "I won't run away. I want to see these people. If I meet them and have a talk, they will understand." Just as he had finished speaking the officers who had been searching for him from room to room entered the dining hall and finally confronted Inukai, now left on his own. Sub. Lt. Mikami Taku, forgetting that he had already shot a guard on the way and had not reloaded, hastily pulled the trigger of his pistol. It failed to fire. At that, Inukai raised his right hand, as he often did on the Diet stand to restrain hecklers, and waved it slowly up and down. "Please! Wait! You can shoot anytime. Let's sit down and talk," he told them. Wearing loose Japanese robes, his arms folded close to his chest in a gentle self-embrace, he calmly led them into a nearby sitting room. Mikami, pistol at the ready, followed close behind.

Inukai took a seat with his back to the alcove and quietly looked up at the circle of officers surrounding him. "Do you have to keep your boots on? How about taking them off?" he asked, in reproof for this breach of domestic etiquette. He took a cigarette from the box on the table and motioned to the officers to join him. "What's the point of talking about boots? Surely you know why we have come. Haven't you any last words?" interjected Mikami. Nodding in assent, both elbows on the table, Inukai began to talk. As he did so, Sub. Lt. Yamagishi Hiroshi barked, "No discussion! Fire!" Inukai again raised his hand to remonstrate, saying, "Wait! Wait! There is no need to shoot!" but almost immediately Mikami and one of the others fired in quick succession and Inukai's body slumped forward. Yamagishi then ordered, "Out! Out!" and they all ran off. A maid hurried into the room after they had gone and found Inukai, still with both elbows on the table, bleeding profusely from the head and temples. Inukai asked her to light the cigarette still between the fingers of his right hand. Three times in succession he repeated, "Call back the young people who were here a moment ago. I want to talk with them."

Having made an escape, Inukai's son Takeru returned to the prime minister's residence shortly after the commotion had died down. Inukai was still clearly conscious and told him, "They shot from just a pace away, so even with their bad aim, they couldn't miss." His voice was calm and quite normal. Six hours later Inukai died. He was seventy-eight years old.

On Inukai's death, Ozaki Yukio became the only person continuously elected to the Diet since its first session in 1890. Ozaki had gone on an overseas tour in August 1931, one month before the Manchurian Incident. On that fateful 15th of May he was in Britain. When he set out on his journey Ozaki had hoped he could do something to help improve international relations, but the situation grew steadily worse, both in East Asia and worldwide. During his stay in Britain, Ozaki's English wife died,

[173]

and in February 1933 he returned to Japan with her ashes. By then, party cabinets had come to an end, and as the military stranglehold on politics tightened, freedom of speech was progressively curtailed. As for Ozaki's hopes for better relations abroad, in March 1933 an imperial edict was issued announcing Japan's withdrawal from the League of Nations.

On his return home, as a liberal politician Ozaki was put under strict surveillance by the authorities. His autobiography published in 1937 describes his feelings at that time: "Throughout my life, I did all I could to promote constitutional government, political organization, and party discipline." But in all these things he had failed. The parties were rife with corruption, and now, looking at the situation around him, he felt that in Japan constitutional government was not, after all, a viable proposition. "Sixty years of giving all my heart and effort had ended up in utter ignominy." He could not ward off the sinking feeling that his life had been spent in vain. Then one evening he suddenly realized that he was being very poor-spirited, and that failure until now was training for future success; it was a preparation. Thereupon, "I suddenly felt as if my whole world had been transformed." As an avalanche of dark ruin thundered down, Ozaki lived quietly from day to day in loneliness and isolation, looking toward a better future like a hopeful prophet.

Inukai's natural bent toward pragmatic politics had eventually led him to become Seiyūkai president, and then to meet a violent death while prime minister. In Ozaki's case, too, the situation of his later years seems to be consistent with his past. Now an old man in his late seventies, though destined to live until 1954, Ozaki lamented the days of his youth in the poem: "What, alas, has become of my dream that, given the opportunity, I could inspire and enliven the common people all over the world?" While the stormy seas of fascism raged around him, Ozaki continued to mount the Diet stand with this swansong in his heart and boldly proclaim his belief in individual freedom and parliamentary government. Surely, this was because the innermost being of his youth was still vibrant, in spite of it all.

An article by journalist Miyake Setsurei written in 1931 contrasted Inukai and Ozaki as follows: "Now he has become prime minister, Inukai Tsuyoshi's stock tops the market. People love

[174]

him, and his spirits are irrepressible. He does not force himself on people and cannot be manipulated by others. That is the hallmark of a great political leader. In contrast to Inukai, where is Ozaki and what is he doing? He gives the impression of being a miserable loner. . . . Ozaki was last in office as justice minister in the second Ōkuma cabinet; he is divorced from practical politics and simply proclaims his personal ideals. . . . Both men were once in the same class; now Inukai is a party leader heading the government, while Ozaki lurks in the wings of the Diet as an isolated independent. Is this a trick of fate? Or should one call it something else? The two men certainly present a curious contrast. Yet the real test will be what the Inukai cabinet achieves.'' If it does nothing, Miyake continued, "Ozaki's capacity to frame ideals and present them to a wide audience will be vindicated, clearly demonstrating his faithful adherence to political convictions and principles. . . . What is the respective proportion of idealism in Inukai and Ozaki? At the moment Inukai is an outright realist and has no ideals while Ozaki has an equally strong commitment to idealism and is far removed from reality. The future will decide which of these positions is correct.''[21]

Are we better placed today to compare Inukai and Ozaki? The path the two men followed as politicians certainly presents a striking contrast, but to assess their relative merits and demerits would be tedious. More immediately, when we recall Inukai's long political career, an old proverb comes to mind: "Character is destiny." Perhaps it is more useful to reflect on the way national politics were conducted in those years, leading him on to such a fate. When we recall both sides of Inukai's life—the pure and the impure, the light and the dark—it seems all the more important to ponder anew the actual condition of politics in Japan since the Second World War.

SAIONJI KIMMOCHI

Last of the Genrō

1849–1940

Saionji Kimmochi was born in Kyoto toward the end of 1849. His family was one of the nine Seiga, emperor-related court nobles of the highest pedigree. A little over three years after his birth, Commodore Perry's squadron of Black Ships arrived off Edo Bay to demand that seclusionist Japan open its doors, ushering in the agitated final years of the Bakufu. The imperial court, for centuries a political cipher whose very existence had been half forgotten by the people, was quickly thrust into the focus of national attention by the movement to "Honor the Emperor, Expel the Barbarians" and the succeeding movement to overthrow the Bakufu. In time, this led to the Meiji Restoration of 1868, when the emperor resumed his place as sovereign, a brilliant figure at the center of the historic stage.

Young Progressive

Growing up in this stormy period of commotion and change, the young Saionji could not help feeling stimulated and excited. He took up horse riding, then began to practice swordsmanship until ordered to give this up by the Kampaku, the emperor's chief adviser. He read Rai Sanyō's *Nihon Gaishi* (Uofficial History of Japan), a famous work completed in 1826 tracing the central role of the imperial institution in Japan's history and lamenting the loss of actual governing power by the emperor to military rulers. Like so many other loyalists, he was captivated by this book and began to advocate the restoration of imperial rule. Restless, young, imaginative, Saionji came to see day-to-day life at the imperial court as tedious and anachronistic, in thrall to old conventions and precedents, engrossed from morning to

[177]

evening in complicated traditional ceremonies and customs. In later years he described his state of mind at that time as a "kind of general despair."

Saionji was not alone in his frustration; such feelings were shared by many of the young, public-spirited court nobles during the final years of the Bakufu. But compared with most of the others, Saionji's opinions were noticeably progressive. For example, he maintained that archery was now a futile pursuit, since the rifle was the weapon of the future. After reading Fukuzawa Yukichi's *Seiyō Jijō* (Conditions in the West), an immensely popular and influential account of Western institutions and society published in 1866, he felt that if only he had been born in that part of the world, life would really be interesting.[1] Saionji's dream was not just for a restoration of imperial rule; he was fascinated by the Western world. In late Bakufu and early Restoration years the imperial court was pervaded by an atmosphere of icy hostility to foreigners and determination to expel them, so Saionji's views were quite exceptional. Confucian scholar Itō Yusui, who taught Chinese classics to the sons of court nobles, regarded Saionji and Yanagihara Sakimitsu, later a distinguished diplomat, as the most brilliant of his pupils. But Saionji was not only clever; he was also a young man with progressive ideas.

Tokugawa Yoshinobu, the last shogun, resigned his office and returned governing power to the emperor in a memorial of late 1867. By the end of the year, a Restoration edict announced the formation of a new Meiji government. Just nineteen years old, Saionji was immediately made a junior member of the Council of State, the highest executive and deliberative body of the government. When the war against the pro-Bakufu rebels began early in 1868, Saionji as an imperial commander set out with an army to control the provinces north of Kyoto. Clad in helmet and war tunic, mounted on horseback, his imperial standard fluttering in the breeze, he advanced to Tamba province at the head of troops from the Satsuma and Chōshū domains. The horsemanship he had practiced so diligently in his early years now served him well. His soldiers are said to have congratulated him on how ably he rode his horse. After a triumphal return to Osaka, he was then posted to Echigo province as imperial commander for the pacification of the northern provinces. When he had put down the rebels in that area, he fought at the siege of Aizu castle northeast of Tokyo.

Before he set out for the front, Saionji appeared at court in Western dress, causing a great outcry and commotion among the anti-foreign nobles. Saionji believed that if Japan was going to change over to Western-style military weapons and tactics it should be done thoroughly, beginning with uniforms. He later recalled that he was not only the first court noble to wear Western clothes at the palace, but first to have his hair cut short in the foreign style.

After Aizu castle fell, Saionji again went north to Echigo province. Later in 1868, when rebel resistance ended, he returned to Tokyo and lodged at the annex of Nakamurarō restaurant in Kōtō district, thoroughly enjoying himself in the nearby red-light quarters. The tendency toward social equality after the Restoration met with his hearty approval. His first name, Kimmochi, he felt, was constricting and a burden, with its connotation of noble status. So, as an admirer of the seventeenth-century dramatist Tamiya Bōtarō, author of the colorful *Kompira Rishōki* (A Record of Blessings from the Kompira Shrine), for a while he called himself Bōichirō.

Student in Paris

For some years, Saionji had wanted to study overseas. He expressed this desire to government leaders just after his appointment as junior councillor, but civil war had broken out, and he was sent on military duty. When he returned from Echigo province, he pressed his demands to go overseas with renewed eagerness. Long afterward, Saionji recalled a conversation of this time with Councillor Kido Takayoshi. "He told me that I was the best man in the government, but I was not especially impressed. He then suggested that perhaps I hoped to be the best man in all Japan, but still I kept silent. How about being the best man in the world? Kido asked. No, I replied, it was not a matter of being first or second. It didn't matter to me where I worked. I just wanted to be a useful person. 'Well said!' exclaimed Kido, slapping his thigh with delight and congratulating me."[2] The progressive and broad-minded character of Saionji in his youth comes through clearly in this conversation. Not only Kido, but Council of State Vice-president Iwakura Tomomi and Councillor Ōkubo Toshimichi also saw great promise in Saionji. At length, his petition to go overseas was approved, and he set sail from Yokohama at the end of 1870, passing through the United States and England on his way to France. His arrival at Paris coincided with an interesting event: the Commune had just proclaimed a revolutionary government.

In Paris, he studied under the liberal lawyer Emile Accollas. His life there was free and easy, and he enjoyed it to the full. Japanese friends of this time included the famous novelists Nakae Chōmin and Kōmyōji Saburō. At Accollas's house he became acquainted with the future president of France, Georges Clemenceau, and mixed with literary figures like the Goncourt brothers and Théophile Gautier, and with the musician Liszt. Gautier's daughter helped him to translate the tenth-century classic, *Kokin Wakashū* (Collection of Japanese Poems Ancient and Modern), published into French under the title *Poèmes de la Libellule*. He ended up staying in Paris for ten years, a period in his life that always remained an unforgettable and delightful memory.

Liberal Aristocrat

Saionji returned to Japan in 1880. He was now thirty-two years old. By then the Freedom and People's Rights movement had stirred people throughout the nation to a high pitch of political enthusiasm. The *Tōyō Jiyū Shimbun*, a newspaper dedicated to expounding liberal principles, had been founded in spring 1879, and Saionji became its president on the recommendation of journalist Matsuda Masahisa, a fellow law student of Paris days and later a famous Jiyūtō and Seiyūkai leader. That someone of Saionji's illustrious family should join the Freedom and People's Rights movement provoked considerable public astonishment. Naturally, government leaders were perturbed and embarrassed. They appealed to the imperial court, and as a result an order was issued, and Saionji had no alternative but to leave the paper.

Nevertheless, Saionji determined to challenge the government's action in a written memorial to the emperor. The reason for the recent imperial order, he conjectured, seemed to be, first, that demands for liberty confused the people and hurt the government. But such a view ran counter to the imperial proclamation of 1875 promising gradual progress toward constitutional government. Or perhaps the reason was that nobles should not be involved in the newspaper business. But if newspapers were so damaging to the government, this prohibition should apply to former samurai and ordinary citizens as well. If the emperor had time to grant him an audience, Saionji concluded, he would like to report his views more thoroughly. However, Emperor Meiji made no response to the memorial, and the matter lapsed.

Saionji's conduct throughout this *Tōyō Jiyū* episode provides many a vivid glimpse of his character. It is quite clear that he was motivated by liberal views, but his own account of why he joined the newspaper is very revealing. Later in life he confessed, probably in all sincerity, "I was not a strong advocate of people's rights, and I had no deep commitment to the newspaper business. It was all just a bit of fun, a chance to buy myself a moment of pleasure."[3]

Saionji's temperament can be summed up as aristocratic. Such a person puts a high premium on freedom of action and hates any kind of restriction from others. At the same time, his attitude toward the world is detached, unenthusiastic, and basically cold-hearted. His view of human affairs is either playful or aloof. Saionji's account of his motives in becoming a newspaper president illustrates this very well. To give another example, early in 1868 Saionji shocked people by announcing his intention to take as his wife someone from the *burakumin* outcast community. As he later recalled, "I had no profound thoughts of attacking old customs or breaking down family privilege. It did not occur to me to make great exertions or sacrifice myself for such things; it was just a reflection of my personal style."[4] He also recalled that on his return from France, people seemed to have become apathetic, and he felt discontented and unhappy himself. Nevertheless, "I had no anger about the way things were going, no hopes or ambitions, no courageous urges to promote progress, no strong feelings of any sort. I am just the same today." And as for the depraved human heart, "the enormous spirit and effort required to overcome and improve it is beyond me. Maybe I can be called

[181]

cold and unfeeling, but I don't think that is true. I don't go against the trend of the times, and I don't follow it."[5]

Secure in his noble birth, Saionji had no urge to seek further fame. Especially after 1893, when his younger brother succeeded by adoption to Sumitomo Kichizaemon, one of Japan's wealthiest merchants, he never had to care about money. He also had little desire for power. Added up, the circumstances of his life allowed him free reign to indulge the aristocratic side of his temperament. On the other hand, a liberal way of thinking was a fundamental part of his makeup. This was due principally to his intellectual bent and love of rational thought, enabling him to arrive at logical, fundamental principles. Nevertheless, he could be willful, moody, or perverse in speech and conduct, behaving quite like the selfish nobleman, especially in his private life.

In tastes, as well as temperament, Saionji was thoroughly aristocratic, as many of his conversations show. For example, when discussing the splendid mansion recently built by politician Koizumi Sakutarō, Saionji told him: "If nobody lives in a large house with spacious grounds, things will become painfully cramped. Having to crouch is not good. One needs to be free and easy. I hope the rich will never get scared and become petty."[6] Talking with his private secretary Harada Kumao in June 1936, Saionji said, "These days people are forever going on about 'the masses'; if that expression is used too much, progress will come to a halt. In many ways, luxury leads to progress and improves culture. Government leaders should remember that, too."[7]

When compelled to resign from the *Tōyō Jiyū* newspaper, Saionji's reaction was true to form: he submitted a memorial directly to the emperor. Restriction from others was something he fought against all his life. When it came to imposing his will on others, he was very disinclined to do so, and this made him appear rather passive. But if others attempted to impose their will on him, he reacted fiercely. At such times his character was very positive and vigorous. Hence he was not content to obey the directions of government leaders on the newspaper issue without making a protest.

His appeal to the throne also illustrates the very close ties between Saionji as a Seiga court noble and the Imperial House. Saionji and Emperor Meiji were childhood playmates; they took drawing lessons together. The *biwa*, a kind of lute, was the traditional artistic specialty of the Saionji family. Even after becoming prime minister, he sometimes played it at informal banquets when requested to do so by the empress. The friendly relationship between Saionji and Emperor Meiji was noted by several observers. For example, when Yamamoto Tatsuo, finance minister in the second Saionji cabinet, presented an opinion on fiscal policy to Emperor Meiji for the first time, Prime Minister Saionji was also present. Long afterward, Yamamoto described this occasion to Koizumi Sakutarō. Yamamoto was guided to the audience chamber by a master of ceremonies who opened the door for him. "When the emperor noticed my entry," Yamamoto continued, "he turned to look directly toward me. Saionji drew his chair to one side and suddenly grew totally serious and attentive. I had a vivid impression that until then they had been talking together without reserve and completely at ease. Saionji was a boyhood friend of the emperor, and in view of the historical links between the Seiga families and the Imperial House, it seemed to me that he and the emperor must have had a bond of mutual affection, one where all distinction between high and low was absent. It was something quite different from what we generally think of as the ruler-subject relationship."[8]

Quite the opposite from Itō, who Saionji in later years described as trying hard to make life at the imperial court solemn and dignified, Saionji wanted it to be more friendly and informal. Both naturally and as a liberal, he respected the throne, but he wanted to make it more accessible.[9] On another occasion, Saionji observed that "since our present sovereign, Emperor Hirohito, pays great attention to national affairs, I think that not only cabinet ministers but vice-ministers and bureau heads should be received in audience to discuss official business." Cabinet ministers, Saionji continued, were too restrained when in audience with the emperor. If they had a difference of opinion about routine government affairs, they should feel quite free to submit memorials giving their reasons for this. When Emperor Meiji had disagreed with his views, Saionji had sometimes told him quite frankly how certain matters ought to be handled, and after heated argument had managed to overcome the emperor's

[183]

objections. That was the true role of an adviser to the throne. "The deference a subject shows to the sovereign and other marks of respect shown by inferiors to superiors are just formal courtesies. They do not mean that one must submit to all the views of the emperor."[10] Saionji's deep emotional affinity with the Imperial House and his liberal convictions are equally evident in these words.

Japan in the World

After giving up the presidency of the *Tōyō Jiyū* newspaper, Saionji was appointed to an advisory post in the Council of State, resuming his career as an official. When Itō Hirobumi went overseas in 1882 to make investigations for the constitution, Saionji was included in his entourage. A Peerage Law was promulgated in 1884, and Saionji was given the title of marquis, second in the five grades of nobility. Next, he became minister to Austria-Hungary, and later, to Germany. He spent about six years as a diplomat in Europe, but during his period of residence abroad he had very little work to do. When he lived in Berlin, he is reputed to have spent much of his time lolling in bed, immersed in reading *gidayū* traditional dramas. Bored with this existence, he dreamed up odd diversions. Hearing that a woman convicted of murdering a Japanese diplomat in Belgium had become a Paris prostitute after release from prison, Saionji decided to go there to enjoy her company himself, but when he broached the idea, his startled colleagues finally prevailed on him to desist. There were many such stories he told in the reminiscences of his later years.

When he returned to Japan in 1891, one of his first projects was to build a villa in Ōmori Iriarai, a coastal resort on the southwest fringes of Tokyo. He drew up the plans and directed the carpenters himself. His estate was over 6,000 square meters in area, and flowing through the garden were two streams each four meters across. It also had a grove of plum trees. In spring, the snowy egrets flocked to the nearby rice fields. He named this villa Bōrokusonsō and there lived a leisurely life, indulging his many interests and enjoying the peaceful rural surroundings.

On his return from Europe, Saionji had been appointed president of the Board of Decorations, and in the following year he became vice-president of the House of Peers. In October 1894, he joined the second Itō cabinet as education minister. He was then forty-six years old.

As education minister, Saionji had to give speeches on various occasions: in March 1895 to the graduation ceremony of the Tokyo Higher Normal School, and in June he addressed a conference of headmasters at the education ministry. His speechmaking commitments were much the same the following year. In the speeches he made around that time, he spoke on educational matters, stressing the need to promote education and apply the sciences if Japan aspired to rank with the Western Powers. Special effort must be put into English-language education, he believed, and to balance the burden on students, it would be wise to abolish Japanese literature from the curriculum, or at least reduce the time spent on it. Education for women was most important also, both to make Japan a civilized nation and to ensure that the next generation was raised by capable mothers. In spirit, the people should be lively and exhilarated, balanced and capable, and must avoid declining into lugubrious anger or grotesque eccentricity. It is currently fashionable among our youth, he continued, to admire and imitate patriot-heroes at a time of national disaster. That bodes ill for the future; the prosperous Japan of today requires quite different qualities in its citizens. Above all, a solid education must pay careful attention to the major trends in the world and the reasons behind the rise and decline of civilizations.

Saionji's opinions were very enlightened for the time. Too much so, for some. They were ill-received in a nation gripped by the feverish nationalism whipped up during the Sino-Japanese War of 1894–95, and Saionji was bitterly criticized by some sectors of the population. By then, educational policy, too, had acquired a strong overlay of nationalism. Saionji even thought of issuing a second Imperial Rescript on Education to counteract this trend, and the emperor gave his private assent. But the second Itō cabinet fell before such a rescript could be drafted, and the proposal lapsed.

In 1896, toward the end of the second Itō cabinet, Mutsu Munemitsu, Saionji, and others launched a new magazine,

Sekai no Nihon (Japan in the World), with the politician and historian Takegoshi Yosaburō as editor-in-chief. The journal's title was suggested by Saionji, who always had an instinctive fondness for the phrase "Japan in the World." To him, it rang of the greatness of Western civilization that he so deeply admired and heralded the day when Japan would rank with Britain and the United States as one of the leading nations of the world. Underlying it all was his vision of universal peace. Progress in civilization was bringing the world ever closer to international harmony, Saionji believed. If Japan was to become one of the leading civilized nations, it must move with this current in world history. Saionji, in short, stood for internationalism. Thus during the Sino-Japanese War and its aftermath, when a surge of national self-confidence inspired clarion calls for Japan to become the leader of Asia, Saionji heartily detested such ideas, regarding them as narrow-minded and ignorant. Proposing to call the new magazine "Japan in the World" was no mere momentary whim; its title summed up one of his most cherished ideals.

When Itō formed his third cabinet in 1898, Saionji was again appointed education minister. This time, however, he resigned after just over three months on a plea of illness.

Retreat to Ōiso

Saionji had been closely associated with Itō Hirobumi since the trip to Europe in 1882, and twice he had been asked to serve in an Itō cabinet. Then in 1900 Itō organized the Seiyūkai, and Saionji became a member of the party founding committee. But soon afterward, Saionji was appointed president of the Privy Council and had to sever all connections with the party. However, when Itō replaced Saionji as president of the Privy Council by imperial order in 1903, he asked Saionji to take over for him as Seiyūkai president. Saionji later recalled that "when Itō asked me to do this, I considered it a duty that I ought to take on."[11]

In a critical essay written just after these events, Toyabe Shuntei observed that Saionji was not consumed by the feverish desire for fame seen in contemporary politicians; this was a reflection of his personality and was reinforced by his profound wisdom. But he lacked the enthusiasm to challenge society and battle through to victory for the sake of realizing his principles and beliefs. Actually, he did not seem to have a particularly strong penchant for politics. Toyabe reported how Saionji was often compared as a political leader with Lord Rosebury. But while Rosebury had the curiosity to participate in politics as a drama, Saionji was content to remain a critic or spectator. He showed no signs of aspiring to play a leading role. "To direct a political party requires stamina rather than knowledge, courage rather than wisdom, and in some circumstances incitement rather than instruction. Saionji is rich in knowledge and very wise, but when it comes to stamina and courage, many people have private doubts about him." Saionji, continued Toyabe, had the intelligence to know others and to know himself as well, and was probably fortified by self-confidence more than ambition when he consented so readily to become party president; but "whether he had the ability to lead and control its members is a doubtful proposition that must be left for the future to decide."[12] The answer to Toyabe's doubts became clear quite quickly.

In his inaugural address as the new Seiyūkai president, Saionji promised, "I shall, to the limit of my strength, act with courage; I shall, to the best of my ability, exercise wisdom. You can count on me to do my best. In pursuing my objectives, I shall act with sincerity of heart and mind, fairly and openly. If one carefully studies how things work in the political world, it is clear that stratagems, devices, and tactical ploys are now out of date. They turn out to be quite useless. Intelligent people laugh them off as worthless efforts. I hope you will all understand that I am not the type of person who can resort to such things. I mention this because I intend to work hard for you and hope to receive your help in matters that are beyond me, your new president." Despite these promises, Saionji thereafter entrusted practically all party business to Hara Takashi and Matsuda Masahisa. He retired almost permanently to his villa at Ōiso, further down the coast from Tokyo, having transferred his domicile there from Ōmori. On the rare occasions when he visited the capital, he stayed at his residence in Kanda Surugadai.

Saionji built the Ōiso villa to his own specifications and once again supervised the construction with great care. An elegant and

[187]

tasteful house, he called it Tonarisō and spent quiet and un-
disturbed days there, indulging his many pastimes. As a man of
great knowledge, he enjoyed reading Japanese and Chinese books,
of course, but he was also well read in Western literature, especially in French. He had an appreciative eye for Japanese and
Western painting, and he enjoyed the theater and *sumō* wrestling.
He also played the checkerboard games of *go* and *shōgi* and took
pleasure in raising *bonsai* dwarf trees. Composing *haiku* verses
was another of his interests. One day after returning from a visit
to Itō's villa, Sōrōkaku, he wrote the verse: "What a joy to come
home and recover my view of Mt. Fuji, neglected in my absence
by locals who take it for granted!" Other poems composed at
Ōiso include: "Gentle waves, don't rise up and pound against
us! We mustard flowers" and "Blowing in from across Hana-
mizu river, an early summer wind storms through the fresh
greenery." From his young days, Saionji was a habitué of the red-
light quarters, where he was known as Otera-san (Mr. Monk).
There is also a story that he delighted in wearing a *haori* jacket
lined with red silk and decorated with playing-card motifs, tailor-
made at Chikusen, a shop favored by men of informed taste. He
liked traditional ballad dramas such as *kiyomoto*, Edo-style *jōruri*,
and *tambai* short lovesongs. In culinary tastes, Saionji's palate
was most refined and difficult to please. Just to prepare his daily
meals taxed the best of chefs, and he was known to not touch
food he disliked. Even after he arranged for chefs from the famous
restaurant Nadaman to serve him in yearly rotation, pleasing him
was so difficult that they frequently asked to leave their jobs.

With such broad-ranging interests, he inevitably entertained
a wide variety of friends and visitors at his house. Saionji's modesty
and politeness toward others was renowned throughout his life.
His household members all had firm instructions that whoever
called on him—whether cabinet minister, businessman, actor,
jester, or geisha—each one was his guest and on no account should
anyone be treated with less than full respect. He was a good listener, and since he had so many interests he could converse on a
wide variety of topics. His guests received the impression of sharp
intelligence as he exchanged witty and ironic remarks with them.
Nevertheless, he was very irritable and petulant toward those in
his domestic entourage. Hashimoto Saneaya, a relative, recalled

Saionji's peevishness as being most marked in his days as education minister, Seiyūkai president, and through to the Paris Peace Conference. During these twenty-five years there was scarcely a single person in Saionji's household who was spared the lash of his tongue; the servants bore the brunt of it. He became more tranquil in his latter years, however, and rarely displayed anger. "Even so, now and again, he would flare up just as he did when he was younger."[13]

War with Russia

The Russo-Japanese War broke out in 1904, about a year and a half after Saionji's appointment as Seiyūkai president. From its outset, the succession of battles and victories fueled an already fervid nationalism in Japan. The spectacle of people seeming to be intoxicated by chauvinism and to have lost all reason and moderation was, to Saionji, a debasing one. In March 1904, addressing the Seiyūkai party rally just before the opening of the 20th Diet, Saionji said that during this war, on which the fate of the nation hung in the balance, the people had to pull together with the aim of final victory. He noted that the phrase "national unity" was being used everywhere. "But is it not true that the public tends to use the word 'unity' in a narrow sense, taking it to mean blind obedience to the views of others? . . . Suppose that the Diet simply did whatever the government said, ostensibly in the interest of promoting national unity; or that the government thoughtlessly acted upon what it believed was the view of the people without considering the outcome—that would be very unfortunate, and disaster would be sure to follow." On a later occasion, Saionji warned the Seiyūkai party rally against the danger of unthinking antiforeignism and extreme hostility becoming rife among the people. Under today's circumstances, we must do our duty in a calm and rational frame of mind, Saionji continued, adding that "in this present time of danger to our country we must strive all the more to behave like a civilized nation."

Peace negotiations between the two belligerents were concluded in September 1905 at the Portsmouth Conference held in the United States. When a draft outline of the peace treaty became known in Japan, a large number people were outraged at the

[189]

humiliation of what seemed to them a spineless, unfair settlement, particularly when Russia refused to pay any indemnity for what had been a costly war. The most hostile critics demanded that the draft treaty should be rejected out of hand and the war continued until satisfactory peace terms were obtained.

In the midst of this public agitation, Saionji told the Seiyūkai standing committee that the leading nations of the world hoped to establish international peace and to end the hostilities in a humane way. The Portsmouth Conference had not been called to compel the defeated side to submit to the victors and sue for peace. What kind of impression would it make on the leading nations if Japan were to demand continuing the war on the grounds that specific peace conditions must be obtained before consenting to peace? After all, he said, our national interests had been secured: Japan had punished the violence of the Russians and purged them from Manchuria and Korea.

Three months after this speech, public anger against the Treaty of Portsmouth exploded. After an initial demonstration at Hibiya Park, rioting spread throughout Tokyo on 5 and 6 September 1905, as several thousand agitators attacked and burned official residences, government offices, police stations, and Christian churches. Finally, martial law was declared and soldiers moved in to restore order. Considering the mood of the infuriated public, Saionji had courage to speak the way he did. His words were a very clear expression of his internationalism and proof that he would stick by his convictions.

A Languid Prime Minister

The first Saionji cabinet was formed in June 1906, in an agreement that he and Katsura would alternate in power in the foreseeable future. As prime minister, he often invited prominent literary people to his residence in Kanda Surugadai to pass the whole of late spring evenings in talk. Since the gatherings tended to become regular, a name was found, and the group began calling itself the Useikai (Pattering Rain Society). Saionji's high level of culture was fully displayed at these famous gatherings. One caught a glimpse of his liberal ideas as well, for during his first cabinet the strict controls previously exercised over the socialist

[190]

movement were relaxed a little, allowing rather more margin for expression. But in the policies of his first and subsequent cabinet, there is nothing that can be positively attributed to Saionji, either as prime minister or party leader.

As Seiyūkai president, Saionji had entrusted almost all party business to Hara and Matsuda; as prime minister, he left important affairs chiefly to Hara. That he was asked to form a second cabinet in August 1911 was in fact largely the result of Hara's negotiations with Katsura. The political strategy of his cabinets was managed by Hara, both times his home minister. Saionji found forming a cabinet and handling government business infinitely tedious. His patent lack of enthusiasm and drive aroused anger and frustration in Hara. A lack of will and languid indifference to honors and power was always part of Saionji's character, and as prime minister he displayed these qualities to the full.

When Saionji's second cabinet collapsed, Katsura was ready to take over. He had resigned from his post as Lord Keeper of the Privy Seal a few months previously, and promptly formed his third cabinet in February 1912. In opposition to this, a Movement to Protect Constitutional Government was launched, whipping up public opinion against the cabinet and putting it in a very difficult position. Katsura's last resort was to persuade Emperor Taishō to send a message to Seiyūkai President Saionji encouraging him to withdraw the motion of no confidence then before the Diet. Saionji called a meeting of Seiyūkai Deit members and told them that he himself must comply with the imperial message, out of his duty as a subject. But it was quite proper for them, as representatives of the people, to hold fast to their opinions. Saionji simply asked them to act with all due prudence. Well aware that Katsura was on the brink of resigning, the Seiyūkai members unanimously resolved to continue their support for the no-confidence motion. Public agitation peaked as huge crowds stormed the Diet compound shouting for the cabinet's overthrow, and Katsura was forced to resign with all his ministers.

Saionji made this the occasion to renounce the party presidency, and he withdrew to Seifūsō, his Kyoto villa. Thereafter, he refused to have anything to do with party business and firmly rejected all pleas by Seiyūkai members to remain president. Many years later he described his feelings at that time in words that have an authentic ring: "Quitting the Seiyūkai presidency had no great significance. I was not taking responsibility for failure to control the Seiyūkai after the imperial message, or anything like that. Orders from the emperor must be obeyed, but his message was not all that emphatic. My inability to control the Seiyūkai was very regrettable, but I did not believe it would improve matters to attempt a forcible change in the atmosphere of the Diet or to clamp down on public agitation. From the Seiyūkai's point of view also, it did not matter if I retired. It was probably best for the Seiyūkai if I did so. As you know, I have always made it a habit to leave a little room for maneuver and to act before a situation becomes too tight. If I had thought it would do any good, I would have gone on trying, but there was no point. Anyone else could do the job in my place, and I was glad to be relieved of as much responsibility as possible. It seemed a good opportunity, and so I gave up the party presidency. But it is quite wrong to say that I felt compelled to do so because I had failed to obey the emperor's message. I simply thought it was time to put Hara in charge of affairs. Things had also become rather tiresome."[14]

After the cabinet resigned, the genrō met at the palace to confer about Katsura's successor. Saionji was also summoned to attend, and from then on he was ranked as one of the genrō. Yet even then the Seiyūkai would not accept his resignation and kept pressing him to remain party president. But he stubbornly refused and would not even look at party business, so Hara and Matsuda ran the Seiyūkai for him. When Matsuda died in 1914, Hara was appointed party president on Saionji's recommendation.

The Paris Peace Conference

After Terauchi's cabinet collapsed in September 1918, Yamagata asked Saionji to be prime minister. Saionji declined, so Yamagata turned to Hara instead. At last, Hara achieved his ambition to form a Seiyūkai cabinet. Two months later, the First World War ended in victory for the Allies. The peace conference opened in Paris in January 1919, and Yamagata and Hara were intent upon having Saionji attend as Japan's chief delegate. At first Saionji refused, but as he confessed in later years, "Well, I wasn't really obstinate; I thought it might be good to go abroad for a time and enjoy myself," and so he agreed.[15] Now in his seventieth year, Saionji embarked from Yokohama with his mistress Okumura Hanako, known to all as Ohana-san, his two physicians Miura Kinnosuke and Katsunuma Seizō, a nurse, and the head chef of Nadaman restaurant. This mission with its large entourage became a lively topic of conversation, inspiring such colorful epithets as "the snowdrop voyage," suggestive of a pleasure trip.

At the Paris Peace Conference, Saionji renewed his acquaintance with Georges Clemenceau, the friend of his student days. Now president of France, Clemenceau was basking in the glory of a victorious leader. His memoirs refer to "amiable Saionji, impetuous once, today quietly ironical, and an old comrade of mine at the lectures of our law professor, Emile Accollas."[16]

Saionji and his fellow delegates said very little during the conference on any matter not directly related to Japan. However, when the issue of Japan's continued occupation of Shantung came up in the conference program, they were forced to defend the stiff conditions for withdrawal, against strong protests from China. There were rumors that the Japanese delegates would walk out of the conference if their conditions were not met, and some of them did indeed want to do so. So Saionji set out to dissuade them. He called a meeting and told his fellow delegates that establishing the League of Nations was of greater importance to Japan than the Shantung issue. Nothing could be more stupid, he said, than to lose our heads over a petty imbroglio about Shantung, abandon the impending League of Nations, and withdraw from the conference. "However, if you want to withdraw, do so! All of you! I will stay here on my own, so you can go straight-away."[17] In any event, Japan's conditions on Shantung were accepted and the matter ended peaceably. As a convinced internationalist, Saionji set great store by the League of Nations and was most eager for Japan to take part in its launching. His resolute challenge to the other delegates on behalf of the League was reinforced by his hatred of being dominated by others, one of the strongest points in his character.

Just after Saionji returned from Paris, he attended Prime Minister Hara's farewell banquet for Admiral Saitō Makoto, who was about to take up his post as the new Korea resident general.

Saitō gave an address and as it ended, the whole assembly fell silent. At that moment, it is said, Saionji suddenly raised his cup and called out to Saitō in a loud voice, "Your Excellency, please conduct a civilized administration!"[18] What Saionji meant by civilized is clear enough, perhaps, when his past words and actions are considered.

Saionji was now at leisure and could concentrate on building a new villa at Okitsu, a favorite coastal resort of his in Shizuoka prefecture. He continued to stay at his Kanda Surugadai residence when in Tokyo, but henceforth Okitsu became his preferred abode, and he spent the better half of his life there. Fronting on the wave-lapped shore of Suruga Bay and abounding in simple elegance, Saionji's new home was called Zagyosō, at the suggestion of his friend Viscount Watanabe Chifuyu. The name was derived from a famous episode in ancient China. According to tradition, King Wen of Chou once went on a hunting expedition, for which the oracles promised a great prize. The king was disappointed in his quest for game, but unexpectedly came across a retired minister of great renown, Lü Shang, as he sat in a reed hut, fishing. The delighted King Wen greeted Lü with profuse courtesy and immediately appointed him chief counselor. Watanabe drew on this story to show a parallel between Saionji and the venerable Lü Shang; enjoying a life of quiet contentment while looking out on the waters, Saionji all the while bore heavy responsibility as a genrō to advise the emperor. In the year following the peace conference, Saionji was raised from marquis to prince, the highest grade of nobility, in reward for his distinguished services.

"Constitutional Normality"

When Saionji first became a genrō, there were five others: Yamagata Aritomo, Inoue Kaoru, Matsukata Masayoshi, Ōyama Iwao, and Katsura Tarō. By November 1921, however, after Hara's assassination, the only genrō still living were Yamagata, Matsukata, and Saionji. Saionji was now seventy-three years old; Yamagata was eighty-three and Matsukata eighty-six. Saionji felt apprehensive that sometime soon the heavy burden of responsibility he shared with these two colleagues would come to rest entirely on his own shoulders.

[194]

To succeed Hara, the genrō recommended his finance minister Takahashi Korekiyo as next prime minister. It was Saionji who had proposed Takahashi, on the grounds that if a cabinet change followed whenever the prime minister died in office, this would set a dangerous precedent.[19] In February 1922, shortly after Takahashi's cabinet took office, Yamagata died. He had been the most powerful of the genrō for many years and to the end of his days held party cabinets in great disdain. The genrō were now reduced to two, Matsukata and Saionji. A few weeks later, Saionji told Matsumoto Gōkichi, a confidant on matters of politics who often visited his house, that now, with Yamagata's death and Matsukata in advanced old age, he would find himself compelled to take on all the genrō's responsibility and get embroiled in palace affairs and politics. Later, he told Matsumoto that he wanted to live a little longer and apply himself to important matters now facing the imperial family and the nation. The crown prince was still young, but since November 1921 had been acting as regent during the illness of Emperor Taishō, so Saionji especially wanted to watch over affairs for the next four or five years.[20]

Saionji had played an important part in setting up the Hara and Takahashi cabinets, but this did not mean that he advocated carrying on government by party cabinets in the future. At the time of the Takahashi cabinet, Saionji told Matsumoto that people were talking more and more about the pure theory of parliamentary government, constitutional normality, and so on, suggesting that the proper way to govern was by cabinets alternating between the two major political parties. However, continued Saionji, "Although we speak of a Seiyūkai cabinet, that is not correct; it is the emperor's cabinet." He then asked, "In what books can you find the terms 'pure theory' or 'normality' in relation to constitutional government? In what countries are such things practiced at present? Sometime soon I want to call in some scholars and consult them about this. What do you think?"[21]

Saionji did not at that time fully comprehend the principle of party cabinets. He supported the Takahashi cabinet, even though he believed nobody in the Seiyūkai had sufficient ability to be prime minister, because of his determination to keep Katō Takaaki, president of the rival Kenseikai, out of office. Katō had been foreign minister in the second Ōkuma cabinet and bore respon-

[195]

sibility for the abrasive Twenty-One Demands on China in 1915, a fact that made Saionji very uneasy about Katō's diplomacy and its international repute.[22] As Saionji turned over in his mind who should be the next prime minister after Takahashi, his preferred choice was Den Kenjirō, a Privy Councillor and protégé of Yamagata. In other words, Saionji wanted to set up a so-called neutral cabinet headed by a non-party prime minister and then get the Seiyūkai to support it.

The Takahashi cabinet collapsed in June 1922 after several months of internal feuding, upon which Saionji first consulted his fellow genrō Matsukata on whom to recommend. Backed by the Satsuma clique, Matsukata suggested Admiral Katō Tomosaburō, navy minister in the previous cabinet and Japan's chief delegate at the Washington Conference of 1921–22. Saionji agreed, and Katō formed a transcendence cabinet.

In autumn that year, Saionji bought a villa in Gotemba at the foothills of Mt. Fuji. Thereafter, he spent his summers at this mountain retreat with its profusion of wildflowers, enjoying the gentle breezes, reading, and going for walks.

Prime Minister Katō died in office in August 1923, and Saionji recommended Admiral Yamamoto Gonnohyōe as his successor. Saionji believed that neither the Seiyūkai nor Kenseikai president was up to taking office and that internal feuds had made both parties divided and weak. So he hoped that Yamamoto would form a national-unity cabinet, drawing support from all sections of the official and political world. After Yamamoto had disposed of current business and set government finance and administration in order, Saionji wanted him to preside over a fair and impartial general election. But just over three months later, a young radical fired a shot into the prince regent's limousine at Toranomon, just outside the palace. Prime Minister Yamamoto took responsibility for this incident, and resigned with all his cabinet.

The Last Genrō

All too quickly, Saionji had to recommend another candidate. With Matsukata's agreement, he proposed Privy Council president Kiyoura Keigo as next prime minister, expecting him to continue Yamamoto's policies. Saionji assumed that Kiyoura would give a due share of power to the Seiyūkai, which in return would find it advantageous to support Kiyoura's cabinet. Thus it came as a surprise when in January 1924 Kiyoura formed a transcendence cabinet with most of its ministers drawn from various factions in the House of Peers. A chorus of angry opposition came hard on the heels of its formation, denouncing the cabinet as anachronistic. Opinion was split within the Seiyūkai about what position to take toward the new cabinet. Those who maintained that the cabinet should be supported broke away to form a new party called the Seiyūhontō. That spurred the Seiyūkai remnants, together with the Kenseikai and Kakushin Club, to launch a second Movement to Protect Constitutional Government. Backed by public opinion, they set out to overthrow the Kiyoura cabinet.

The number of Diet seats held by the pro-cabinet Seiyūhontō was nowhere near a majority, so the party urgently needed a general election to gain more strength. Saionji was very worried that the Kenseikai would gain more seats in the next election and that the resulting balance of power would force him to recommend Katō Takaaki as the next prime minister or that at any rate a coalition cabinet with Kenseikai members would emerge.[23] In the general election of May 1924, the Seiyūkai, Kenseikai, and Kakushin Club—the so-called Three-Party Alliance to Protect Constitutional Government—together gained a majority of Diet seats. The Kenseikai with 150 seats also became the leading party. With no hope of controlling the House of Representatives, Kiyoura promptly resigned with all his cabinet. Even after the election, Saionji still hesitated and pondered, but he could not think of a suitable person to form a "neutral" cabinet. Resigned to the situation, he steeled himself and recommended Kenseikai president Katō Takaaki. Thus, with Katō as prime minister, a three-party coalition cabinet was set up in June 1924.

In July, Matsukata died and Saionji finally became the sole genrō. The role of the genrō was above all to act as makers and guardians of the cabinet. Always careful to avoid being hemmed in by external forces and determined to keep his freedom of action, Saionji was now alone in the exercise of enormous powers and responsibilities. This was not just a matter of politics—as in all else he did, his whole personality was at stake.

[197]

Saionji found Katō's performance as prime minister clumsy, typical of the incompetence of party presidents in general. He despaired of ever finding a party leader worthy to be prime minister. In future changes of government, he thought, if the circumstances demanded, neutral cabinets might still be the best choice. Confidently expecting to form the next cabinet, the Seiyūkai appointed General Tanaka Giichi party president in April 1925, and then began negotiations for an alliance with the breakaway Seiyūhontō. Katō had formed a coalition cabinet supported by the three major parties, but the Seiyūkai and Kenseikai had been at loggerheads for some time, and internal disunity finally forced his cabinet to resign in July 1925. The Seiyūkai and Seiyūhontō promptly announced that they had formed an alliance. Since these two parties together held 227 out of 464 Diet seats, a workable majority, they felt sure that the next cabinet was in their grasp. Not so Saionji, who had watched these machinations with wry contempt. Ignoring this rash attempt to force his hand, he advised the emperor to reappoint Katō prime minister. Katō accepted and reconstructed a cabinet based solely on the Kenseikai. Although it did not have a majority, the Kenseikai still held more seats than any other single party and managed to survive for the next six months by exploiting divisions among its rivals.

When Prime Minister Katō died of illness in January 1926, the Kenseikai immediately appointed Wakatsuki Reijirō its new president. Thereupon, Saionji recommended Wakatsuki as next prime minister, and he formed his first cabinet. Saionji felt that the Katō cabinet's policies were not yet deadlocked, and also wanted to reaffirm the precedent set after Hara's death while in office that such an event need not result in a cabinet change. But he did not think much of Wakatsuki's ability as a political leader, and later complained to his confidant Matsumoto Gōkichi that Wakatsuki was simply not cut out to be prime minister. More than ever, Saionji felt depressed at the lack of able leaders in the political parties. Although he had supported a number of party cabinets in the last few years, he had by no means abandoned his belief that neutral cabinets were still an attractive alternative.

The Wakatsuki cabinet barely managed to keep in office, limping on with a slender majority in the House of Representatives. The Kenseikai (165 seats) faced mounting rivalry from the Seiyūkai (161 seats), and the Seiyūhontō (87 seats). Attempts by Wakatsuki to form an alliance with the Seiyūhontō proved abortive, and the political world fell into a state of confused stagnation. However, the Kenseikai and its two main rivals were all in a difficult quandary. A manhood suffrage law had been passed in 1925 under the first Katō cabinet, quadrupling the electorate to 12 million voters. All three major parties could not predict the results of the next election with any certainty, so they wanted to postpone dissolving the Diet for as long as possible. Consequently, the political intrigues over who should form the next cabinet became even more murky and contorted. The 52nd Diet of December 1926 opened just after the funeral of Emperor Taishō; the Seiyūkai and Seiyūhontō put up motions of no confidence in the cabinet, and it looked as if a Diet dissolution was at last inevitable. Prime Minister Wakatsuki requested the emperor to order a Diet suspension and met with Seiyūkai President Tanaka Giichi and Seiyūhontō President Tokonami Takejirō. He told them that with the coronation of the new emperor pending, he wished to avoid stirring up political warfare for the moment. Tanaka and Tokonami demanded that Wakatsuki and his cabinet should give careful consideration to the circumstances that had prompted their no-confidence motions. Wakatsuki agreed to do so. Tanaka and Tokonami interpreted this reply as a promise from Wakatsuki of an early cabinet transfer, and they dropped their opposition.

That compromise between the three rival parties astounded the public. Saionji, also, hoping for a dissolution that would get the political logjam moving again, was most disappointed. Wakatsuki had previously sent Harada Kumao, Saionji's private secretary, to Okitsu to inform Saionji that he had requested a Diet suspension as a preliminary step and would carry out a dissolution if the opposing parties showed no real change of heart. Saionji was bitterly frustrated to hear news of this sudden compromise that had dashed his hopes for dissolution. "So it won't take place," he regretted to Harada. "I was really counting on a quick and decisive dissolution. . . . Is there any real connection between an imperial funeral and dissolving the Diet? How could

[199]

a Diet dissolution be an act of disrespect toward the emperor's funeral? The politicians, of course, must be held responsible. Very few of them can step back and see the larger picture as a whole. The common people with their low level of political awareness are also partly to blame. How unfortunate, but I suppose such a thing just had to happen. . . Ah, well! So the dirty political struggle at the present will just go on and on!"[24] Neutral cabinets continued to seem a future possibility for Saionji, as he grew ever more disenchanted with the political parties.

Diplomatic Complexities

Shortly after the three-party compromise, the Wakatsuki cabinet clashed with the Privy Council over countermeasures to the current financial panic and collapsed in April 1927. This time, Saionji's choice fell on General Tanaka Giichi, president of the Seiyūkai. Despite gaining added strength after union with the Kakushin Club in May 1925, the Seiyūkai still held only 166 out of a total of 464 seats. A few months after he formed his cabinet in April 1927, Tanaka faced a powerful challenge from the Minseitō, formed after a merger of the Kenseikai and Seiyūhontō. The Minseitō elected as its president Hamaguchi Osachi, an able leader of good reputation, and with 219 seats the new party now topped the Seiyūkai.

Tanaka barely managed to restore the lead of the Seiyūkai in the general election early the next year, but his cabinet was soon in trouble over an ominous diplomatic incident. On 4 June 1928, the Chinese warlord Chang Tso-lin, who had controlled Manchuria since 1920, was blown up by a bomb explosion while traveling on a train just outside Mukden. Chang's assassination had been secretly plotted by rightist officers of the Japanese Kwantung Army, seeking to head off the China reunification movement as it advanced in concert with Chiang Kai-shek's Northern Expedition. It was the historical prelude to the Manchurian Incident of three years later.

Receiving news of the bombing, Prime Minister Tanaka visited Saionji and told him in strict confidence that Japanese army officers seemed to be responsible. If that was clearly established, Saionji replied, they must be firmly punished and military dis-

[200]

cipline upheld, not only to maintain control over the army, but also to preserve Japan's good reputatiō abroad. In the long run, furthermore, such a response would help build good will on the Chinese side. Saionji told Tanaka that as an army general he ought to be able to control the military. The Seiyūkai was a powerful party and could certainly take effective action if resolved to do so. A firm stand now would be very good both for Tanaka and the party alike.

However, as the facts became clear, both cabinet ministers and Seiyūkai leaders began to maintain that if Japanese army officers were indeed responsible, the incident should be consigned to oblivion. Tanaka began to waver, but Saionji repeatedly urged him to report all the details of the incident to the emperor. When Tanaka went to the palace to report, he told the emperor that Japanese army officers were suspected of instigating the bombing, and that this was currently under investigation.

Meanwhile many army leaders began to hail the officers responsible as patriots and vehemently objected to any talk of a court-martial. Little by little, Tanaka was enmeshed in a tangle of conflicting interests. Under the pretext of carrying out investigations, things dragged on inconclusively, much to Saionji's disgust. He quietly promised himself, as Harada listened, "While I am alive, I swear that this incident will not be shrugged off inconclusively."[25] The emperor repeatedly asked Prime Minister Tanaka for information on how the investigations were progressing, until finally Tanaka went to the palace to report. This time he told the emperor that fortunately Japanese army officers were not to blame, and that the railway guards would be dealt with by administrative measures. But the emperor, who already knew the true facts, probed further. Could Tanaka explain, he asked, why this report was very different from his previous one? Realizing how displeased the emperor was with him, Tanaka was overawed and immediately resigned, followed by all his entire cabinet.

Saionji next recommended Minseitō President Hamaguchi Osachi, who formed a cabinet in July 1929. A few months later, Tanaka died suddenly, a disgraced and disappointed man. In September, Inukai Tsuyoshi was appointed to succeed him as Seiyūkai president.

Just after Tanaka's death, Seiyūkai leader Uchida Nobuya, a supporter of Inukai's nomination to party president, had called on Saionji. He described this visit many years later: the reason for calling, he told Saionji, was that when Uchida urged him to stand for party president, Inukai had said, "Go and seek Saionji's opinion." Inukai had for many years advocated the radical view that the genrō should be abolished, and had kept strictly aloof from them. As a result, he felt very diffident about approaching Saionji, so Uchida had come to speak for him. When Uchida had finished, Saionji drew himself up and replied forcefully, "What kind of a man is Inukai? He has always been a strong advocate of abolishing the genrō, and now he asks my opinion!" Uchida was flustered and tried to patch things up by replying, "No, Inukai is consulting you not as a genrō, but as a former Seiyūkai president; that is what matters to him." Saionji looked as if he had seen through Uchida's lame excuse, but did not pursue it. Uchida felt relieved and returned to Tokyo.[26]

A major item in the Minseitō's platform was to support diplomacy based on international justice, as a necessary foundation for world peace. Japan participated in the London Naval Disarmament Conference which began in January 1930 during Hamaguchi's cabinet. At the time, Saionji spoke at length about the disarmament issue to Harada: "The Paris Peace Conference has given us a new opportunity, and a striving for peace and happiness prevails; no nation in the world is making aggressive preparations." The new opportunity was in fact a manifestation of the spirit proclaimed by Rousseau and other philosophers centuries ago, he went on; "treaties of disarmament and non-aggression have a respectable history." The policy of disarmament "aimed to promote human happiness, out of a love for peace."[27] Saionji naturally hoped that whatever the Japanese navy might demand at the conference, Chief Delegate Wakatsuki could be counted on, by all means, to succeed in the treaty negotiations. He remembered his own frame of mind at the Paris Peace Conference. In March, Saionji contracted influenza and pneumonia, which caused great alarm because of his advanced age. Feverish and very ill, he babbled deliriously about "disarmament," "Italy," "France," unable to contain his anxiety about the success of the conference even in his semi-conscious state.

By April 1930, the disarmament treaty had progressed to the signing stage. It first went before the Privy Council for scrutiny. In collusion with the Naval General Staff, which had strong objections of its own, the Privy Council put some harsh strictures on the Hamaguchi cabinet and for a time forced it on the defensive. The Seiyūkai, now under Inukai's leadership, echoed the Privy Council, and threw itself into ousting the Hamaguchi cabinet. Saionji found this discouraging. He fumed to Harada that all the political parties, whether pro-cabinet or opposition, should be putting aside their differences in a unified effort to oppose the continual high-handedness of the navy. But the Seiyūkai, in aligning itself with the Naval General Staff, was in fact supporting the military—out of a sheer hunger for power. Saionji regarded this as a most dangerous and worrying matter.[28]

This year, 1932, Saionji turned eighty-three. He recovered from his illness in the spring and began to take better care of himself. He spent most of the day at Zagyosō reading Japanese, Chinese, and French books. He also enjoyed activities such as engraving seals and cultivating *bonsai*. On still, warm days he walked in the garden and then took an afternoon nap. In the evening, he sat alone at his desk in the study and read his fortune from a pack of cards. At dinner, painstakingly prepared by his anxious cook, he poured himself prime quality *saké* from Nada. His table was never without Vichy water, imported from France by Meijiya department store, right up to the Pacific War when it could no longer be obtained. He liked Havana cigars, but as he grew older he developed a taste for Egyptian cigarettes, too. When he went out on visits or traveled, he usually wore tasteful Japanese dress. His socks were always of dark blue calico from exclusive Tokyo shops, such as Sanoya in Owarichō; his clogs were from Awaya in Nishi Ginza. In summer, he wore a straw boater, but in winter he preferred a soft cap. When in Western dress, his collar studs, cuff links, and tie pins were made of gold, and he wore them in combination with red. His gloves and wallet were of French make. For toilet articles, such as scent, toothpaste, and mouthwash, he preferred those produced by the Ubigan Company of Paris, probably reminders of his student days there. Even on reaching old age, Saionji still presented all the appearance of a Western-style man of fashion.

[203]

Onrush of Military Fascism

In November 1930, Prime Minister Hamaguchi was shot and severely wounded at Tokyo station by a rightist youth, and died later the following year. His cabinet lingered on for a few months but resigned in March 1931. Wakatsuki Reijirō had replaced Hamaguchi as Minseitō president, and following the precedents set by Hara and Katō, Saionji recommended him as the next prime minister. Five months after the formation of the second Wakatsuki cabinet, the Manchurian Incident of September 1931 precipitated Japan's politics into a period of great turbulence. But not without warning. The assassination of Chang Tso-lin in 1928 had been followed by an abortive coup in March 1931 by young army officers of Sakurakai, an ultranationalist society formed in September 1930. A tidal onrush of military fascism centered on young army officers was now well on its way, although the scene of action again shifted overseas.

The Manchurian Incident was sparked off by an explosion on the railway several kilometers north of Mukden. Officers of the Japanese Kwantung Army had planted the bomb themselves, and then used this as a pretext to retaliate by putting into motion prearranged military plans to occupy key areas of Manchuria. Badly shaken, the Wakatsuki cabinet tried unsuccessfully to impose restrictions on the military and contain the situation. Wakatsuki called on several important government and political leaders to seek their opinion on what to do, but only Saionji sympathized with him and pledged support for any measures he resolved to take. Then, in December 1931, internal disunity forced the Wakatsuki cabinet to resign. This time, Saionji turned to Seiyūkai president Inukai Tsuyoshi, who became prime minister in the same month.

Before the imperial mandate had been formally issued, however, Saionji summoned Inukai to inform him that the emperor was deeply concerned by the cabinet's inability to control the army and by the unauthorized military actions in Manchuria. Saionji made it clear that the new cabinet must do everything possible to regain control. But the Inukai cabinet also found restraining the military virtually impossible. In March 1932, the army announced the formation of an independent state of Manchukuo;

[204]

Puyi, the last descendant of the deposed Ch'ing dynasty, took office as regent, until proclaimed emperor in March 1934.

When Konoe Fumimaro, vice-president of the House of Peers, visited Okitsu early in 1932, Saionji quoted the famous aphorism of the twelfth-century Chinese general Yüeh Fei: "If its civil officials do not covet money and its military officers do not fear death, a realm can expect peace." But today, Saionji continued, turning this around seemed more appropriate: "If the civil officials do not fear death and the military officers do not covet money. . . ." In other words, "Right now our civil officials are overawed by violent gangs, and military officers are greedy for wealth." This was a sad state of affairs, he added with a sigh.[29] As the conversation went on, Saionji told Konoe that recently the political situation had turned in a direction that totally confounded his hopes and better judgment. When government changes occurred, he would find it very hard to recommend a military officer as prime minister. Given the present circumstances, he had to reflect carefully and act with resolution, or risk disgracing himself in the eyes of posterity. So he was now thinking about giving up his privileges and titles of nobility and relinquishing his post as a genrō.[30]

Saionji felt impotent and beleaguered. He feared that under the pressure of present and future developments, he would be forced to compromise or betray his role as a genrō. But precisely because the situation was so serious, and no longer within the capacity of the nation to handle, he could not bring himself to resign just yet.

Anxiety robbed Saionji of any peace of mind during these ominous days. Unable to contain his concern about the future, in early spring 1932, despite the bitter cold, he decided on a visit to Tokyo. He sent for Harada, telling him, "The other day the Lord Chamberlain called and told me the emperor is so distraught over the arrogance of the army that he finds it difficult to sleep at night. His Majesty has even felt compelled to do such things as sending a messenger to the Lord Chamberlain's house at 11 P.M. asking him to come to the palace at once. It is disrespectful of me to say so, but I am even more worried than His Majesty. The emperor's anxiety is understandable, but he need not be alarmed to that extent. I shall go to Tokyo to pay my respects and advise

[205]

him not to worry. The nation faces no real danger of startling changes in the future, and if my visit to Tokyo can set the emperor's mind at rest a little, it will be worthwhile. Right now, that is all I can do, so I will make the trip. While I don't think I can achieve much, in my capacity as genrō, I want to meet Takahashi, for one thing, and discuss government finance, and also to hear General Ugaki's views, both as army minister and as executive head. I think this is what I should do. If I tell Dr. Katsunuma, my chief physician, he will no doubt discourage me from going in this cold; so I have not told him about the trip yet. Anyway, on the 5th I intend to go to Tokyo and after seeing several people, pay my respects to the emperor."[31]

All the while, fomented and spearheaded by the military, fascism continued its violent advance. On the very day that Saionji went to Tokyo, the director-general of the Mitsui combine, Dan Takuma, was shot and killed by members of the Ketsumeidan, a right-wing terrorist group led by Inoue Nisshō, a renegade Buddhist priest. A month earlier, a Ketsumeidan member had murdered Inoue Junnosuke, former finance minister and currently chief manager of the Minseitō.

Saionji arrived at Tokyo under the strictest guard. On the day he was due to visit the palace, he told Harada that although he was to be received in audience by the emperor, he had nothing special to report. He wanted to tell His Majesty, " 'The situation does indeed warrant anxiety, but there is no cause for despair. Many of us have witnessed great upheavals in our lifetimes, and looking from a broader perspective, I think it is most important that Your Majesty not worry so much and remain calm.' That is basically what I want to say, but is it enough? Should I say more?"[32] Thus on that day, 14 March 1932, Saionji, now eighty-three, visited the palace to console a young emperor sick with worry.

Two months later, in broad daylight at his official residence, Prime Minister Inukai was shot to death by uniformed army and naval officers. That outrage, soon to be known as the May 15th Incident, meant that Saionji had to leave Okitsu once more to advise the emperor on the appointment of the next prime minister. Every station on his route was placed under strict guard, creating a truly awe-inspiring spectacle.

[206]

The young officers who assassinated Inukai had hoped that their act would precipitate a military coup d'état. Deep hostility toward corrupt party cabinets had long been festering in the military, especially among the young officers, making the choice of the next prime minister a critical one. This time Saionji was assisted in making a choice by an informal group of senior palace advisers, consisting of the Lord Keeper of the Privy Seal, the president of the Privy Council, and previous prime ministers. After consultations with them, Saionji recommended Admiral Saitō Makoto. Saionji seems to have hoped that when the shock of recent events had subsided, the government would return to a more normal course.

Toward the end of 1932, Chief Private Secretary to the Privy Seal Kido Kōichi visited Saionji at Zagyosō. As they talked, Saionji repeated his wish to be relieved from his post as genrō. Kidō's diary contains a record of their conversation: Saionji said, "I am now at the age of decline; my body is weak, and I cannot shoulder responsibility. It is painful having to be constantly involved in politics and so I want to resign as genrō." Kidō replied, "I think that in our situation now there is a greater need than ever for a genrō. I know it is a great burden for you, but in many instances the military is acting on its own initiative and the politicians are being all too acquiescent. I think, therefore, that there is no one but the genrō who can shoulder the task of government." Saionji answered, "I know that is true, which makes the pain unbearable. I dislike what is called semi-retirement, but can I not be allowed even that?" Kido replied, "Even if as genrō you went into semi-retirement, there is no guarantee that the emperor would not consult you again." Saionji said this made him feel even more depressed.[33] Once again, Genrō Saionji found it impossible to escape from his responsibilities. For as long as he remained in this role, he would have to brave the onrushing tides of military fascism.

Prime Minister Saitō visited Okitsu in April 1934 and reported that allegations of corruption were now rocking the cabinet, so he now wanted to step down to make way for a new head of government. Saionji would not listen. Shaking his head, he urged Saitō to stay: "No matter what, I ask you at this time to make an even greater effort," he said and persuaded Saitō to

[207]

remain in office. A little later, pleading illness, Kuratomi Yūzaburō tendered his resignation as president of the Privy Council. Saitō considered putting up Privy Council Vice-president Hiranuma Kiichirō to succeed him, but Saionji rejected that choice out of hand. As head of the ultranationalist Kokuhonsha society, Hiranuma had long-established connections with rightist groups and was a supporter of the military. To appoint such a man Privy Council president, this would provide a dangerous loophole for military fascism to worm its way into inner palace circles, Saionji thought, and he was determined to prevent that at all costs. Saionji therefore recommended former Lord Chamberlain Ichiki Kitokurō for the post. When he summoned Ichiki to obtain his formal assent, Saionji urged him to be ready to sacrifice himself for the nation.

It was during the Saitō cabinet that in March 1933, under military pressure, Japan withdrew from the League of Nations. The League had commissioned the Lytton Report, whose findings were highly critical of Japan's actions in Manchuria. Withdrawal from the League greatly saddened Saionji. In autumn 1934, a year afterward, he told Privy Seal Secretary Kido Kōichi that if Japan did not constrict itself in East Asia by Pan-Asianism and other such slogans, and worked to solve world problems together with Britain and the United States, it could probably attain world status as one of the three leading nations. But abandoning the League made this impossible, he sighed in disappointment.[34]

26 February 1936

Saitō resigned with all his cabinet in July 1934, taking responsibility for a graft scandal involving the Teijin Rayon Company. Amid a strident public outcry, several high-level politicians, including his vice-minister of finance, were accused of stock market manipulation. Although debilitated by the oppressive heat, Saionji left Gotemba for Tokyo and went straight to the palace. After consultations with senior colleagues—the previous prime minister, the president of the Privy Council, and the Privy Seal— Saionji then recommended Admiral Okada Keisuke as the next prime minister. Saionji had been scandalized by the behavior of the political parties under the Saitō cabinet, as they played up to the military, plying their masters with ingratiating ploys in their thirst to gain a little more power. When Okada formed his cabinet, ugly rumors were current that the party leaders were steeped in corruption, and he was expected to do something about it. Saionji advised him that while constitutional government had to be upheld, there was no need to take the parties too seriously in their present rotten condition. Saionji later told Okada that it would be all to the good if the cabinet stuck firmly to its principles and if necessary dissolved the Diet two or even three times in succession to force the parties into line.[35]

Just after taking office, Prime Minister Okada visited Saionji at his summer retreat in Gotemba. Saionji recalled a palace audience some years ago when he had advised the emperor: It is quite in order to suspend the constitution or to revise it. But violations of the constitution can on no account be allowed, regardless of the cost in lives or disorder. Of course, there are times when treaties must be revised, and it is quite in order to abrogate them. But a truly great empire must never violate treaties. "The emperor," continued Saionji, "found this advice most acceptable." Okada replied that he understood what Saionji expected of him and agreed to act accordingly.[36]

Saionji remained on guard against Hiranuma. In spring 1935, Privy Council President Ichiki made known his wish to resign on grounds of poor health and suggested that Hiranuma succeed him. The Privy Seal Secretary Kido Kōichi went to Okitsu to discuss the matter with Saionji, who insisted that Ichiki must stay in office until he died and flatly refused to consider Hiranuma as a possible successor. However, later in 1935, Hiranuma's name came up again as a likely candidate. Several groups suggested that he would be able to conciliate the military and right wing. Saionji would hear none of it, telling Harada: "Hiranuma's appointment to Privy Council president is absolutely out of the question. If that type of person is not kept as powerless as possible, there is no hope for the world." In the end, Ichiki remained in his post. When Privy Seal Makino Nobuaki had visited Okitsu in early summer 1935 to report that his health was failing, Saionji pressed him to continue in office: in times like these both of them must be resolved to stay at their posts until they died. For the sake of the nation, they must try harder than ever before.[37]

Pressure from the military induced the Okada cabinet to terminate the Washington Naval Arms Limitation Treaty in December 1934 and to boycott the London Naval Conference in January 1936. At home, violence and confusion continued. In November 1934, two rightist officers of the Army Academy were arrested and detained for plotting a coup d'état. Several cadets were also expelled. The incident escalated a confrontation within the army between field officers of the ultranationalist Imperial Way faction and a Control faction centered on military bureaucrats. Throughout 1934 and 1935, Minobe Tatsukichi, emeritus professor of Tokyo University's Faculty of Law and a member of the House of Peers, was fiercely criticized by rightists for his academic theory that the emperor was simply one of several organs of the state and did not embody all sovereignty in his own person. As a well-known advocate of liberalism and democratic progress, Minobe was singled out for special intimidation by fascist critics. Meanwhile, military pressure on politics continued, until finally on 26 February 1936 several hundred soldiers attempted to force a Shōwa Restoration. They occupied key sections of Tokyo for several days, while their assassination squads hunted down and shot to death former prime minister Takahashi Korekiyo, Lord Keeper of the Privy Seal Saitō Makoto, and Inspector General of Military Education General Watanabe Jōtarō. Lord Chamberlain Suzuki Kantarō was severely wounded, and several other prominent people were lucky to escape with their lives.

At Okitsu, as in Tokyo, 26 February was a cold winter day. Sometime after 7 A.M., while the snow fell incessantly, Saionji emerged from Zagyosō. Muffled in a scarf, his frail form supported by private secretary Nakagawa and the head maid, Saionji got into an automobile waiting at the front door. He took refuge for a time at the prefectural police headquarters and was then driven to the governor's official residence. There he spent the night. Upon leaving his house, Saionji is reported to have told Nakagawa, "I am placing myself in the care of you and the others. But my registered domicile is at Okitsu, so I mustn't stay away for very long." Saionji returned home on the next day, 27 February. But for some time afterward, the prefectural authorities kept a launch anchored in the bay near the Saionji house and continued to mount a careful guard. Saionji had been on the conspirators' hit list, marked down as an "evil adviser to the emperor," but just before the rebellion took place the plans were changed and he escaped attack.

Incensed at news of this military rebellion, the emperor insisted that prompt measures be taken to suppress the rebels. But Saitō Makoto was dead, and the severely wounded Suzuki Kantarō was unable to attend at court; the emperor had lost his two closest advisers. Having barely escaped assassination himself, Prime Minister Okada Keisuke assumed responsibility for the rebellion, and a week or so later resigned with all his ministers. The emperor ordered Saionji, although in poor health, to come to the capital immediately to discuss the next cabinet. Saionji arrived in Tokyo under strictest guard, just after the rebels finally surrendered, and went straight to the palace. He conferred with Privy Council President Ichiki Kitokurō, Lord Chamberlain Yuasa Kurahei, and Chief Private Secretary to the Privy Seal Kido Kōichi, and after careful reflection recommended Konoe Fumimaro. But Konoe adamantly refused to accept, pleading illness. The choice then fell on Hirota Kōki, foreign minister in the previous cabinet and an ex-diplomat with rightist political connections. After much difficulty coping with military interference in the selection of his ministers, Hirota finally formed a cabinet in March 1936.

From the start, the Hirota cabinet was so hemmed in by the military that it was virtually powerless. Saionji told Harada that they simply had to get a cabinet in office with the will to combat the military, or all was lost. But things had now come to such a pass that in any conflict with the military, "constitutional government will be swept away. Even today it is barely in operation." Saionji sympathized with Hirota—he had no choice but to act as he was doing.[38]

The Hirota cabinet was pushed by the army into signing the Anti-Comintern Pact with Germany in November 1936. Saionji predicted to Harada, "We will be nothing but a tool of Germany, with no benefit whatsoever to ourselves." In December, when Seiyūkai politician Koyama Kango visited Saionji, the aged genrō was beside himself with anxiety over Hirota's diplomacy. The cabinet was pursuing a line, he told Koyama, that in effect ignored Britain, the United States, and China; Germany and Italy had no stake in East Asia, so moving over to their side simply amounted to being exploited for nothing in return. Finance Minister Baba Eiichi's fiscal policy was simply to go along with all the demands of the military, added Saionji, and Hirota was just an opportunist.

In January 1937, Saionji celebrated entering his eighty-eighth year with his family. At that time, looking back over the past, he said to Harada, "When I think of it now, Kido Takayoshi, Ōkubo Toshimichi, Itō Hirobumi, and Katō Takaaki—even the less talented Hara Takashi—they were all such able men...," bemoaning the lack of competent leaders at a time of grave national crisis.[39]

That same month, Seiyūkai member Hamada Kunimatsu made a speech in the 70th Diet criticizing the military, who retaliated with angry demands for a Diet dissolution to punish the parties for such presumption. The cabinet was divided on whether to comply, so it resigned. Saionji recommended General Ugaki Kazushige as prime minister, but opposition from the military made it impossible to form a cabinet. Then he proposed Hiranuma Kiichirō as his first choice, with General Hayashi Senjūrō as his second. When Hiranuma declined, Hayashi set up a new cabinet in February 1937.

Resistance and Retreat

Some time before, Saionji had confessed to Kido Kōichi, "I have tried to achieve numerous things in politics, but in the end one can only do as much as the level of public awareness permits. Recently, I have become quite convinced of this."[40] He also told Harada many times, "Whatever one says, the people's understanding is at such a low level that there is probably no way to improve them, unless by providing a thorough political education."[41] For Saionji to see education as the only hope for reform was a clear revelation of how far he believed the political breakdown had gone. Military fascism by its violent onslaught had now almost completely crushed party politics and any resistance Saionji might put up could only end in failure. In the matter of key appointments, he had already lost ground. Despite Saionji's earlier objections, Hiranuma had been appointed president of the Privy Council during the Hirota cabinet's term of office. To cap it further, Saionji had proposed Hiranuma as his first choice to succeed Hirota as prime minister.

By this time, Saionji's earlier resolve to keep military men out of high office had long since eroded. In 1932, just after the Manchurian Incident, he had told Konoe that he would find it very hard to recommend a military man as prime minister, and wished to avoid disgracing himself in the eyes of posterity. Yet he had recommended Admiral Saitō Makoto as prime minister later the same year and Admiral Okada Keisuke in 1934. He had some good reason for these choices: his aim was to control the military by means of its more moderate and enlightened leaders. Even so, when he later recommended General Hayashi Senjūrō in 1937 after the fall of the Hirota cabinet, Saionji had no such expectations. As army minister in the Okada cabinet, Hayashi had tried to purge ultranationalists of the Imperial Way faction from key posts and that was probably why Saionji recommended him. After the formation of the Hayashi cabinet, when Harada remarked to Saionji that the prime minister seemed to be understanding things better, Saionji retorted: "Oh, no! He won't understand a thing! Military men simply cannot comprehend the meaning of such concepts as 'the welfare of a nation and its people.' "[42]

As the political crisis deepened, Saionji continued to request relief from his duty to recommend prime ministers and from acting as genrō. But Lord Keeper of the Privy Seal Yuasa and his secretary Kido held him back. At a time when certain people outside the palace were intent on severing the emperor from his close advisers, they argued, Saionji with his influence at court could perform a valuable role in resisting such attempts. If Saionji retired, what would happen? They were adamant that he remain in his post. Finally, as a concession to Saionji, a new procedure was devised whereby future prime ministers were to be recommended by the Lord Keeper of the Privy Seal after consulting Saionji's opinion. Faced by a mighty tide of military fascism, the emperor's closest advisors clung desperately to Saionji, now eighty-eight years old, as one of the last reliable supports they had.

The Hayashi cabinet collapsed in June 1937, deadlocked over how to handle the Diet. Following the new procedure, Konoe

[213]

Fumimaro was nominated as prime minister. Konoe's background was impeccable. Even the Saionji family, one of the nine Seiga aristocratic families, were ranked below the five Sekke. The Konoe were, in fact, the leading Sekke family and thus at the very top of the aristocratic tree. Saionji first became acquainted with Konoe when he was a student at Kyoto Imperial University. His intelligence and personality impressed Saionji, who saw great promise in him. Konoe first rose to prominence in the House of Peers, finally becoming its president in 1933. Then rumors began that sooner or later he would be a candidate for prime minister. Saionji assisted Konoe to advance his career, but he also urged him to move with caution. In 1934, when his cabinet was in its last days, Saitō Makoto suggested Konoe as the person best qualified to succeed him. On hearing of this from Harada, Saionji said he thought Konoe should follow his own wishes at that time and go to the United States. It would be a good chance for him to take a careful look at Japan from overseas; he could become prime minister at some future time. His amicable relations with the military notwithstanding, Konoe had the advantages of an untarnished reputation and high social status. Apart from such qualities, what else could be used to resist the military, Saionji asked.

When the Hirota cabinet was about to collapse in mid-1937 and the question of the next prime minister came up, Saionji said to Harada, "The time is not right for Konoe. He would end up becoming a puppet, which would be very unfortunate. Anyone else who comes forward right now will probably become a puppet, too, but it is best for Konoe to be prudent." One of the problems was that since the time of the Manchurian Incident, Konoe had grown increasingly sympathetic toward the demands and actions of the military and rightists, and as a result had gained considerable popularity in those quarters. Saionji had serious doubts and fears about Konoe's course. In August 1936, a few months after the February 26th Incident, Saionji told Harada that Konoe had visited the other day, but talked as if he were a spokesman or defending lawyer for the military. Saionji found it difficult to understand why Konoe said what he did. Was it out of conviction? Did he feel compelled to talk like that? Or was he frightened? Or seeking to enhance his present position? Saionji added,

"I think it such a shame for someone of his ability and birth to act as he does. Isn't there some way of gently guiding him toward a more reasonable course?" Harada suggested that Konoe might be amenable to persuasion if they remonstrated with him about his behavior, but that he seemed to lack courage and was worried too much about his popularity. Perhaps it would be a good thing if the emperor also encouraged him to be a little more prudent? Saionji agreed, and it seems that they decided to approach the emperor through Lord Keeper of the Privy Seal Yuasa.

Nevertheless, when Harada visited Okitsu after Hayashi's resignation in June 1937, it was Saionji who had changed his mind and recommended Konoe to form his first cabinet. Saionji admitted that he had hesitated about recommending Konoe in the past, and had tried to avoid doing so if at all possible. But if the emperor sought his opinion, he could only recommend some-one in whom he had complete confidence, and there was no one but Konoe. It appeared to Harada that Saionji had really made up his mind on the matter. Perhaps Saionji believed that Konoe's appointment would ease friction with the military and rightists, and provide some guarantee against any major departure from present courses.

Betrayed Hopes

On 7 July 1937, a month after the Konoe cabinet took office, Japanese troops on maneuvers near Marco Polo bridge outside Peking clashed with local Chinese forces. A cease-fire was arranged a few days later, but Japan announced its intention to mobilize and three weeks later occupied Peking and Tientsin. Thereupon, China and Japan finally plunged into a full-scale conflict. The China Incident, as it was called, continually escalated with each new demand of the military, and Saionji's anxiety took on the quality of a deepening nightmare.

Konoe's actions as prime minister quickly made things worse. To begin with, Konoe seriously considered granting a general amnesty to all young officers and rightists convicted of acts of violence since 1932. Army spokesmen had been lobbying for this for some time, and Prime Minister Konoe responded, thinking that such a move might produce greater national unity at a time

[215]

when Japan faced a momentous crisis in international relations. Privy Seal Yuasa and President of the Board of Royalty and Peerage Kido pleaded with Konoe to reconsider. But Konoe had thought hard about the matter and was not to be dissuaded. Yuasa then turned to Saionji for support. When he first heard of Konoe's plans for an amnesty, Saionji was very angry. He told Harada, "If he is going to do such irrational things, then he had better resign. There is no special reason why he has to stay in office."

Konoe called on Saionji at Gotemba to explain his views on the general amnesty, in the hope of winning him over by friendly persuasion. But Saionji only hinted at his own stand and would not be drawn into details. Afterward, Saionji told Harada that any attempt to issue an imperial order for a general amnesty must be stopped at all costs. If Konoe went ahead with it, he was cutting off his future. How unfortunate if he became a mere puppet of the military! Konoe must become more mature and "hoist the banner of civilized government." It was most improper for a prime minister to act so irresponsibly; not in the public interest at all. A general amnesty would render the constitution meaningless, Saionji fumed. Konoe subsequently dropped his proposal for a general amnesty, probably as a result of Saionji's strong opposition.

Always hoping in his innermost heart that the conflict with China would not expand, Konoe nevertheless was dragged along by the military, unable to apply brakes. Hostilities spread and escalated. A tortuous process of peace negotiations ended in failure by late 1937, whereupon Konoe issued his famous Declaration of 1938: "Henceforth we shall no longer negotiate with the Chinese Nationalist government," it stated, transforming the incident into a long-term war.

Shortly afterward, the Konoe cabinet published an outline of a National Mobilization Law. It was in fact the military that had demanded such a law as a preparation for total war. By granting the government extensive powers to issue legislation, the law reduced the basic civil rights of the people and the powers of the Diet to names without substance. Despite the Diet's virtual impotence under military pressure, a few members stood up to challenge the draft law when it came before the 73rd session of December 1937 to March 1938. But the draft was defended by

[216]

people such as Privy Councillor and legal scholar Shimizu Kiyoshi, who denied that the proposed law could be interpreted as
an infringement of the constitution. When Harada reported on
this, Saionji exclaimed, "What on earth do people like Shimizu
know about the constitution!" In substance, continued Saionji,
this law suspends the constitution, and it never should be passed
by the Diet. Was there no means of blocking it? But the Diet,
intimidated by the military and rightists and manipulated by
their allies in the Seiyūkai and Minseitō, finally passed the law
without amendment.

Saionji could not contain his growing disappointment with
Konoe. As prime minister, he seemed to have lost all sense of
responsibility and was showing poor powers of leadership, Saionji
thought. Konoe's behavior was servile; he needed more self-confidence as the head of government. Saionji wanted him to be
more independent and to lead more positively. He told Harada,
"Konoe carries on like someone's lackey; isn't that utterly hopeless?" Even so, when Konoe intimated that he wanted to resign,
Saionji pressed him to stay in office. The problem was that Saionji
could not think of anyone better to succeed him. Saionji later
lamented to Harada, "The omens are very bad. When the Ming
dynasty of China was collapsing, just as in Japan today, there
were plenty of wise men but they all kept silent. Their weakness
was that they never got together in organized groups, and so they
could not interact."[43]

In autumn 1938, with no visible prospect of resolving the conflict in China, Konoe again expressed his intention to resign. He
hoped to escape from responsibility for the political situation by
becoming Lord Keeper of the Privy Seal as successor to the ailing
Yuasa, who also wanted to relinquish his post. On hearing this,
Saionji told Harada that the Konoe cabinet was kept in power
by army support. If Konoe became Privy Seal, the army would
be able to extend its power into the palace. "Almost everything
in politics is already controlled by the army, but the palace must
be kept free of its influence," Saionji insisted. For that reason he
was absolutely against appointing Konoe as Privy Seal and wanted
Yuasa to be told this in strict secrecy. If Konoe wanted to resign,
he should consider what would happen after he left office. If he
departed with dignity, in a way that could not be called irre-

[217]

sponsible, that would be quite acceptable. At the same time, Saionji asked Harada to tell Yuasa that "although it may be a great hardship, he should stay in his post until he dies. He must serve the emperor at all costs."[44] By now, all Saionji's hopes in Konoe had been betrayed.

A month later, in November 1938, Koyama Kango visited Saionji at Okitsu. Koyama related how helpless he felt as events kept taking completely unexpected turns; he and others could not even begin to frame an opinion, but simply looked on, dumb with amazement. Saionji responded, "You are all young, so you can still go out and fight. But as for myself. . . ." As the words trailed off, his despair filled the silence.[45]

A short time later, Vice-President Wang Ching-wei defected from the Nationalist government in Chungking and began negotiations with Japan for setting up a puppet government. This stratagem had been plotted by the military and reeked of intrigue and treachery. Hearing the news, Saionji deplored the depths to which Japan's foreign relations had fallen. To Harada he declared, "Plotting is quite out of place in civilized diplomacy." He then murmured reflectively, "Where on earth are they taking this nation? What do they intend to do? It's incomprehensible to me." In December 1938, Konoe followed up Wang's defection by issuing a Declaration on China-Japan Relations, foreshadowing a New Order in East Asia. He then made this the occasion to resign with all his cabinet in January 1939. Saionji heard of this in advance and asked Harada, "Since Konoe became prime minister, what has he done in government? I certainly have no idea. What more can one say?" He added, "But I suppose that is the way things are nowadays, and it cannot be helped. I am profoundly sorry for the emperor. Precisely because he understands so much, my sympathy for him is unbearable. I am also very sorry for the Lord Keeper of the Privy Seal, and even for Konoe, too; their predicament is a product of the times and cannot be remedied."[46] Saionji's tone of hopeless resignation seemed to apply to his own situation as well.

Yuasa consulted Saionji about the next cabinet and on his own responsibility recommended Hiranuma Kiichirō. Just after the new cabinet was formed in January 1939, Saionji commented to Harada about the choice of Hiranuma, "The reason is that he's elastic." Harada thought Saionji meant that if Hiranuma was put in a position of responsibility he was too pliable to do much harm. Hiranuma took over from the previous cabinet the problem of strengthening the Anti-Comintern Pact, but the diplomatic negotiations proved to be very difficult. At the time, Saionji told Harada, "After all, Japan is being treated by Germany and Italy like a small Balkan nation, isn't it? If by any chance Germany and Italy go to war with Britain and France—or, to put it another way, if Germany and Italy win—we must realize that Japan will be even more under their thumb than now. It is so very distressing that the cabinet could not see this in advance." Saionji later commented, "The prime minister constantly speaks of moral diplomacy, but what on earth is he talking about? Diplomacy is nothing more than promoting the national interest, so all talk of morals amounts to no more than hot air." When Harada asked how he defined the national interest, Saionji replied that this was "interest framed on the basis of correct concepts."

While the negotiations for the Anti-Comintern Pact were dragging on, Germany suddenly announced the signing of a Non-aggression Pact with the Soviet Union. Left completely in the lurch by this diplomatic volte-face, Hiranuma resigned with all his cabinet in August 1939. At his summer retreat in Gotemba, Saionji informed Harada that he had absolutely no suggestions about a successor cabinet, simply insisting that "I want the next prime minister to ensure, at all costs, that the emperor's wishes are clearly established." From the outset, Saionji had been completely opposed to strengthening the Anti-Comintern Pact, and he said of the negotiations, "We now face the biggest failure in our diplomatic history. The influence of the military today is a real nightmare. Anyone in charge of affairs will find things very difficult. Japan should, no matter what, act in concert with Britain, the United States, and France."

After the fall of Hiranuma's cabinet, Saionji agreed to Yuasa's nomination of General Abe Nobuyuki. The Abe cabinet had just taken office when war broke out between Germany and Poland. That was in September 1939, and precipitated the Second World War. From the very beginning, the Abe cabinet was a puppet of the army. Quickly forsaken even by its master, the cabinet collapsed after a mere four months. This time, Yuasa, with Saion-

[219]

ji's approval, recommended Admiral Yonai Mitsumasa as the next prime minister. However, the army had never liked the Yonai cabinet, and in July 1940 brought it down after a short six months.

Life's End

In 1940, Saionji reached the age of ninety-two. His health was poor that year, so he did not spend the summer at Gotemba but remained at Zagyosō, where air-conditioning had been installed.

When the Yonai cabinet fell, Kido Kōichi, who had just succeeded Yuasa as Privy Seal, undertook to recommend the next prime minister. He first consulted previous prime ministers and then sought the opinion of Privy Council President Hara Yoshimichi. They all proposed Konoe. A few weeks previously, Konoe had given up his post as Privy Council president and launched the Movement for a New Political Structure, an attempt to form a new, nationwide party organization. He was now at the summit of his popularity, a handsome and impressive figure, drawing the attention and hopes of the people toward himself amid wide acclaim. Hearing from Harada that Konoe would certainly be the next prime minister, Saionji was not impressed. "The concept of governing on the basis of popularity is quite out of date," he said.[47] Thereafter, on behalf of the Privy Seal, his chief secretary Matsudaira Yasumasa visited Okitsu to ask Saionji's opinion about recommending Konoe. Saionji replied that he was now a very old man and had been ill recently; he did not really understand the present political situation, and to respond in such a state of ignorance would be disloyal to the emperor. He therefore declined to venture any opinion at all. When Konoe formed his second cabinet in July 1940, Saionji had long since given up all hopes of firm, decisive leadership from him.

One of the first acts of Konoe's new cabinet was to issue an Outline of a Basic National Policy. This document announced that a New Order in Greater East Asia would be established, as a first step in Japan's mission to extend its empire across the world. As a sequel to this, the Imperial Headquarters-Cabinet Liaison Conference drew up a policy statement entitled, "Main Principles Governing Japan's Response to Changes in the World."

[220]

The alliance with Germany and Italy must be strengthened, the statement declared, in order to settle the China war, to determine Japan's policy toward Southeast Asia and the Pacific, and to achieve a significant improvement in relations with the Soviet Union. Both these documents were drawn up and issued in compliance with military demands. They clearly demonstrated that the second Konoe cabinet was simply a puppet of the military. Saionji commented to Harada that, all things considered, Konoe seemed destined for a miserable fate, "like a beggar who dies by the roadside." When Harada repeated this remark to him, Konoe replied, "No. My fear is that I shall come to a much worse end than that."

In September 1940 a Tripartite Pact was signed in Berlin between Japan, Germany, and Italy. It was then triumphantly hailed as the stepping stone toward a New Order in Greater East Asia. All the while, Foreign Minister Matsuoka Yōsuke kept bombastically proclaiming a forthcoming Greater East Asia Co-prosperity Sphere and was heartily applauded by the crowds as a hero of the epoch. Immediately after the Tripartite Pact was signed, Harada told Saionji that some people thought Matsuoka must be insane. Saionji smiled sardonically and replied, "If he really is mad, all the better. At least that gives us the hope of him one day returning to his senses."[48]

Konoe's Movement for a New Political Structure took firm shape in October 1940 with the formation of the Imperial Rule Assistance Association. A few months previously, the Seiyūkai, Minseitō, and smaller parties all dissolved and joined Konoe's new movement, hoping, as ever, for a greater share of power. A subservient Diet in December 1940 extended the National Mobilization Law of 1938, imposing rigid control over politics, society, and the economy. These events dealt the coup de grace to constitutional government. With the Diet now at its last gasp, political freedom was swept clean away.

On 10 November 1940, the nation celebrated the 2,600th anniversary of the founding of the Japanese empire, with ceremonies attended by the emperor and empress, higher officials both civil and military, and a wide range of popular representatives. That evening in the public square before the palace, the autumn air resounded with the voices of over 50,000 people chanting, "Long

[221]

Live the Emperor!'' All the while, Saionji lay on his sickbed at Zagyosō. His condition had deteriorated seriously as a result of kidney inflammation. When Harada visited Okitsu on the evening of 13 November, Saionji's physician Katsunuma Seizō told him, "I have treated the prince for several decades, but this is the first time on becoming ill that he had spoken to me about politics. Anxiety about the political situation at home and abroad seems to be greatly undermining his health. He murmurs a lot to himself, saying things like, 'They talk of a New Order but the nation has become painfully divided,' or, 'Diplomacy will also prove difficult.' If Harada had any good news for Saionji, continued Katsunuma, please would he tell him of it now, it could revive his spirits. On 18 November Harada again visited Saionji at his bedside. Recalling Katsunuma's suggestion, Harada reported that to avoid a war if at all possible, General Nomura Kichisaburō would be posted as ambassador to the United States, taking with him the good will of the army and navy. Saionji seemed very happy, asking "Will he really go? Please give Nomura my best wishes." When Harada went on to report that Prime Minister Konoe was making great efforts to negotiate with Chiang Kai-shek to end the China war, Saionji murmured, "Whatever can Japan say now that Chiang will listen to?"[49]

Saionji's disappointment and anxiety was now beyond endurance. Lying on his sickbed, he seemed to have lost all will to live, much to Katsunuma's regret. On the evening of 24 November 1940, Saionji's ninety-two years of life came to an end, as rain cast a misty shroud over Zagyosō.

The Meiji Constitution is worded in spare and concise language. While authoritarian in some respects, it was nevertheless a modern constitution with a certain measure of liberalism. Saionji always hoped in his heart that these liberal potentials would expand and develop. His dream, which remained constant throughout his long life, was that under the emperor's reign and equipped with a liberal political structure, Japan would play an important role in world politics alongside Britain, the United States, and the other great nations of the West.

In his final years, when military fascism imposed its control by violence, Saionji as a genrō put up as much resistance as he could.

[222]

But his resources were too few, and he failed. The political parties of the time could not be expected to put up much resistance. The vast majority of party politicians played along with, even lauded, the military; their only concern was to gain a greater share of power. Finally, around the time of Konoe's second cabinet, the parties went into voluntary dissolution, one after another, and vanished. The people, too, were not equipped to resist. Naive and gullible, they believed what they were told by military and government propaganda, most of them eager conformists in obedience to orders and support for nationalistic goals. Saionji saw only one sure base for resistance: the palace. That was the final irony. Only the palace remained firm against the tidal wave of military fascism that seemed to inundate everything else. But it could never become a force in politics. Powerless to save anything but itself, Saionji's last bastion still left him miserably broken. The contempt of fascist ideology for international peace and its denial of political freedom were totally incompatible with Saionji's liberal principles and, more fundamentally, with his innermost feelings and character. A fierce hatred of fascism was almost instinctive to someone of his aristocratic temperament.

Saionji's youth in Paris and his long years of self-sufficiency were hopeful and serene, but he ended his days in times of raging storm. Was the tragedy his alone? The course of Saionji's life as an individual somehow seems to epitomize modern Japan's fateful progress from early promise to a catastrophic disaster.

NOTES

ITŌ HIROBUMI

1. Ashikaga Yoshimitsu (1358–1408), Toyotomi Hideyoshi (1536–95), and Tokugawa Ienari (1773–1841) were military rulers on friendly terms with the reigning emperors of their day.

2. Ozaki Yukio, *Kindai kaiketsu roku* (Tokyo: Chikura Shobō, 1934), pp. 169–70.

3. Kumada Ijō, ed., *Kanju shōgun jūō dan* (Tokyo: Jitsugyō no Nihonsha, 1924), pp. 34–36.

4. Furuya Hisatsuna, *Tō kō yoei* (Tokyo: Minyūsha, 1910), pp. 207–8.

5. Fang Hsüan-ling (578–648) and Tu Ju-hui (585–630), chief ministers at the T'ang court, restored the dynasty by means of their strategic and executive abilities.

6. Yamaji Aizan, *Omou ga mama ni* (Tokyo: Shunyōdō, 1914), pp. 192–93.

7. *Tokyo Asahi Shimbun*, 9 November 1909, Goan, "Itō kō no enzetsuburi."

8. Mutsu Hirokichi, ed., *Hakushaku Mutsu Munemitsu ikō* (Tokyo: Iwanami Shoten), pp. 609–10. Mutsu Munemitsu, "Sho genrō danwa no shūheki."

9. Shumbō Kō Tsuishōkai, comp., *Itō Hirobumi den*, vol. 2 (Tokyo: Shumbō Kō Tsuishōkai, 1940), pp. 1047–48.

10. Tsuda Shigemaro, *Meiji seijō to shin Takayuki* (Tokyo: Jishōkai, 1928), pp. 727–28.

11. Ozaki, *Kindai kaiketsu roku*, pp. 166–67.

12. *Tokyo Asahi Shimbun*, 28 October 1909, "Inukai Tsuyoshi dan."

13. Kaneko Kentarō; Hiratsuka Atsushi, ed., *Itō kō o kataru* (Tokyo: Kōbunsha, 1939), pp. 58–59. Furoku, Zadankai sokki.

14. Ozaki, *Kindai kaiketsu roku*, pp. 167–68.

15. Koizumi Sakutarō; Kimura Tsuyoshi, ed., *Saionji Kimmochi jiden* (Tokyo: Dai Nihon Yūbenkai Kōdansha, 1949), p. 102.

16. Hinonishi Sukehiro, *Meiji Tennō no go nichijō. Rinji teishitsu ni okeru danwa sokki*, (Tokyo: Shingakusha Kōyūkan, 1952), p. 61.

17. Furuya, *Tō kō yoei*, pp. 213–15.

18. *Tokyo Asahi Shimbun*, 9 November 1909, Goan, "Itō kō no enzetsuburi."

19. Kaneko Kentarō, *Yo no shirareru Itō kō*, part 2 (Tokyo: Kaigun Keiri Gakkō, 1928), pp. 17–18.

20. Toyabe Shuntei, "Itō kō wa tōshu no utsuwa naru ya," *Shuntei zenshū*, vol. 1 (Tokyo: Hakubunkan, 1909), p. 15.

21. Furuya, *Tō kō yoei*, pp. 157–59.

22. Toyabe, "Daiyōji no Itō naikaku," *Shuntei zenshū*, vol. 1, p. 39.

23. Tokutomi Sohō, *Waga kōyū roku* (Tokyo: Chūō Kōronsha, 1938), p. 79.

24. *Yomiuri Shimbun*, 2 February 1922, "Kikuchi Ashigarashimo gun gunchō dan."

25. *Tokyo Asahi Shimbun*, 28 October 1909, "Inukai Tsuyoshi dan."

26. *Taiyō* (October 1908). Tenraisei, "Rekidai shushō no kantei seikatsu."

27. Toyabe, "Kojin to shite no Itō kō Ōkuma haku," *Shuntei zenshū*, vol. 1, p. 5.

28. Uematsu Takaaki, *Kōshaku Itō Hirobumi. Kōshaku Saionji Kimmochi* (Tokyo: Tōkaidō Shoten, 1912), p. 246.

ŌKUMA SHIGENOBU

1. Tsumaki Chūta, ed., *Kido Takayoshi monjo*, vol. 4 (Tokyo: Nihon Shiseki Kyōkai, 1930), p. 102.

2. Watanabe Ikujirō, ed., *Ōkuma Shigenobu kankei monjo*, vol. 1 (Tokyo: Nihon Shiseki Kyōkai, 1932), pp. 440–42.

3. Ichijima Kenkichi, "Ōkuma kō no tokusei," *Bummei Kyōkai Nyūzu*. Ōkuma kō tsuibo gō (1932), p. 22.

4. Enjōji Kiyoshi, ed., *Ōkuma haku sekijitsu tan* (Tokyo: Shinchōsha, 1914), p. 15.

5. Mutsu Munemitsu, "Ōkuma haku shusshin shimatsu," *Hakushaku Mutsu Munemitsu ikō* (Tokyo: Iwanami, 1929), pp. 653–55.

6. Ozaki Yukio, "Ōkuma Shigenobu kō to watakushi," *Ōkuma Kenkyū*, no. 2 (October 1952), p. 196.

7. Mumeishi, *Seitō to shuryō* (1915), pp. 256, 269.

8. *Tokyo Asahi Shimbun*, 8 January 1922, "Kume Kunitake dan."

9. Fukumoto Makoto, *Nichinan sōrō shū* (Tokyo: Tōadō Shobō, 1912), pp. 383–84, 385.

10. Emori Yasukichi, ed., *Ōkuma haku hyakuwa* (Tokyo: Jitsugyō no Nihonsha, 1909), pp. 110–19, 119–23.

11. Mutsu, "Shogenrō danwa no shūheki," *Hakushaku Mutsu Munemitsu ikō*, p. 611.

12. Nakano Seigō, *Shichikin hachijū* (Tokyo: Tōadō Shobō, 1913), pp. 38–39. Uzaki Rojō, *Katsujinken satsujinken* (Tokyo: Tōadō Shobō, 1913), pp. 67–69. Kojima Kazuo, *Seikai gojūnen Kojima Kazuo kaikoroku* (Tokyo: Sangensha, 1951), pp. 25, 28–29.

13. Yamada Ichirō, "Ōkuma haku wa tōshu no utsuwa ni arazu," *Taiyō* (May (1896).

14. Ikeda Ringi, ed., *Waikō kanwa* (Tokyo: Hōchi Shimbunsha Shuppanbu, 1922), p. 195.

15. Gorai Kinzō, *Ningen Ōkuma Shigenobu* (Tokyo: Waseda Daigaku Shuppankai, 1938), p. 469 ff. Tokutomi Sohō, "Ōkuma kō no henrin," *Jimbutsu Keikan* (1939), pp. 220–22.

16. *Tokyo Asahi Shimbun*, 8 January 1922, "Kume Kunitake dan."

17. Ozaki Yukio, "Seikai ni okeru kyojin Ōkuma kō no shōgai," *Jitsugyō no Nihon*. *Ōkuma kō aitō gō* (February 1922), pp. 45–46.

18. *Tokyo Asahi Shimbun*, 11 January 1922, Miyake Setsurei, "Yukeru waikō."

19. Yokoyama Kendō, *Haku Ōkuma* (Tokyo: Jitsugyō no Nihonsha, 1915), pp. 221, 428–29.

20. Toyabe Shuntei, "Saikin no Ōkuma haku," *Shuntei zenshū*, vol. 1 (Tokyo: Hakubunkan, 1909), pp. 119, 121, 124–26.

21. *Tokyo Asahi Shimbun*, 27 January 1913.

22. *Shin Nippon*, April 1914. Also published in Waseda Daigaku Henshūbu, ed., *Ōkuma haku enzetsu shū kōen no risō* (Tokyo: Waseda Daigaku Shuppanbu, 1915).

23. Ibid.

24. Reply in the House of Representatives, 18 December 1915.

25. Matsue Yasuji, ed., *Ōkuma kō sekijitsu tan* (Tokyo: Hōchi Shimbunsha Shuppanbu, 1922), p. 229.

HARA TAKASHI

1. Hara Keiichirō, Hayashi Shigeru, eds., *Hara Takashi Nikki*, 6 vols. (Tokyo: Fukumura Shuppan, 1965, 1967), III, 387 (6 February 1914).

2. Ibid., IV, 313 (8 September 1917).

3. Ibid., I, 246 (24 August 1897).

4. Ishikawa Hanzan, "Hara shi no sōnan," *Taikan* (December 1921).

5. *Hara Takashi Nikki*, II, 67–68 (13 June 1903).

6. Ibid., II, 221–22 (13 January 1907).

7. Ibid., II, 286 (25 January 1908).

8. Ibid., II, 348–50 (7 April 1909).

9. Ibid., III, 76 (25 December 1910).

10. Ibid., III, 21 (6 April 1910).

11. Ibid., III, 134 (8 June 1911).

12. Ibid., III, 201 (23 December 1911).
13. Ibid., III, 197 (16 December 1911).
14. Ibid., IV, 8 (11 June 1914).
15. Ibid., IV, 19–20 (9 June 1914).
16. Ibid., IV, 233ff (11 November 1917, *passim*).
17. Ibid., IV, 432 (20 August 1918).
18. Mochizuki Keisuke, "Hara sōsai no omoide," *Shuchō*, vol. 1, no. 5 (November 1922).
19. Kataoka Naoharu, *Taishō shōwa seijishi no ichi dammen* (Kyoto: Nishikawa Bunko, 1934), pp. 210–11.
20. Ozaki Yukio, *Kindai kaiketsu roku* (Tokyo: Chikura Shobō, 1934), p. 95.
21. Tokutomi Sohō, *Daiichi jimbutsu zuiroku* (Tokyo: Minyūsha, 1926), pp. 93–94.
22. Yokoyama Kendō, "Hara Takashi to Chōroku sensei," *Chūō Kōron* (December 1921).
23. Tokutomi, pp. 92–93, 98.
24. Yokoyama, "Hara Takashi."
25. Sōma Motoi, ed., *Chichi no eizō* (Tokyo: Tōkyō Nichi Nichi Shimbunsha, 1937), p. 63.
26. Maeda Renzan, *Hara Takashi den*, vol. 2 (Tokyo: Takayama Shoin, 1943), p. 365.
27. Matsunami Niichirō, ed., *Mizuno hakase koki kinen ronsaku to zuihitsu* (Tokyo: Mizuno Rentarō Sensei Koki Shukugakai Jimusho, 1937), p. 558, "Hara Takashi shi o omou."
28. *Hara Takashi nikki*, V, p. 200 ff. (21 October 1920).
29. Reply in House of Peers, 28 January 1921.
30. *Hara Takashi nikki*, V, 454, 461 (3, 21 October 1921).
31. Ibid., V, 293, 294, 297 (9, 14 October 1920).
32. Ibid., V, 265 (5 August 1920).
33. Ibid., V, 369 (4 April 1921).
34. Maeda, vol. 2, p. 366.
35. Baba Tsunego, *Gendai jimbutsu hyōron* (Tokyo: Chūō Kōronsha, 1930), pp. 31–32.
36. *Hara Takashi nikki*, V, 314 (23 November 1920).
37. Baba Tsunego, *Kaiko to kibō* (Tokyo: Yomiuri Shimbunsha, 1948), p. 97.
38. Oka Yoshitake, Hayashi Shigeru, eds., *Taishō demokurashii ki no seiji: Matsumoto Gōkichi seiji nisshi* (Tokyo: Iwanami Shoten, 1959), p. 60 (27 March 1921).
39. *Tōyō Keizai Shimpō*, 16 July 1921, "Shōhyōron: Kensei yōgo undō no yume."

INUKAI TSUYOSHI

1. Inukai Tsuyoshi, *Bokudō dansō* (Osaka: Hakubundō, 1922), pp. 140–47.
2. For example, Washio Yoshinao, ed., *Inukai bokudō shokan shū* (Tokyo: Jimbunkan, 1940), p. 355.
3. Inukai, *Bokudō dansō*, pp. 302–4.
4. Kojima Kazuo, "Inukai bokudō o kataru," *Chūō Kōron* (July 1932).
5. Yokoyama Kendō, "Gendai jimbutsu kanken," in Bokudō sensei denki kankōkai, comp., *Inukai bokudō den*, vol. 3 (Tokyo: Tōyō Keizai Shimposha, 1939), p. 478.
6. Toyabe Shuntei, "Inukai Tsuyoshi shi," *Shuntei zenshū*, vol.1 (Tokyo: Hakubunkan, 1909), p. 501.
7. Washio, *Inukai bokudō shokan shū*, p. 137.
8. Kojima Kazuo, "Seikaku gōdō temmatsu," in Koichinenkai, ed., *Kojima Kazuo* (Tokyo: Nihon Keizai Kenkyūkai, 1949), p. 903.
9. Washio, *Inukai bokudō shokan shū*, p. 162.
10. Miura Gorō, "Semmannen ni hitori shika umarenu otoko," in Nukada Shōnan, *Tateru Inukai bokudō ō* (Osaka: Tateru Inukai Bokudō Kankōkai, 1930), p. 63.
11. Washio, *Inukai bokudō shokan shū*, pp. 257–58.
12. "Teikoku no kikin," in Dai Nihon Yūbenkai, ed., *Inukai bokudō shi dai enzetsu shū* (Tokyo: Kōdansha, 1927), pp. 239–40.

13. Ibid., p. 243.
14. Inukai, *Bokudō dansō*, pp. 72–103.
15. Koizumi Sakutarō, *Kaiō jidan* (Tokyo: Chūō Kōronsha, 1935), p. 13.
16. Ozaki Yukio, *Gakudō hōdan* (Tokyo: Konnichi no Mondaisha, 1939), pp. 286–87.
17. Kojima Kazuo, "Unkan sunkan," in Koichinenkai, *Kojima Kazuo*, p. 324.
18. Kojima Kazuo, *Seikai gojūnen Kojima Kazuo kaikoroku* (Tokyo: Sangensha, 1951), pp. 176–78.
19. Inukai Takeru, "Yamamoto Jōtarō to Inukai Tsuyoshi, Mori Kaku," *Shin Bummei* (July 1960).
20. Sources used in this account of the incident include: court-martial records (*gumpō kaigiroku*); Inukai Takeru, "Tsuisō," *Chūō Kōron* (July-August 1932); Inukai Takeru, "Bōfu no isshūki," ibid. (June 1933); *Inukai bokudō den*, vol. 2. Also, communications with people involved and letters of the late Inukai Takeru to the author.
21. Miyake Setsurei, *Jimbutsu ron* (Tokyo: Chikura Shobō, 1939), pp. 308–11.

SAIONJI KIMMOCHI

1. Koizumi Sakutarō, Kimura Tsuyoshi, ed., *Saionji Kimmochi jiden* (Tokyo: Dai Nihon Yūbenkai Kōdansha, 1949), p. 24.
2. Kido Kōichi, *Kido Kōichi nikki*, 2 vols. (Tokyo: University of Tokyo Press, 1966), I, 216, (27 January 1933). Also, Harada Kumao, *Saionji kō to seikyoku*, vol. 3 (Tokyo: Iwanami Shoten, 1951), pp. 6–7.
3. Kimura, *Saionji Kimmochi jiden*, p. 81.
4. Ibid., p. 50.
5. Ibid., pp. 73–74.
6. Ibid., pp. 214–15.
7. Harada, *Saionji kō to seikyoku*, vol. 5, p. 99.
8. Koizumi Sakutarō, *Zuihitsu Saionji kō* (Tokyo: Iwanami Shoten 1939), pp. 230–31.
9. Kimura, *Saionji Kimmochi jiden*, p. 102.
10. Ibid., pp. 174–75.
11. Ibid., p. 139.
12. Toyabe Shuntei, *Shuntei zenshū*, vol. 1 (Tokyo: Hakubunkan, 1909), pp. 536–37, 541.
13. Hashimoto Saneaya, "Saionji kō no omoide," part one, *Kokoro* (September 1954).
14. Kimura, *Saionji Kimmochi jiden*, pp. 164–65.
15. Ibid., pp. 168–69.
16. Clemenceau, Georges, *Grandeurs et misères d'une victoire* (Paris: Plon, 1930), p. 126.
17. Harada, *Saionji kō to seikyoku*, vol. 1, pp. 20–21.
18. Ibid., p. 21.
19. Ibid., p. 220.
20. Oka Yoshitake, Hayashi Shigeru, eds., *Taishō demokurashii ki no seiji: Matsumoto Gōkichi seiji nisshi* (Tokyo: Iwanami Shoten, 1959), p. 161 (8 May 1922).
21. Ibid., p. 142 (9 March 1922).
22. Ibid., p. 295 (19 January 1924).
23. Ibid.
24. Harada Kumao, *Tōan kō seiwa* (Tokyo: Iwanami Shoten, 1943), pp. 101–2.
25. Harada, *Saionji kō to seikyoku*, vol. 1, p. 10.
26. Uchida Nobuya, *Fūun gojūnen* (Tokyo: Jitsugyō no Nihonsha, 1951), p. 119.
27. Harada, *Saionji kō to seikyoku*, vol. 1, p. 88.
28. Ibid., p. 210.
29. Ibid., vol. 2, pp. 229–30.
30. *Kido Kōichi nikki*, I, 134 (26 February 1932).
31. Harada, *Saionji kō to seikyoku*, vol. 2, pp. 232–33.
32. Ibid., p. 240.

33. *Kido Kōichi nikki*, I, 207–8 (15 December 1932).
34. Ibid., I, 351 (9 August 1935).
35. Harada, *Saionji kō to seikyoku*, vol. 4 (1951), pp. 5, 12.
36. Ibid., p. 30.
37. Ibid., pp. 276–77.
38. Ibid., vol. 5 (1951), pp. 156–57.
39. Harada, *Tōan kō seiwa*, p. 98.
40. *Kido Kōichi nikki*, I, 497 (4 July 1936).
41. Harada, *Saionji kō to seikyoku*, vol. 5, p. 135.
42. Ibid., p. 264.
43. Ibid., vol. 7 (1952), p. 84.
44. Ibid., pp. 171–73.
45. Koyama Kango, *Koyama Kango nikki* (Tokyo: Keiō Tsūshin, 1955), p. 212.
46. Harada, *Saionji kō to seikyoku*, vol. 7 (1952), p. 252.
47. Ibid., vol. 8 (1952), p. 291.
48. Ibid., p. 360.
49. Ibid., pp. 396–98.

INDEX

Attitudes, Qualities, and Relations

ITŌ HIROBUMI

cliques, 25–26
conceit, 16–22
constitutional government, 7–9,13, 26–29
conversations, 19
diplomacy, 4–6, 12–14, 15, 17, 29–31, 40–42
emperor, 3, 20, 22–26, 183
family, 21
home, 33–35
honors, 21–25
Inoue Kaoru, 3–4, 31–32, 34, 35
money, 35, 37
party leadership, 13, 29, 92–93
patriotism, 3–4, 20–21
speeches, 26–27
tastes and interests, 32, 35–37
women, 37–39
Yamagata Aritomo, 14–16, 19, 26, 32–33, 34, 38

ŌKUMA SHIGENOBU

cliques, 60–61
conceit, 49, 56–59, 65, 70–71, 80–81
constitutional government, 50, 76–78
conversations, 49, 61–68
democracy, 59, 83–84
diplomacy, 46, 52–53, 62, 81
education, 46, 62–63
emperor, 46, 56, 59, 69, 82
family, 69
genrō, 55, 77, 78, 79, 80, 81–82, 84, 100
home, 64, 67, 69–70, 72
honors, 58–59, 83–84
Hara Takashi, 60
Itagaki Taisuke, 56, 62, 74–75, 83, 84
Itō Hirobumi, 48, 50, 52, 60, 61, 62, 63, 64, 69, 72, 76

money, 69–70
party leadership, 52, 57, 59–61, 80–82, 147
speeches, 60, 61–62, 64, 76–77
tastes and interests, 63–64, 66–73
women, 66, 73
Yamagata Aritomo, 81, 148, 151

HARA TAKASHI

conceit, 101, 112–13
corruption, 118–20, 122
diplomacy, 121–22
education, 87–88
family, 85, 87, 89, 95, 110–11
genrō, 101–2
home, 105, 107, 110
honors, 97, 107–8, 115–16
Inoue Kaoru, 88, 89, 90, 91
Itō Hirobumi, 91, 92–93
money, 105–8, 120
Mutsu Munemitsu, 89–91, 109
party leadership, 92–93, 100–101, 104–9, 115
political principles, 98, 101, 109–10, 116–18, 136, 142, 151
Saionji Kimmochi, 93–98, 100–101
speeches, 109–10
tastes and interests, 112
Yamagata Aritomo, 93–94, 96, 98, 101–2, 103, 104, 113–14, 116, 117–18, 120–21, 136

INUKAI TSUYOSHI

corruption, 139, 145–46, 170
conversations, 126, 130
diplomacy, 165–71
education, 125–28
family, 125, 137, 138
genrō, 136, 159, 202
Hara Takashi, 119, 125, 136, 142

[231]

home, 164–65
money, 139
Ōkuma Shigenobu, 128–29, 131, 147, 148
Ozaki Yukio, 125, 127–28, 134–35, 146, 148, 157, 161, 164, 173–75
party leadership, 131, 133–34, 151–54
political principles, 128–30, 132, 147–48, 149, 151–57, 162–63, 167–69
Saionji Kimmochi, 202, 204
speeches, 126, 130
tastes and interests, 126, 172

SAIONJI KIMMOCHI

aristocratic temperament, 181–82, 223
constitutional government, 195, 209, 222
conversations, 182, 188, 190
democracy, 182
diplomacy, 186, 189–90, 192–93, 202, 204–5, 208, 211–12, 218–19, 221, 222
education, 177–78, 180
emperor, 180–84, 192, 205–6, 218
family, 177, 181, 188
home, 184, 187–88, 191, 194, 196
honors, 182, 184, 186, 191
Itō Hirobumi, 183, 184, 186
liberalism, 180, 182–83, 190–91, 223
money, 182
party leadership, 93, 94, 96–97, 100, 186–87, 191–92
speeches, 185, 189–90
tastes and interests, 177, 180, 188, 190, 203
women, 179, 184, 188
Yamagata Aritomo, 121, 192